OUR ARMY

OUR ARMY

SOLDIERS, POLITICS, AND AMERICAN CIVIL-MILITARY RELATIONS

Jason K. Dempsey

PRINCETON UNIVERSITY PRESS   PRINCETON AND OXFORD

Copyright © 2010 by Princeton University Press
Published by Princeton University Press, 41 William Street,
Princeton, New Jersey 08540
In the United Kingdom: Princeton University Press, 6 Oxford Street,
Woodstock, Oxfordshire OX20 1TW

Library of Congress Cataloging-in-Publication Data

Dempsey, Jason K., 1972–
  Our army : soldiers, politics, and American civil-military
relations / Jason K. Dempsey.
      p.   cm.
  Includes index.
  ISBN 978-0-691-14224-1 (hardcover : alk. paper)—
  ISBN 978-0-691-14225-8 (pbk. : alk. paper) 1. Civil-military relations—
United States. 2. Soldiers—United States—Attitudes. 3. Soldiers—United
States—Political activity. I. Title.
  JK330.D46 2009
  322'.50973—dc22   2009021741

British Library Cataloging-in-Publication Data is available

This book has been composed in Sabon

Printed on acid-free paper. ∞

press.princeton.edu

Printed in the United States of America

10 9 8 7 6 5 4 3 2 1

To my wife, Laura, who has edited, assisted with, and tolerated this project beyond all reasonable expectations. And to my children, Jack and Mary Frances: I sincerely apologize that I spent so much of your first years working on a book that makes no mention of either fire trucks or dolphins.

Contents

Illustrations

Tables

Preface

WE PROJECT OUR PREJUDICES onto people we do not know. We fill gaps in our understanding of others with stereotypes and assumptions. The American army is especially susceptible to this dynamic, as few Americans have direct experience with military service. Because of this, a formation of soldiers can become a blank slate upon which we might imagine the best, or worst, of America.

In recent years it has been commonly assumed that the American military is overwhelmingly Republican and conservative. For some this has been a point of pride, as the military is generally one of the most respected institutions in the United States. For others this perceived affiliation with the Republican Party has been a point of concern. Many have wondered about the professionalism of a force wholly associated with one side of the political spectrum.

This book presents a comprehensive assessment of the political and social attitudes of members of the U.S. Army. The evidence suggests that while a great many officers feel comfortable identifying themselves as conservative and/or Republican, the sentiment is not consistent across the army. However, it is clear that the perception of the army as overwhelmingly Republican is widespread, both in and out of the military. This perception has led political parties to adjust their voter-targeting and campaign strategies. It has also generated extensive discussion among scholars of civil-military relations. In some respects it has been a case of too much theorizing, or overreacting to incomplete data.

There are two purposes to this book and two intended audiences. The first purpose is to add some depth to our understanding of the people who serve in the American military. I want to replace the stereotype of the American soldier with a more nuanced understanding of how soldiers think about social and political issues and a better understanding of the ways in which they are similar to, or different from, the civilian population. One half of the audience for this book is therefore the American public, who are entitled to a richer understanding of their army.

The second purpose is to highlight to members of the army the dangers, and impropriety, of conflating identification with a political party or political ideology with military service. The perception of the military as a monolithic voting bloc may be inaccurate, but it was not created out of whole cloth. A generation of military leaders grew up in a military education system that forgot to teach the importance of political neutrality. As a result, an unacceptable number of army officers have comfortably combined their political and professional identities. This not only leads outsiders to question the nature and utility of military advice to civilian leadership, but introduces another, unnecessary, impediment to team building within the institution. Officers cannot, and should not, be expected to not have opinions on social and political issues, but they must proactively separate their political attitudes from their professional responsibilities.

This is not a call for officers to avoid thinking about politics. On the contrary, officers need to spend more time thinking about how to balance their rights as citizens with their obligations as commissioned officers. And in doing so they must think about internal army relations and how their personal political views may not be representative of the soldiers they lead, and therefore carefully separated from their identity as officers. They must also think about the effect that overt partisanship has upon the army's interactions with civilian leadership. There is a fine line between engaging the political process for the health and most effective use of the armed forces and becoming a centerpiece for partisan debate. Temporary gains derived from expressions of party loyalty will always be outweighed by long-term costs to the army's professional reputation.

With multiple messages and audiences, this manuscript avoids simplistic classification. On the one hand, citizens should be reassured that their military reflects America to a greater degree than they may have believed. On the other hand, there is room for improvement in how army officers approach the political process. Neither the public's perception of the military nor the political activities of army officers have thus far led to any crisis in civil-military relations. However, the combination of a changing political landscape and a turbulent security environment requires that Americans engage in a serious and informed discussion of the future of American civil-military relations. Such a discussion is necessary to ensure that our army, the army of all Americans, maintains the trust and confidence of the people it serves.

Acknowledgments _____

OVER THE COURSE OF COMPLETING this book I have unintentionally learned quite a bit about bureaucratic politics and public relations. But as painful as those lessons were, they have only deepened my understanding of the army as a public institution and heightened my respect for those who have responsibility for managing it.

This book would not have been possible without a long list of educators and mentors. Beginning at West Point in the early 1990s, Colonel (Ret.) Frederick Black, Colonel (Ret.) Robert Gordon III, Colonel (Ret.) Jay Parker, and Major Dana Isaacoff each challenged me to think critically about the institution I was about to enter. At Columbia University I had the great fortune of working with Robert Shapiro, the rare professor who is both a first-rate scholar and a tremendous teacher. I was also fortunate that Robert Erikson, Erik Gartzke, Colonel Michael Meese, and Allan Silver all agreed to be on my dissertation committee. This work has benefited tremendously from their suggestions and insights. Thanks also to Ira Katznelson for reviewing early outlines of this research as part of his seminar at Columbia and for putting me in touch with Princeton University Press. Chuck Myers at Princeton put together a great review and production team, including Ole Holsti and an anonymous reviewer, who provided a wealth of constructive suggestions.

Gary Langer at ABC and Mark Blumenthal at *Pollster.com* were gracious enough to air some of my findings as the research progressed, and I am thankful for the opportunity as well as for their perspectives on public opinion polling generally. Peter Scoblic at *The New Republic* was extraordinarily helpful in distilling this research for a larger audience.

This research was made possible through the financial backing of the Tomás Rivera Policy Institute; I am grateful to Rodolfo O. de la Garza for his initial support. I would also like to thank the Eisenhower Foundation for fellowship support during the final phases of this project. Additional funding was provided by the Academic Research Division of the United States Military Academy. Support at Columbia came from the Saltzman Institute for War and Peace Studies, the School of Arts and Sciences, and the Institute for Social and Economic Research and Policy.

For assistance in coding and managing the survey mailings, I am indebted to Jo May at West Point as well as fellow students John Delano, Sam Dryzmala, Mat Krogulecki, Marty Lachter, and Yoshiko Toriumi. Thanks also to Jeffrey Herman, Sue Zayac, and Jay Goodwin for their computing assistance and to Doug Gallagher for his work on the online surveys. Major B. J. Bailey was an exceptional help in assisting with some of the printing tasks. The research would not have been possible without the data-management wizardry of Major Marc Wehmeyer and Luke Gallagher. I am also grateful for the support of Major David Lyle and Colonel Casey Wardynski, who, as economists, were probably ashamed to be associated with such pedestrian research on "attitudes" but were nonetheless tolerant of my efforts.

For supporting this research through the approval process and creating a great working environment, I am indebted to Brigadier General (Ret.) Daniel Kaufman and Brigadier General (Ret.) Russell Howard, as well as the rest of the faculty of the Department of Social Sciences at the United States Military Academy. Particularly I want to thank an exceptional community of scholars of civil-military relations including Colonel (Ret.) Don Snider, Lieutenant Colonels Isaiah Wilson III and Suzanne Nielsen, and Major Darrell Driver. Colonel (Ret.) Don Connelly deserves credit as the torchbearer for the study of civil-military relations at the army's Command and General Staff College. I also thank Elizabeth Samet in the Department of English for taking an interest in the research on cadets and offering her insights into life at West Point. All of these officers and scholars have helped make this a better manuscript.

I am especially grateful to my colleague Major Craig Cummings, who sat next to me in my first class on American politics at West Point and has been an invaluable friend and study partner ever since. Most important, I thank my family for always supporting my efforts. Ultimately, I must thank my parents, Jack and Linda, and my sister Danita—my first military family.

OUR ARMY

Chapter 1 _____

Introduction

AMERICANS ARE WELL AWARE of the example George Washington set for the relationship between the fledgling American state and its military. The image of Washington as victorious military commander grandly announcing his retirement and abruptly departing Annapolis by horse, thereby forgoing any Napoleonic aspirations to power, is indelibly inked in the American psyche.[1] The idea that the uniformed hero would ride away from the army he almost single-handedly maintained and led through the Revolution, *his* army, to return to his home on Mount Vernon, voluntarily relinquishing a very good chance of becoming America's first monarch, was a stunning precedent in American civil-military relations. In this, Washington emulated Cincinnatus and demonstrated how members of the armed forces in America should not attempt to directly translate military power into domestic political power.

Despite his refusal to assume power on the basis of his military position, Washington became America's first president—due in no small part to his military service. The prestige that Washington had gained through his sacrifice during the Revolution was a valuable asset for those trying to determine the course of the new nation. Planning for the Constitutional Convention, Henry Knox and James Madison worked diligently to secure his attendance to lend legitimacy to the idea of a major transformation of government.[2] Washington ultimately agreed and served as the president of the convention. This allowed him to remain above the debate and made him a natural choice for the newly created position of president. Washington thereby set the first example of how military service could still be a valuable asset for elected public office without violating the premise of civilian supremacy.

Since the time of Washington's successful transition from military commander to president, more than a few men (and, increasingly, women) with military experience have attempted to translate their service into political power. And a greater number without a background of military service have tried to draw upon the support of members of the military

---

[1] This was the second of his notable exits, the first being his departure from his fellow officers at Fraunces Tavern in New York in November 1783. Ellis, *His Excellency*, 146.

[2] Ibid., 173–78.

as a political asset. In recent years, these efforts have become more acute. As the stature of the military rises, so does its appeal as a political force. However, this basic relationship represents a paradox.

The reputation of the military has steadily increased since the late 1970s.[3] Today a higher percentage of people state that they have "a great deal of confidence" in the military than they do in medicine, religion, the press, or Congress.[4] Much of this gain in prestige has come from the army's performance on the battlefield, as in the aftermath of the first Gulf War, and the rally effect of the attacks on the United States in 2001. But aside from these spikes in confidence during and after armed conflict, there has been a steady increase, which many attribute to the growing professionalism of the American military since the advent of the all-volunteer force.[5] There are many dimensions to military professionalism, but one key aspect has been the apolitical nature of military service.

Military service is fundamentally about protecting the state—not just a fraction of the state. Military sacrifice is implicitly for the greater good and has never been conceptualized as sacrifice for a specific political agenda. This dynamic of representing collective interests over specific interests is among the reasons that people often have more confidence in the presidency than they do in Congress. If we take the example further, we note that the judiciary generally ranks higher than both the presidency and Congress due to its perceived position "above the fray" of most political squabbles, and the military typically ranks above all three branches of government.[6] A significant portion of the military's prestige comes from its reputation as one of the most apolitical American institutions.

And thus the paradox of prestige. The more members of the military build a reputation for apolitical service to the country the greater a political prize the military becomes. As the military gains in prestige, the political backing of members of the military, either implicit or explicit, becomes an advantage in electoral politics. In the view of political operatives, the military is therefore a valuable "prestige vote" whose capture translates into much more than the actual votes of members of the military.[7]

---

[3] For trends over time, see Torres-Reyna and Shapiro, "Trends." A Gallup poll from June 4, 2006, reported confidence rates for the military, the Supreme Court, the presidency, and Congress at 73%, 40%, 33%, and 19%, respectively.

[4] For a brief overview of trends over time by the General Social Survey, see Schott, "Op-Art."

[5] Nielson, "Civil Military Relations of the US." Also King and Karabell, *Generation of Trust.*

[6] This is clearly a simplification of the dynamics around public opinion and the Supreme Court. More nuanced views can be found in Cummings and Shapiro's "Studying the Effect of Elite Leadership." Also Mondak and Smithey's "Dynamics of Public Support."

[7] Frum, speech to cadets at West Point.

The 2004 election highlighted how central military service and the political preferences of the military can be to political campaigns. Against
the backdrop of wars in Afghanistan and Iraq, the military service of both
presidential candidates was a major component of each campaign. Both
candidates aggressively sought to win the votes of military personnel
and their family members. Each candidate invited retired generals to
speak on his behalf during the campaign and at the nominating conventions.[8] At times it seemed as if a virtual arms race had been initiated as
both parties sought retired members of the armed forces to sit onstage
behind their candidate.

A decisive moment in this struggle involved retired General Tommy
Franks. Fresh out of uniform as the combatant commander for the geo-
graphic region covering Afghanistan and Iraq, Franks stepped onto the
stage of the Republican National Convention and endorsed George W.
Bush for president. This was notable because his endorsement appeared
explicitly designed to highlight the apolitical nature of military service
and, by extension, the "purity" of Franks's endorsement of Bush. Franks
began his speech by noting, "I'm not a Republican. I'm not a Democrat.
But I believe in democracy. I believe in America. After almost four decades
as a Soldier I've been Independent. But, here I stand tonight, endorsing
George W. Bush." He then spent the remainder of his speech talking about
war, ending with a reference to George W. Bush not as president but as
"Commander-in-Chief."[9] In doing so, Franks translated the reputation of
the military for apolitical service into a strong endorsement of the Republican candidate for president.

This dramatic endorsement from a newly retired general and the steady
drumbeat of debates over the meaning of military service and attitudes of
service members spurred survey researchers to take notice. Unfortunately,
there was a dearth of information about the general public's attitudes
toward military issues and an almost complete absence of surveys of military personnel. Survey questions about military service largely vanished
with the end of the draft in 1973, and comprehensive data on the social
and political attitudes of active-duty members of the military were virtually nonexistent.[10] As late as 2000, many surveys omitted military installa-

---

[8] General (Ret.) Wesley Clark spoke in support of John Kerry, and General (Ret.) Tommy
Franks spoke in support of George W. Bush. General Clark was also joined on stage at the
DNC Nominating Convention by nine retired generals and admirals.

[9] Franks, "Text of Gen. Tommy Franks."

[10] One indicator of how little the academic world paid attention to the military during
this period is that military sociology consistently ranked last among sociological specialties
after 1965. This dynamic was replicated across academia and included history and political
science. Rustad, "Review of the Political Education of Soldiers." Coffman, "Course of Military History." Walt, "Renaissance of Security Studies."

tions from their sampling procedures.[11] In 2004 survey researchers scrambled to fill the gap.

The most notable of these efforts were made by the Annenberg Public Policy Center and the Military Times Media Group.[12] Using their extensive database of respondents contacted for the 2004 National Annenberg Election Survey (NAES), the Annenberg Center conducted a special survey of 656 households with an active-duty service member.[13] The Military Times newspapers capitalized on a series of surveys begun in 2003 which utilized their subscriber rolls to identify and survey members of the military. For the 2004 election they were able to survey 1,498 of their subscribers who were also active service members.[14]

These polls from the Annenberg Center and Military Times Company reported significant support for the incumbent Bush and high rates of Republican Party affiliation among members of the military. Of the 372 respondents in the Annenberg Center survey who were members of the military, 47% identified themselves as Republicans and 15% identified themselves as Democrats. The Military Times Company reported that 60% of their respondents described themselves as Republican and only 13% identified themselves as Democrats. Seventy percent of their respondents approved of the job being done by President Bush. These findings were well publicized but did not cause a significant stir, as they appeared to confirm the findings of a study conducted in 1998 and 1999 by the Triangle Institute for Security Studies (TISS).[15]

[11] This was probably due to the difficulty of gaining access to military installations. Given this military base exclusion, the members of the military whom surveyors typically were able to reach were the older and higher-ranking service members, who are more likely to live off of military reservations. There were not, however, any efforts to target the military or summarize the views of military personnel as a unique subgroup.

[12] The Military Times Media Group publishes a weekly newspaper for each of the four services. These four papers are the *Army Times, Navy Times, Air Force Times*, and *Marine Corps Times*. Hodierne, "Military Times Poll."

[13] The final sample consisted of 372 members of the military and 284 people who were immediate family members of a service member. The average age of service-member respondents was thirty-nine, and almost 50% reported having ten or more years of military service, indicating that the typical survey respondent was much older than the average member of the military. It also appears that at least 129 of the 372 members of the military surveyed were no longer on active duty as of October 2004, although the data on this are incomplete. See the Military Cross-Section Study in Romer et al., *Capturing Campaign Dynamics*.

[14] Subscribers to these types of professional publications can naturally be assumed to have a greater interest in the military as a career than other service members. Respondents to the Military Times surveys in 2004 were disproportionately officers and were older than the average member of the military. More discussion of the Military Times surveys can be found in chapter 9 and appendix C.

[15] For more details on the Triangle Institute for Security Studies' Survey of the Military in the Post Cold War Era, see Feaver and Kohn, *Soldiers and Civilians*.

The TISS project was an attempt to assess whether an attitudinal "gap" existed between the military and civilian populations. The authors of the TISS study were interested in the attitudes of military elites and limited their analysis to midlevel and senior-level officers who were currently attending professional military schooling. The surveys did not include junior officers or the enlisted ranks. However, the study was the most comprehensive analysis of the attitudes of senior military leaders to date, with 723 active-duty service members included in their surveys. The findings of the TISS study appeared to confirm widespread anecdotal evidence that the military had become overwhelmingly Republican, with 64% of officers in the survey choosing to identify with that party. Only 8% identified themselves as Democrats.[16] Although the TISS study is very useful as a starting point for quantifying the gap between the military and society, the project's focus on senior military leaders meant that the TISS survey sample represented only about 6% of the army.[17]

While each of these studies made valuable contributions to our understanding of the social and political attitudes of the military, many questions remain. This book seeks to fill the gap in our understanding of the active military population by examining one branch of service, the army, in detail. Focusing on one branch of service allows for the first in-depth look at the attitudes of enlisted personnel as well as a careful analysis of various subgroups within the service, such as junior officers, women, and racial and ethnic minorities. This analysis is made possible by the first and only random-sample survey of the army that addresses the social and political attitudes of active service members.

Citizenship and Service: A 2004 Survey of Army Personnel

The Citizenship and Service Survey (hereafter C&S Survey) was designed to collect data on each respondent's (1) general attitudes toward the army, including morale, career intentions, and opinions about army leadership; (2) reasons for joining the army; (3) personal attitudes toward social issues and political issues, including foreign policy; and (4) experiences of discrimination and opinions concerning gender and racial and ethnic relations in the army and civilian society.[18] Wherever useful and possible, the

[16] Ricks, "Widening Gap." For TISS data, see Holsti, "Of Chasms and Convergences," 28.

[17] As of February 2004, majors and above made up approximately 29,000 of the army's 487,000 personnel.

[18] The primary purpose of the survey was an analysis of Hispanic integration in the army. However, the study included questions on attitudes toward foreign policy, social issues, political ideology, and participation. For an analysis of attitudes across races and the state of Hispanic integration, see Dempsey and Shapiro, "The Army's Hispanic Future."

survey replicated questions in existing American national surveys to allow for comparisons with the civilian population.[19]

In addition to gathering this baseline information on attitudes, the survey included extensive demographic information. Survey questions concerning respondents' demographic characteristics focused on data that the army had not normally collected. These included questions on language proficiency, the military service of family members, and the immigration status of the soldiers' parents and grandparents.

Every soldier and officer on active duty whose name was in the army's personnel database as of February 2004 was eligible for inclusion in the survey, with the exception of personnel deployed in combat zones; those in units deploying to and from Iraq and Afghanistan during the months of April and May 2004; and soldiers and officers in a few select ranks.[20] Due to the high turnover and sustained deployment of forces into Iraq and Afghanistan, the exclusion of soldiers currently in a combat zone did not prevent combat veterans from being included. A large number of respondents (375, or 32% of the sample) were veterans of either Operation Iraqi Freedom (2003–4) or Operation Enduring Freedom in Afghanistan (2001–4); and 143 indicated that they had been involved in direct ground combat in the previous two years.

The survey excluded sergeants major and generals due to the small population size of these ranks and the high visibility of generals.[21] The survey also excluded the lowest two enlisted ranks, private E1 (PV1) and private E2 (PV2), because of the very high mobility of these soldiers. Soldiers entering the army generally serve in these ranks for less than a year, spending the majority of their time in basic and advanced individual training before arriving at their first regular unit. The soldiers and officers in the four rank categories just cited make up approximately 10% of the army on active duty, which left 90% of the army population, by rank, eligible to be included in the survey.

The design of the survey sample focused on the dimensions of race and rank and included oversamples of certain groups based on projected return rates. Specifically, the sample included additional white, black, and

[19] These national surveys include the National Elections Study, the NORC General Social Survey, the Latino National Political Survey, the Chicago Council on Global Affairs Survey (formerly Chicago Council on Foreign Relations), the National Annenberg Election Study, and the Triangle Institute for Security Studies survey.

[20] Potential respondents were randomly drawn from a February 2004 database. Mailing addresses for those soldiers came from a separate December 2003 database, which reportedly contained more accurate contact information.

[21] In analyses that might report on survey respondents from small populations, it may be difficult to protect fully the anonymity of such respondents as required by rules regarding the use of human subjects, to which the C&S Survey conformed.

Hispanic officers as well as additional black and Hispanic enlisted soldiers in an attempt to get close to two hundred respondents in each category.[22] In the end, responses from the basic sample plus the oversample, taken together, yielded a final sample size for analysis of 1,188, including responses from 563 enlisted men and women, 90 warrant officers, and 535 officers.[23] The composition of the final sample, broken down by rank, gender, and race and ethnicity, is shown in table 1.1.

The survey was conducted primarily via mail questionnaires between April 3 and July 24, 2004. Each respondent received an introductory letter that was followed, in sequence, by the primary survey mailing, a reminder postcard, and then a second survey mailing.[24] The last contact was a fifth letter offering respondents the option of completing the survey online. The response rate for the survey was 45% among those soldiers and officers whose mail was not returned as undeliverable.[25] All reported data in this book are weighted to reflect the army population on the dimensions of race, rank, and gender, except where noted.[26]

In sum, the C&S Survey provides a baseline and comprehensive view of social and political attitudes across one branch of military service, the army. This baseline allows for the examination and testing of previous findings based on anecdotal or incomplete evidence. By closely examining the possible determinants of these attitudes and the role of the military in shaping political views it also allows for a clearer picture to emerge of how members of the military form their political views.

The 2004 West Point Preelection Survey

Although the bulk of the analysis in this book focuses on the attitudes of members of the active-duty army, these findings are augmented in chapter 8 with the results of a survey of West Point cadets conducted on the eve of the 2004 election. Data from this survey provide another angle from which we can explore the reason for any differences between soldiers and officers. By examining future officers in precommissioning training, the survey also provides a window into the way the army may or may not socialize its future leaders.

---

[22] The six primary groups we wanted to compare were white officers, white enlisted soldiers, black officers, black enlisted soldiers, Hispanic officers, and Hispanic enlisted soldiers.

[23] See chapter 3 for a detailed explanation of the army's rank structure.

[24] Dillman, *Mail and Internet Surveys.*

[25] See appendix A for a full discussion of the survey methodology and how the response rate was calculated.

[26] See appendix A for more details on the survey design.

TABLE 1.1
Sample Breakdown by Race/Ethnicity, Rank, and Gender

	Rank			
Race	Enlisted	Warrant Officers	Officer	Total
White	197	14	209	420
Hispanic	192	32	173	397
Black	130	37	126	293
Other	44	7	27	78
Total	563	90	535	1,188
Male	*432*	*81*	*407*	*920*
Female	*131*	*9*	*128*	*268*

Source: C&S Survey.

The cadet survey was designed using the C&S survey as a guide and covered many of the same topics. The survey also included questions that might inform the way the political and social attitudes of future officers develop. These included questions on the military service of family members, the political affiliations of family members, and the socioeconomic status of cadets' families. The survey also explored the extent to which cadets feel pressure to identify with either of the two major political parties.

The survey was administered through a secure Web site from Saturday, October 30, until 5 p.m. on Tuesday, November 2 (Election Day). Responses to the survey yielded a final sample size for analysis of 885, including responses from 738 men and 129 women. The survey response rate was 54 percent. The survey methodology is discussed in more detail in chapter 8.

This study uses the results of both the cadet survey and the C&S Survey in an attempt to answer the following specific research questions:

1. To what degree is the army different from the American public in terms of political participation and political and social attitudes?
2. What role do demographic differences play in explaining any attitudinal differences?
3. How do soldiers and officers differ in their social and political views, and why?
4. What role does self-selection play in explaining the attitudes of those who join an all-volunteer army?
5. Are civilian perceptions of military attitudes accurate? Is the military rightly perceived as a conservative and predominantly Republican institution?

6. What are the implications of the answers to these questions for civil-military relations?

This study sits at the intersection of several disciplines. It relies primarily on an analysis of opinion data but draws heavily from literature on civil-military relations. The bulk of it focuses on the opinions of members of the army but often analyzes how perceptions of these attitudes influence elite-level interaction and the broader relationship between the military and American society. Likewise, the study of civil-military relations does not fit neatly into any academic discipline but has most often been pursued by historians, political scientists, and sociologists. In attempting to answer these questions, I draw on the previous efforts of scholars in these fields.

This book proceeds with a brief discussion of the history of political attitudes and participation among members of the army, followed by a survey of current civil-military relations literature and its application to this study. Following this summary, in chapter 3 I provide the reader with an overview of the army circa 2004 and an explanation of those elements of army life that are discussed later in the book. The heart of the analysis is in chapters 4 through 8. In chapter 4 I outline the views of members of the army on select social and political issues. In chapter 5 I address the ideological self-identification of members of the army and specifically the conventional wisdom that the army is an inherently conservative institution. Chapter 6 takes this analysis further by looking at the party affiliation of members of the army. In chapter 7 I look at how all of this translates into political activity by active-duty members of the army. In all four of these chapters I examine subgroup differences within the army (mostly between soldiers and officers) and compare the attitudes and activities of members of the army with the civilian population. This analysis of the active-duty army is followed in chapter 8 by an examination of how the army may or may not socialize future officers in precommissioning training.

This book concludes with a discussion of the implication of these findings for the future of American civil-military relations. This discussion also includes an analysis of how the outlook of members of the army may have changed over the last four years.

Chapter 2 _____

Soldiers and Politics

Historical Overview

Political participation among members of the military is not a new phenomenon, but several factors place today's military in a unique position in American history. First, it is only in the last fifty years that a large standing military has been a permanent part of the American landscape. We have had large military forces before, but they were typically built up in response to a specific conflict and reduced immediately after the termination of hostilities. Second, the military votes. Officers have often been active in politics, but only in recent years has voting been both accepted as a norm among members of the military and made possible by relatively new laws that allow members of the military to vote via absentee ballot. Third, the linkages between the military and society are more tenuous than they have ever been. In the past, military and political elites were often one and the same, but with the passing of the World War II generation, the proportion of political leaders with military experience has precipitously declined. Simultaneously, the end of conscription has meant that only those who choose to join the military do so. Last, today's military is viewed as a solidly Republican voting bloc. The purpose of this chapter is to place these developments in the context of American history.

From the Revolution to Civil War

The history of the army is replete with stories of officers pursuing political careers following military service and, in at least two cases, while still serving in uniform. But overt political activity and expressions of partisan affiliation by members of the military was most common in the period between the Revolution and the Civil War. During this period there was no such thing as a distinct army profession, and politics and military service often went hand in hand. This phenomenon was not unique to the American experience but was in keeping with the historical norm of having combatants, particularly combat leaders, come from the "most politically relevant strata of society."[1] Samuel Huntington describes the view

---

[1] Segal, *Recruiting for Uncle Sam*, 9.

of the Founders toward the relationship between political and military elites: "Unable to visualize a distinct military class, they [the political elites] could not fear such a class."[2] The fact that six of twelve presidents between 1815 and 1860 served as officers demonstrates how political and military elites were often one and the same.

Evidence of how commonplace it was for officers to be overt in their political attitudes and affiliations in this early era can be seen in a list of all 256 officers in the army as of July 1801. The list was compiled by the chief clerk of the War Department to help identify the eighty-six officers who would be discharged as part of Thomas Jefferson's efforts to reduce the military. What is unique about this list is that it identifies the political affiliations of each officer. As Alexander Hamilton had specifically sought to fill the army's ranks with Federalists, it could be expected that the transition to a Republican administration would involve some type of purge of those who might not support the new administration. However, an analysis of those chosen for discharge conducted by the military historian Edward Coffman shows no evidence that politics played a central role in determining dismissals; however, it is telling that political affiliation was part of an officer's file. Officers were classified on a scale from "Republican" to "political apathy" to "opposed to the new administration" and "active in its vilification." Even within these files, though, there is some evidence that the idea of a professional and apolitical military ideal already existed. The commentary on the politics of at least one officer read, "professionally the soldier without any political creed."[3] Even though involvement in politics was commonplace, an ideal standard already existed for the professional military officer to distance himself from the political process.

The idea that officers should serve the nation without affiliating themselves with any particular faction also began to develop among officers in training at the United States Military Academy at West Point during the 1820s and 1830s. Cadets began to describe the academy as "the National School" or "the school of the Union." They also began to describe themselves as "children of the Union," implying a commitment to the nation, and not any particular faction thereof.[4] Further evidence of the develop-

---

[2] Huntington, *The Soldier and the State*, 168.

[3] Coffman, *Old Army*, 8–10.

[4] Watson, "How the Army Became Accepted," 237. This ties into the larger development of the professionalization of military service. As warfare became more complex, officers simply had less time to become involved in local politics. And, of course, less involvement also meant less interaction with civilian elites, resulting in a separation between military and civilian leaders that was in large part driven by pragmatic concerns. However, this did not mean that once separated, they would not begin to view each other with distrust. The opposite is true—and thus the study of civil-military relations. Unfortunately, a detailed analysis of how the increasing specialization required by war led to increased military pro-

ment of this apolitical ideal came in 1836 with an exchange of letters in the *Army and Navy Chronicle*. In this instance a writer with the pseud-onym of Alcibiades advocated the active involvement of officers in politics following the model of the Revolutionary War, when many of the army's officers were also politicians. Three months later a writer with the pseud-onym of Justice responded to Alcibiades that since, by law, officers were prevented from showing contempt to the president or Congress, they should refrain from involvement in political campaigns.[5]

Justice was clearly in the minority during this era, however, and keeping one's distance from politics was easier said than done, as officers were often compelled to lobby Congress directly on their own behalf for pro-motions and transfers.[6] Congress also became integral to the commission-ing process in 1843 when it mandated that appointments to the United States Military Academy be distributed equally among congressional dis-tricts, making these appointments a formal part of their patronage.

The apex of officer involvement in politics probably came with Winfield Scott's campaign for the presidency while still on active duty. In 1852 he received the Whig Party nomination but ultimately lost to Franklin Pierce. Interestingly, there was no uproar within the army about Scott's political activity. And while many officers hoped he would lose, some wanted him to win, if only because it would free up his position and allow for a few promotions.[7] That there was no significant concern, either within the army or the general population, that Scott's candidacy represented a dan-gerous encroachment of the military on politics is probably due to several factors. First, the practice of famous generals seeking higher office was nothing new and had never resulted in any kind of constitutional crisis. Scott just happened to be running while still on the active rolls. Second, the officer corps was extremely small (generally fewer than a thousand officers during this period) and did not in itself represent a significant voting bloc. Likewise, most officers had difficulty even voting, as the tran-sient nature of military life made it hard to meet local residency require-

---

fessionalism is beyond the scope of this book. The dynamic is nicely encapsulated, however, in a 1948 quote by Field Marshal Earl Wavell:

Interchangeability between the statesman and the soldier passed for ever, I fear, in the last century. The Germans professionalized the trade of war; and modern inventions, by increasing its technicalities, have specialized it. It is much the same with politics, profes-sionalized by democracy. No longer can one man hope to exercise both callings, though both are branches of the same craft, the governance of men and the ordering of human affairs. (Huntington, *The Soldier and the State*, 70)

[5] Coffman, *Old Army*, 88, and Huntington, *The Soldier and the State*, 207. Huntington does not include a reference to the rejoinder from Justice.
[6] Coffman, *Old Army*, 88. See also Huntington, *The Soldier and the State*, 206.
[7] Coffman, *Old Army*, 90–91.

ments. Last, and probably most important, the officer corps was not unified in its political views, making it impossible for any candidate to claim
that he represented the army.[8] One overview of officers during the period
from 1828 to 1852 revealed an almost equal balance between those who
considered themselves Democrats and those who were Whigs or National
Republicans.[9]

This dynamic carried into the Civil War, where George McClellan's
presidential run in 1864 appeared to garner little support from soldiers
serving at the time. Although some members of the army certainly supported McClellan, efforts to mobilize the army and to enable soldiers in
the field to cast votes are considered to have turned the election in favor
of Abraham Lincoln. In 1864 Lincoln won 116,887 votes from soldiers
compared with McClellan's 33,748.[10]

Post–Civil War

In the aftermath of the Civil War, involvement in politics by active officers
began to decline considerably. As debates raged throughout the country in
1866 about the direction of Reconstruction, the *Army and Navy Journal*
published articles on officer involvement in politics. Unlike the debate in
the *Army and Navy Chronicle* in 1836, the journal repeatedly urged all
officers to stay "aloof from all politicians" and avoid "all political meetings."[11] The sentiment of Alcibiades was decidedly on the wane.

The postwar career of General John M. Schofield is representative of
the withdrawal of active-duty officers from overt participation in politics
and the assumption of a nonpartisan outlook. In 1867 Schofield refused
an overture from several Virginians who urged him to run for the Senate.[12]
This instinct would be reinforced throughout the Reconstruction era as
"the intense partisanship of the American political system intensified the
cautious nature of Schofield and most military officers."[13] With the risk
of being subject to partisan criticism at every turn, and often from both

---

[8] Nor was the army viewed as an especially prestigious institution at the time, which
would have made the claim of being supported by the army a dubious asset in a campaign.

[9] Skelton also notes that even when officers did identify with a party, "their party identifications were remarkably 'soft' when compared to the intense partisanship in the larger
society." Skelton, "Officers and Politicians," 38. Further evidence of the split in the political
views of officers can be found in the Civil War, as many West Point graduates and career
officers joined forces with the Confederacy.

[10] Commager, *The Blue and the Gray*. Also Walsh, "The Most Consequential Elections
in History."

[11] Coffman, *Old Army*, 243.

[12] Ibid., 242.

[13] Connelly, *John M. Schofield*, 338.

sides, officers learned to act cautiously and leave larger questions of policy to political elites. As Schofield addressed the West Point graduates of 1892, he urged that they stay abreast of the political questions of the day while "wisely abstain[ing] from active participation in party politics."[14] Schofield's aversion to partisan politics was ultimately so acute that in 1894 he told a correspondent that he did not want to enter into any "partisan contest" and that he would accept elective office only as a "spontaneous gift" of his state.[15]

Although there were certainly counterexamples to Schofield, they were few and outnumbered. Retired officers still ran for elected office, and decorated service in the Civil War was particularly useful for a political résumé, but engaging in political activity while still in uniform was no longer accepted. Some historians estimate that in this period "not one officer in five hundred . . . ever cast a ballot."[16] The idea of subordination to legitimate civilian authority that began in the service academies in the 1820s was now the norm, as the "concept of an impartial, nonpartisan, objective career service, loyally serving whatever administration or party was in power, became the ideal for the military profession."[17]

General Alfred Bates also articulated this view in 1902 in a speech to the New England Society in New York when he said, "The Army is the country's general servant, well-disciplined, obedient, equally faithful in war, executing civil laws, or performing civil functions. *It knows neither parties nor politics*, but simply asks for instructions and follows them without asking any questions"[18] (emphasis mine). This did not mean that all officers avoided politics, but by this era opinion had shifted such that any active officer who did involve himself in politics was likely to be shunned by the army, as was the case with Leonard Wood in 1920.[19]

By the 1920s and 1930s the idea of officers' abstaining from political matters while still in service had become so ingrained in army culture that a minor scandal erupted in 1923 when a group of officers' wives voted in a local election, leading to an appeal from the losing party. The officers themselves were shocked at the breach of etiquette and were criticized by their regimental commander for letting their wives vote.[20] Another scandal indicative of this aversion to politics occurred in 1934 when Lieutenant Colonel Herman Beukema suggested the inclusion of a book

---

[14] Quoted ibid., 341.

[15] Coffman, *Old Army*, 267.

[16] Huntington, *Soldier and the State*, 258.

[17] Ibid., 259.

[18] Quoted in Brown's *Social Attitudes of American Generals*, 375.

[19] Huntington, *Soldier and the State*, 280–82. Also Janowitz, *Professional Soldier*, 152.

[20] Coffman, *Regulars*, 247.

on the New Deal in a course on economics at the United States Military Academy. The superintendent refused the proposal because the New Deal was "a live political issue, and as such, [was] not suitable for study or discussion in this institution."[21] Such aversion to partisan politics and a reputation for honesty led to the regular use of officers for tasks of national importance, beyond military employment, throughout the interwar period.[22]

Post–World War II

After World War II the norm of avoiding political participation in the form of voting began to disappear.[23] The view of the military leader as "an efficient, disinterested, nonpartisan administrator and diplomat"[24] still prevailed, but the expansion of roles in World War II and the pressing needs of the Cold War also pulled officers directly into the political arena. So while senior generals like Omar Bradley and George Marshall made a point of refraining from voting in uniform, a new generation of officers began to be more comfortable in exercising their right to vote.

Some of this may have been a legacy of the government's response to the activation of so many soldiers during World War II. In 1942 the federal government passed the Servicemen's Voting Right Act, which attempted to guarantee access to absentee balloting by military personnel.[25] The later war years also saw President Roosevelt encouraging, and attempting to facilitate, the voting of soldiers deployed overseas.[26]

[21] Ibid., 245.

[22] In addition to work with the Civilian Conservation Corps, individual officers were often appointed to ostensibly civilian positions. General Herbert Lord became the first director of the Bureau of the Budget in 1922. Overseas, General Frank McCoy was appointed to supervise Nicaragua's 1929 election, followed by duty with the League of Nations. During the New Deal, army officers served as government representatives on the code authorities of numerous industries. Of course, this also had the second-order effect of injecting the military into domestic political questions. Brown, *Social Attitudes of American Generals*, 328, 384–85.

[23] The norm of not running for office while on active duty remained.

[24] Brown, *Social Attitudes of American Generals*, 388.

[25] Although largely ineffective in getting states to allow absentee voting by military personnel, this was the first federal attempt to facilitate soldier voting. Frantzich, "Citizens in Uniform," 16.

[26] President Roosevelt ultimately fell far short of his goal of standardizing absentee ballots and making it easier for soldiers to vote from outside of their state of residence. This was primarily due to strong opposition from southern Democrats who feared that federal interference in state laws governing voting would undermine the disenfranchisement of blacks. For a thorough discussion of the debates surrounding the 1944 statute, see Katznelson, *Fear Itself* (forthcoming).

In 1965 Paul Van Riper and Darab Unwalla published a study of the
voting patterns of senior officers across the four services. Surveying 2,077
officers in the rank of colonel and above, the authors found that 25%
reported voting in 1944. From that point on voting rates steadily increased, with 40% reporting voting in 1956 and 49% reporting being
registered to vote in 1959 (the survey was conducted prior to the 1960
election).[27] These voting rates lagged behind the American public by about
30% in 1944 and the gap shrank to 21% by 1956. This would seem to
confirm anecdotal evidence that prior to the war most officers did not
vote, but it also provides clear evidence that the norm of not voting grew
weaker in the postwar period. Looking for determinants of voting within
the officer ranks, Van Riper and Unwalla also found that the military
tradition still worked to inhibit voting, albeit at a decreasing rate. Specifically, those officers with a family history of service, those who had gradua-
ted from one of the service academies, and those committed to a full career
in the military were less likely to vote than other officers.[28]

Unfortunately the Van Riper and Unwalla study did not ask the officers
in their survey whom they had voted for or their partisan affiliations, so
we do not have data on the partisan attitudes of officers in that period.
However, we do have some analysis by Morris Janowitz on the political
ideologies of officers during this time. In a 1954 study Janowitz found
that among 211 army officers in the rank of major and above who were
assigned to staff duty in the Pentagon, 70% described themselves as "conservative" or "somewhat conservative" (25% and 45%, respectively).[29]

Janowitz could only speculate as to the exact meaning of conservatism
among these officers but suggested that the conservatism found in the
military was probably one of form over content. In this era the term *conservative* appeared to describe a cautious and pragmatic worldview that
put more faith in existing structures and institutions than in any particular
ideology. Likewise, conservatism was not associated with any partisan
identification, making it difficult to discern party preference from this
stated self-identification (although there were indicators that some of the
military's conservatives in the interwar period may best have fit within
the "right wing" of the Republican Party).[30] Janowitz did, however, suggest that increasing demands on the military, begun during the Great De-

---

[27] Van Riper and Unwalla, "Voting Patterns," 51. In rank order, officers in the navy reported voting the most, followed by the Marine Corps, the army, and the air force.

[28] Ibid., 61.

[29] Janowitz, *Professional Soldier*, 237.

[30] Ibid., 242, 236, and 250. For a comprehensive view that places these anecdotes of
right-wing attitudes in the context of a more pragmatic and moderate officer corps, see
Brown's *Social Attitudes of American Generals*.

pression and expanded during the Cold War, significantly raised the level of interaction that officers had with civilian society. This often opened the door to criticism of aspects of civilian society that officers felt were lacking, particularly elements of the economy and the nation's educational system.[31] Such a development could reasonably be expected also to increase the interest of officers in domestic politics.

While there are no data on how members of the military may have voted during this era, Janowitz and fellow sociologist Charles Moskos observed, "From 1945 to 1973, the military establishment of the United States was relatively open-minded and self-critical. The officer corps and especially its elite members had a perspective toward foreign policy and strategic issues which paralleled the divisions in civilian society."[32] Debates over foreign and military policies in the 1950s and 1960s also make clear that the military had significant and often public clashes with Republicans and Democrats alike.

The friction between military leaders and politicians of both parties during this period, and the lack of a clear military bias toward either party, was in many ways a function of the "Cold War Consensus" on foreign policy. As there was general agreement on both the threat of the Soviet Union and the means of containing it, the phrase "politics stop at the water's edge" had some meaning during this era. And when there were differences between the two parties on military issues, it was the Democratic Party that typically supported positions in line with military viewpoints.[33] For much of the Cold War era, the Democratic Party was referred to as the "War Party," as it typically supported an aggressive foreign policy and consistently advocated for greater defense spending.[34] Leadership in this area came from Senator Henry "Scoop" Jackson, who was such a consistent supporter of the military that promilitary Democrats were often described as belonging to the Scoop Jackson wing of the Democratic Party.

The most salient example of the interplay between party politics and civil-military relations during this era was Harry Truman's firing of Douglas MacArthur and the aftermath of that event. Considered by many to be the gravest threat to civilian control of the military since the feud between McClellan and Lincoln, the firing of MacArthur provided an opportunity for Republicans to challenge the Democratic president—with the full support of a five-star general. At the time he was fired, MacArthur had ex-

---

[31] Janowitz, *Professional Soldier*, 246–47.

[32] Janowitz and Moskos, "Five Years of the All-Volunteer Force," 205.

[33] Although the Republican Party was at times more militaristic during this era, it was also strongly isolationist, which prevented full support for a strong military.

[34] Huntington, *Common Defense*, 252–62.

ceeded fifty years of service in the army and was the only five-star general still in uniform. To say he was a hero to the American public would be a dramatic understatement, and the prestige he had accumulated through his military service was used to full effect against Truman.

While the direct cause of MacArthur's firing was the ultimatum he issued to the Chinese in the form of a "military appraisal," thereby scuttling Truman's ongoing efforts to achieve a cease-fire, a contributing factor to Truman's dissatisfaction with MacArthur was his correspondence with members of the opposition party. Republican Joe Martin, then minority leader in the House of Representatives, had been corresponding with the general, and shortly after MacArthur's ultimatum to the Chinese, Martin read a letter from MacArthur that was critical of administration policies as a vehicle for strongly condemning Truman on the floor of the House.[35]

The fact that MacArthur had strong support from key Republicans and was widely respected by the public made his firing more problematic for Truman. Sensing opportunity for the Republican Party, former president Herbert Hoover urged MacArthur to hurry back to the United States as soon as possible after his relief. MacArthur complied and was greeted with throngs of supporters and a 69% approval rating among the American public.[36] Men like Joseph McCarthy and Richard Nixon seized upon the general's popularity to advance their own agendas, further weakening Truman's position.[37]

Indeed, as MacArthur toured the United States, in uniform, the public was presented with a picture of a valiant warrior at odds with his president. And while Truman's reputation was significantly damaged by the episode, he ultimately survived, largely because other military officers presented a counterweight to MacArthur's military stature. George Marshall drafted the orders relieving MacArthur; Omar Bradley and the rest of the Joint Chiefs of Staff were unanimous in their approval of his dismissal. Furthermore, as MacArthur's tour of the United States turned into a campaign against the Truman administration, culminating in the keynote speech to the Republican convention in 1952, officers in the Pentagon provided counterattacks and support for Truman.[38] This politicization of

[35] Manchester, *American Caesar*, 638–40.

[36] Ibid., 645, 649.

[37] McCarthy used the firing as the basis for another charge of treason against Truman, and Nixon won additional support for using the firing as a basis to criticize U.S. policy in Asia. Manchester, *American Caesar*, 651.

[38] Although not quantified in any study, another dynamic probably working against MacArthur was the disdain that many in the military had for him. By the time of the Korean War, MacArthur was dramatically senior to every other officer on active duty (he had been superintendent of West Point when the then-current chief of the air force had been a cadet). Given this seniority, he did not have many natural allies, nor did he have peers who might support him against attacks from this new generation of military leaders. Furthermore, the days were long past when MacArthur fearlessly led from the front and inspired soldiers

military leadership did not come without cost, however; Walter Lippmann described the public clashes between generals as "the beginning of an almost intolerable thing in a republic: namely a schism within the armed forces between the generals of the Democratic party and the generals of the Republican party."[39]

The fact that this episode did not seem to have a lasting effect on the partisan leanings of the rest of the military is probably attributable to this public split between the generals, and it is also likely that it served as a warning about the dangers of overt involvement in partisan politics. Also working against the influence of the MacArthur incident on the attitudes and affiliations of the army was the rise of Dwight Eisenhower to national prominence, eclipsing the aspirations of MacArthur.

At first glance, it seems that Eisenhower's choice to run and serve as a Republican might have led a few members of the military in that direction. However, there was sufficient acrimony between Eisenhower and the military during his tenure as president that it is unclear whether his presidency pushed military voters into the Republican column.[40] In addition to fighting against military leaders over national security policy, Eisenhower found himself fighting against the Democrats in Congress to reduce the defense budget, offering a lower estimate of defense spending in all but one of his years as president.[41] Eisenhower's opposition to the dramatic growth in defense spending also led to his famous farewell speech, in which he railed against "the acquisition of unwarranted influence, whether sought or unsought, by the military-industrial complex."[42]

The presidencies of John Kennedy, Lyndon Johnson, and Richard Nixon were also characterized by tumultuous relationships between civilian and military leadership, and it is not clear that members of the military would have felt especially loyal to either party by the time Nixon resigned in 1974. This was, however, a key transitional period in American party politics. Southern conservatives were leaving the Democratic Party and becoming more Republican. Simultaneously, the war in Vietnam increasingly split the two parties as the Democrats became the "antiwar" party, putting an end to the Cold War consensus that the two parties had shared in regards to American foreign policy.

---

through personal acts of bravery, as he had as a regimental commander in World War I. By 1952 MacArthur was more likely to be remembered as the artistocratic proconsul of Japan. For an interesting later perspective on MacArthur from a marine who had served in World War II and written about Inchon, see Heinl, *Victory at High Tide.*

[39] Quoted in Manchester's *American Caesar*, 675.

[40] See Herspring, *The Pentagon and the Presidency*, and Bacevich and Kaplan, "Generals versus the President."

[41] Huntington, *Common Defense*, 261.

[42] Notably, early drafts of the speech included Congress in the "Military-Industrial-[Congressional]" complex. Eisenhower, "Farewell Radio Address."

Post-Vietnam

In what might be viewed as a perfect storm, several events during the 1970s contributed to an increase in both voting and Republican Party identification among members of the military. The increasing split between the two parties on issues of national defense, the advent of the all-volunteer force (AVF), and changes to laws regulating absentee voting set the conditions for a substantial shift in the military's relationship with partisan politics.

In 1973 the passage of the Uniformed and Overseas Citizens Absentee Voting Act removed the major impediment to voting by requiring states to accept absentee ballots from service members. The act was updated in 1986 and embraced fully by the Department of Defense by 1992, when the Pentagon set a target for the military to produce 1.2 million voters by Election Day.[43]

In terms of how members of the military actually voted, several trends suggested that the military would become more Republican in the coming years. Writing in 1975, Janowitz predicted that shifts in recruiting patterns and an increasing reliance on self-selection into service would produce more officers with "conservative perspectives" and a "right-wing political ideology."[44] Writing about universal service in 1957 Huntington also raised the idea that an army manned that way would be more representative of the country it served, at least in the enlisted ranks. In *The Soldier and the State* he outlined how universal service had created militaries where "the enlisted men became a cross section of the national population—citizens at heart—and officers became a separate professional group living in a world of their own with few ties to outside society."[45] This statement implied that in an all-volunteer era, the enlisted ranks would not be a cross section of the population and that the officer ranks could become even more isolated from society. Many authors shared similar concerns about the end of the draft in 1973.[46]

Looking at the attitudes of military personnel in the years immediately after the end of conscription, Jerald Bachman, John Blair, and David Segal warned that the military risked becoming ideologically distinct from the American public.[47] In their analysis of surveys of military personnel between 1972 and 1975, they found significant attitudinal differences between careerists and noncareerists. As the AVF was more likely to be

---

[43] Gellman, "Pentagon Intensifies Effort."

[44] Janowitz, "All-Volunteer Military," 442 and 444.

[45] Huntington, *The Soldier and the State*, 39.

[46] For comprehensive summaries of the views of scholars at the time, see Janowitz, "All-Volunteer Military," and Moskos, "The Military."

[47] Bachman, Blair, and Segal, *All-Volunteer Force*.

populated with careerists than a conscript force, the feeling was that the views of the military would be less reflective of society in the coming years. Specifically, and understandably, the authors saw the types of people who would self-select into a career of military service as being more promilitary than their noncareerist peers and much more promilitary than civilians. These career military personnel were "a great deal more favorable toward the military organization, more eager for U.S. military supremacy . . . , more willing to make use of military power, much more in favor of enlarged military (versus civilian) influence over U.S. policy affecting the military."[48]

Although these views were not distinctly partisan in the abstract, they tended to match the views of Republicans in the newly divided atmosphere of the post-Vietnam era. Whereas up through the Johnson administration differences in foreign policy views rarely fell along partisan lines, the cleavages between the two parties grew dramatically wider during the 1970s and 1980s. In analyzing foreign policy views, Ole Holsti found that while the two parties were sufficiently close during the pre-Vietnam era that political independents typically fell to the left or right of both parties, in the post-Vietnam era the gap was sufficiently wide that the views of independents now fell between party lines.[49] Furthermore, the views of Republicans became distinctly militant in that they began to view military superiority as the preferred approach to achieving peace. In contrast, Democrats during this era were more supportive of cooperative internationalism, an approach emphasizing diplomacy and the use of international institutions to help resolve disputes.

Given these divergent party views, an increasingly careerist, and consequently promilitary, force began to gravitate toward the party that saw a more central role for military power in international relations. Contributing to this shift was the fact that during this era the terms *liberal* and *conservative* were beginning to correlate more and more with Democratic and Republican Party identification.[50] With the realignment of southern conservatives and the Republican embrace of "traditional values," it is not surprising that an institution that already identified itself as conservative would begin to migrate to the Republican Party.[51]

Survey data from Holsti's Foreign Policy Leadership Project (FPLP) show that by 1976 a third of senior military leaders (majors and above)

[48] Ibid., 140.

[49] Holsti, *Public Opinion*, 168–76.

[50] Between 1972 and 2004, the correlation between party identification and liberal-conservative identification increased from just over 0.3 in 1972 to just under 0.6 in 2004. See Abramowitz and Saunders, "Ideological Realignment." Also Shapiro and Bloch-Elkon in "Political Polarization."

[51] Betros, "Political Partisanship," 509.

identified with the Republican Party, and only about one in ten described him or herself as a Democrat. The remaining 55% stated that they identified either as independents (46%) or as "other" or "none" (9%).[52] This represented the beginning of a substantial realignment, as over the next two decades military leaders would overwhelmingly shift to an identification with the Republican Party.

The symbolic end of the Democratic Party's appeal to military personnel was the defeat of Senator Henry Jackson's bids to become president in 1972 and 1976. Jackson's stance on defense issues stood in stark contrast to George McGovern's, the candidate for peace in 1972, and Jimmy Carter's, a supporter of unilateral arms cuts and the withdrawal of military forces from South Korea.[53] These victories by antiwar candidates cemented the impression among many that the Democratic Party was also antimilitary.

The perception that Democrats were no longer supportive of a strong military and the disastrous relationship between Jimmy Carter, ironically a navy man himself, and the military establishment sped along the alignment of military leaders with the Republican Party. By the end of Carter's term, a full 46% of senior military officers in the FPLP surveys identified themselves as Republicans, and some estimated that only 1% of officers preferred Carter over Ronald Reagan in the 1980 election.[54] The extent of the shift during this period was significant enough that Janowitz felt there were clear signs of a trend to the right among military officers by the end of 1970s.[55]

Building on this momentum, Reagan actively courted the military, making "no secret of his admiration and respect for members of the military" and actively expanding the militarybuildup begun in the last years of Carter's presidency.[56] As a result of this effort, 53% of the military officers in the FPLP surveys reported identifying with the Republican Party in 1984. The extent of the relationship between the military and the Republican Party was such that in the aftermath of the 1984 election it was revealed that the Pentagon had shared data on military personnel with the GOP

[52] Holsti, "Widening Gap." The military sample in 1976 numbered 500, most of whom were from the Naval Post-Graduate School; this population consisted mostly of officers with between 8 and 12 years of service. Subsequent surveys went to the National War College and included 115 to 177 officers. The National War College is a higher-level school that is attended by lieutenant colonels and colonels (generally 16 to 26 years of service).

[53] A general overview of the Democratic Party's evolution on defense issues during this era can be found in Traub's "The Things They Carry."

[54] In Holsti's survey, 10% identified themselves as Democrats. Holsti, "Widening Gap," 11, table 1, and Herspring, *The Pentagon and the Presidency*, 264.

[55] Janowitz and Wesbrook, *Political Education of Soldiers*, 74.

[56] Herspring, *The Pentagon and the Presidency*, 265–77.

just prior to the election, in violation of its own rules on the release of such data.[57] By 1988, 59% of military leaders identified with the Republican Party, and only 9% identified as Democrats and the remaining 27% as independents.

After the Cold War

Whereas events after Vietnam set the conditions for the military's gravitation to the Republican Party, it was in the tumultuous period after the fall of the Soviet Union that this alignment would contribute to significant friction in civil-military relations.

While President George H. W. Bush was to initiate the massive downsizing of the military after the Cold War, his relationship with the armed forces was defined primarily by the war to liberate Kuwait. For most senior military leaders, many of whom had begun their service in the 1960s, the Gulf War waged under Bush was a cathartic event that erased lingering resentment over the Vietnam War. In the eyes of many officers, the Gulf War exemplified the way all wars should be fought—with overwhelming force and little direct involvement from political elites.[58] It is therefore not surprising that members of the military might continue to drift toward the party of the president who had overseen this war and away from the Democratic Party, which was substantially less supportive of the war.[59] By 1992 the FPLP surveys showed that 61% of senior military leaders supported the Republican Party compared with only 6% who favored the Democratic Party.

It was in this environment that Bill Clinton entered as the Democratic candidate for president. As the party's nominee, Clinton began to take criticism for his avoidance of military service during the Vietnam War. Paradoxically, William Crowe, a retired admiral and former chairman of the Joint Chiefs of Staff, stepped out to defend Clinton. Although part of Crowe's rationale for publicly endorsing Clinton was to counter charges that the military would not serve under Clinton as commander in chief, his endorsement opened the door for future endorsements by recently retired generals.[60]

[57] Burnham, "Pentagon Is Faulted."

[58] Kittfield, *Prodigal Soldiers.*

[59] Prior to, during, and after the Persian Gulf War, there was about a twenty-point differential between Republicans and Democrats in the proportion who supported the conflict. Holsti, *Public Opinion*, 173.

[60] In commenting on his decision to endorse, Crowe said, "I was quite upset by the thrust of the campaign rhetoric, particularly regarding the military. While the Republicans never said it explicitly, implicit in what they were saying was 'if this guy's elected, the military shouldn't serve.' I thought that was dangerous." Anderson, "An Admiral at the Court of St. James's." See also Kaplan, "Generals Used to Be Neutral." Crowe and Chanoff, *Line of Fire.*

Despite this endorsement, Clinton had a rocky relationship with the armed forces. In addition to inheriting a military in the midst of a massive downsizing after the Cold War, the contentious issue of whether homosexuals should be allowed to serve defined his early relationship with the military. Top military officers expressed their reservations in private and in public forums about allowing homosexuals to serve openly.[61] The relationship would grow only worse as the Clinton administration committed military forces to missions that many felt the military and the United States should avoid.

The situation was such in the early 1990s that Richard Kohn, a prominent historian and scholar of civil-military relations, declared that the relationship between civilian and military elites had reached the level of a "crisis."[62] Shortly thereafter, the Center for Strategic and International Studies convened a conference to assess whether U.S. civil-military relations were in "crisis or transition."[63] The conferees generally agreed that there was no crisis in civil-military relations and that the level of conflict remained within historical norms.[64] Unfortunately, the authors did not address the social and political attitudes of the military directly. They did, however, note the increased prestige of the military vis-à-vis civilian elites and made passing mention of the increasing divide between civilian and military leaders in the AVF era.[65]

The fact that participants in the CSIS study did not feel there was a crisis did not mean they did not recognize points of friction in civil-military relations. This friction, and the military's apparent shift rightward, would continue through the rest of the 1990s. By 1996 it appeared that senior military officers had become a decidedly Republican voting bloc, with 67% reporting Republican Party identification in the FPLP surveys compared with only 7% who identified as Democrats. It appeared that after 1996 the divide continued to grow, as the revelation of Clinton's affair with Monica Lewinsky led many in the military to criticize the president openly and call for his removal.[66]

---

[61] See comments by Powell in Herspring, *The Pentagon and the Presidency*, 339, and Cushman, "Top Military Officers."

[62] Kohn, "Out of Control."

[63] Snider and Carlton-Carew, *U.S. Civil-Military Relations*.

[64] Feaver, "Civil Military Conflict," 129.

[65] Snider and Carlton-Carew noted in the introduction of *U.S. Civil-Military Relations*: "It is perhaps ironic that at a time in U.S. history when we have demonstrably the most effective military leaders in decades, they are challenged to maintain their ethical bearings amidst tensions and conflicts with civilian leaders whom the public holds in lower esteem than the military." In his essay in the volume, Michael Desch mentioned the "changing social and political character of the all-volunteer force" but offered only anecdotal evidence and previous assertions by Huntington. Desch, "United States Civil-Military Relations."

[66] Myers, "Testing of a President."

These developments led more than a few observers to conclude that the military was becoming overly politicized and that a problematic "gap" was developing between the military and American society. The most prominent of these observers was Thomas Ricks, a journalist who wrote about these developments in 1997.[67] Ricks wrote primarily about his observations of the Marine Corps, but he was quickly followed by many scholars from the CSIS forum, who sought to study comprehensively the attitudes of senior military leaders across the services through the TISS surveys discussed in chapter 1. The TISS surveys confirmed the general trend of Republicanization among senior military leaders but, in keeping with the CSIS conference, found no evidence of an impending crisis in civil-military relations.

Many others felt that this shift in attitudes should not have been unexpected and questioned whether these developments warranted major concern. Military Historian (and Colonel) Lance Betros felt that the increase in Republican identification among officers reflected a natural conservative alliance and the perceived advantage of the Republican Party on issues related to national security.[68] Joseph Collins, then a retired colonel and fellow at CSIS, responded to Holsti's FPLP data by observing that "liberals . . . disappeared in the military [between 1976 and 1996], something no doubt related to Franklin Roosevelt, Harry Truman, and John Kennedy fading from current memories." He also asked, "Given the sad record of the Carter years and the unique problems of the Clinton administration, is it any wonder that Republicans did as well as they did in a poll of military officers?"[69] In 2007 a former sergeant succinctly summarized the internal army narrative about the Democratic Party:

After that [Vietnam], Democrats abdicated national security to the Republican Party. What was Bill Clinton's very first foray into defense policy? "Don't ask. Don't tell." Well done, that. You wonder why the military votes overwhelmingly for the GOP? I'd suggest that for years they had little choice: the Democratic Party gave up and left the room, and didn't even pretend to want the votes.[70]

[67] See Ricks, "Widening Gap" and *Making the Corps*. Ricks was a reporter for the *Wall Street Journal* at the time of these stories.

[68] Betros, "Political Partisanship," 502.

[69] Collins was surely referring to the invasion of Afghanistan by the Soviets and the Iran hostage crisis, although, ironically, Carter's handling of the crisis and his hands-off attitude toward military planning for the rescue attempt increased his reputation among senior military officers. Collins and Holsti, "Civil-Military Relations," 201. For a discussion of the reaction of senior officers to Carter's handling of the hostage rescue crisis, see Herspring, *The Pentagon and the Presidency*, 263.

[70] This quote was made in the context of an article highlighting how the perspective of members of the military is changing after the Iraq War. Douglas, "Elect More Jim Webbs."

Questions of causes and implications aside, by this period it was accepted as conventional wisdom that the military was predominantly composed of Republicans. During the presidential election of 2000, the Republican Party scrambled to ensure that the absentee ballots of military personnel were included in any Florida recount, on the assumption that these votes were for Republican candidate George W. Bush. The efforts even included charges from Norman Schwarzkopf, retired commander of forces in Desert Storm, that the Democratic Party was unfairly disenfranchising military voters.[71]

After the close Florida recall and the events of September 11, 2001, it was a certainty that the military would again play a prominent role during the 2004 election. The election did not disappoint, and the attitudes of members of the military and military issues took center stage during the campaign. In addition to heated debates over the military service records of the Democratic candidate John F. Kerry and Bush, the question of which candidate had the support of the military was a repeated theme. With U.S. forces engaged in a controversial war, the sentiment of those carrying the burden of the conflict became symbolically important. The military votes themselves were also deemed important due to the potential effect of absentee ballots in closely contested states.[72] In the end Bush managed to obtain the endorsement of a greater number of retired generals than the Kerry campaign, and the limited data on military attitudes that existed at the time gave Bush an advantage over Kerry among members of the military.[73]

It is here that this book offers a unique perspective on the conventional wisdom of the political attitudes and activities of the armed forces in 2004. Specifically, this book analyzes the results of the C&S Survey to assess political attitudes and inclination toward political participation of the active-duty army in 2004, with sufficient data to distinguish between the attitudes of officers and soldiers. An analysis of these data will enable us to confirm or refute conventional wisdom about the political and social attitudes of members of the military in addition to providing a baseline with which to analyze other, less representative surveys of the military population. In the concluding chapter, I will also bring this historical narrative up to date by analyzing data from the Military Times surveys taken over the last three years to assess the extent to which the army retains the outlook described in detail in the following chapters.

[71] Mazur, "The Bullying of America," 9.

[72] Tyson, "A Strident Minority."

[73] The Military Times surveys reported a 71% approval rating for George Bush among their respondents. In August 2004 the NAES survey asked 7,337 respondents whether they thought Bush or Kerry had more support from retired generals and admirals. About 47% felt that Bush had more than Kerry (the correct answer), and 33% thought Kerry had greater support.

Implications for Civil-Military Relations

Not a single theorist of civil-military relations believes overt partisanship by members of the military is a good idea. The two primary theorists of the last fifty years, Morris Janowitz and Samuel Huntington, disagreed widely about how the military should be structured and utilized, but both were averse to the military's taking sides or being directly involved in partisan political contests. Both wrote their seminal books on the topic at a time when the military was in a historically novel position. Huntington and Janowitz, writing in 1957 and 1960 respectively, addressed the massive growth and permanent nature of the military establishment at the beginning of the Cold War. Instead of drawing down and retreating to stateside posts, the armed forces found themselves on permanent bases in Korea, Germany, Japan, and outposts throughout the world, positioned forward to counter the continuous communist threat. For the first time in its history, the United States would maintain a large standing military. Both Huntington and Janowitz were concerned with how to maintain civilian control over this newly powerful institution.[74]

Huntington's approach to this problem called for a distinct separation between the political and military spheres. Huntington describes the ideal form of civil-military relations as "Objective Civilian Control." In this model civilian and military leaders have distinct areas of responsibility, and the autonomy of each should not be violated. For civilian leaders, this means not interfering with military professionals as they manage the application of violence. For military leaders, it means not getting involved in politics. In Huntington's words, "The antithesis of objective civilian control is military participation in politics," and "The essence of objective civilian control is the recognition of autonomous military professionalism."[75] And while Huntington's view of "politics" is more expansive than partisan political struggles alone, it is clear that this form of political participation is included in the area he marks "off-limits" for military personnel. In his view, "the participation of military officers in politics undermines their professionalism, curtailing their professional competence, dividing the profession against itself, and substituting extraneous values for professional values."[76]

---

[74] It is instructive to know that both also wrote after the release of *The Power Elite*. C. Wright Mills's book was the first to portray the "warlords," or top military officers, on a par with corporate and political elites. Mills, *The Power Elite*. See also summary of Mills in Moskos, "The Military."

[75] Huntington, *Soldier and the State*, 83.

[76] Ibid., 71.

Janowitz did not believe in such a clear demarcation between military and political spheres, but he shared Huntington's view that officers should remain nonpartisan. Janowitz believed that members of the military had largely been able to maintain their honor and remain "above politics" in domestic affairs.[77] He did, however, foresee how the military might begin to violate the admonition to not take sides in partisan politics.

In Janowitz's view, part of the military's ability to remain neutral was due to the "social and political consensus" in American society.[78] Not only had political debates in the United States typically been located within a narrow range of competing views, but views over foreign policy were largely unified during the Cold War.[79] While political leaders argued on the margins of American foreign policy, there was overwhelming consensus that communism presented a serious threat to American security during the Cold War.[80] In this setting, the debate was not over who the enemy was but how best to counter that enemy. As such, military leaders would often find themselves at odds with civilian political leaders over questions of force structure and posture, but these debates rarely broke along partisan lines because there were no significant differences between the two parties during this era.

However, what would happen in the aftermath of the Cold War without a consensus on the broad aims of American foreign policy? Might the military begin to take sides with whichever faction appeared to place a greater emphasis on sustaining a large military? Sophisticated military leaders have always understood that "in seeking to influence the fortunes of their services, in advising on strategic national defense policies, and in spending the bulk of the federal budget, a nonpartisan stance is essential."[81] But Janowitz wrote this in 1960. What if it appeared that one political party consistently favored the military's ideals while an antagonistic relationship arose between the military and the other party?

Such a development, combined with the centrality of the president to the military's view of leadership, may have contributed to the increase in affiliation with the Republican Party. Huntington recognized that after the Civil War the president was central to the military's relationship with the political system. He observed that at the beginning of the twentieth century military officers had an "inbred respect for the integrity of the chain of command stretching from the Commander in Chief to the lowest

[77] Janowitz, *Professional Soldier*, 233.

[78] Ibid.

[79] For a more in-depth view of the relatively narrow range of domestic debates, see Hartz, *Liberal Tradition*.

[80] Zaller and Chiu, "Government's Little Helper," and Dempsey, "Public Evaluation."

[81] Janowitz, *Professional Soldier*, 233–34.

enlisted man."[82] General George Patton probably best encapsulated this sentiment when he said, "I am in the pay of the U.S. Government. If I vote against the administration I am voting against my commander-in-chief."[83] In many ways Huntington argued for strengthening this relationship by increasing the power of the secretary of defense and, by extension, the ability of the president to exercise control over the military services.[84]

Given the role of the president in defining the civil-military relationship, one might expect the military to begin to gravitate to one party if that party's presidents were consistently viewed as more supportive of the military than presidents from the other party. As Joseph Collins noted, and Dale Herspring elaborated in his book *The Pentagon and the Presidency*, since 1976 Republican presidents have typically been perceived as more supportive of the military. Although Carter built up the defense budget in the final years of his presidency, he had already been labeled weak on national security due to the twin humiliations of the Soviet invasion of Afghanistan and the Iranian hostage crisis. Reagan, on the other hand, continued the buildup of military forces and oversaw the largest military spending increase ever to occur while the United States was not engaged in a shooting war. This was followed by the presidency of George H. W. Bush, who presided over the dramatic military victory over Iraq in the Gulf War.

Following the Bush presidency were the strained Clinton years, when the end of the Cold War brought a massive drawdown of military forces.[85] Furthermore, in the absence of the Cold War, the political parties began to stake out distinct views of how American military power should be used. Among Democrats there was fairly consistent support for intervention in places like Bosnia and Kosovo, whereas the Republicans staked out a more noninterventionist stance. This stance also happened to match the frustration of military leaders over these roles and their reluctance to engage in anything less than full-scale conventional war. Combined with heated debates over the integration of homosexuals and the greater integration of women into the armed forces—which Democrats generally favored and Republicans typically opposed—it should not be surprising that members of the military gravitated further toward the Republican Party.

Underlying the changing perceptions of Republicans and Democrats on national security issues was the increasing correlation between the conser-

[82] Huntington, *Soldier and the State*, 259.

[83] Galloway and Johnson, *West Point*, 237.

[84] Huntington, *Soldier and the State*, 428–54. This effort culminated in the passage of Goldwater-Nichols. See Locher, *Victory on the Potomac*.

[85] This drawdown was of course initiated under Bush but presided over by Clinton, in an ironic reversal of the Carter-Reagan buildup.

vative ideological label and Republican Party identification. In the late 1950s and early 1960s, both Huntington and Janowitz viewed "conservatism" as a distinctly apolitical label. Both viewed the label in the sense that Hartz saw it, namely partisan conflict in America was taking place within the confines of liberalism, whereas conservatism was an identification with no direct linkage to contemporary political debates. Officers in this era could therefore describe themselves as conservative without expressing any partisan affiliation.[86] Janowitz, however, did see that even during this period this definition of "conservatism" was becoming more imprecise as a way to describe the outlook of officers. In retrospect, the definition of "conservatism" itself was changing, and officers were changing with it. This migration of the conservative label from a pragmatic and pessimistic worldview to an explicitly ideological and partisan position was another factor contributing to the migration of military officers to the Republican Party.[87]

As officers faced this changing foreign and domestic political landscape, they might be forgiven for neglecting the imperative to remain resolutely neutral. After all, the military education system did not prepare them to understand the nuances and complications of domestic partisan politics.[88] Furthermore, Huntington left the door open for military officers to take positions on political questions and to feel no compunction about sup-

---

[86] Janowitz, *Professional Soldier*, 236.

[87] Shapiro and Bloch-Elkin, "Political Polarization."

[88] Discussion of appropriate norms of civil-military behavior has generally been nonexistent in precommissioning training and only recently has it received any focused attention at the military academies. One of the few exceptions to this has been the widespread dissemination of General of the Army Douglas MacArthur's farewell speech to the West Point Corps of Cadets in 1962. Toward the end of the speech, MacArthur dedicated two paragraphs to civil-military relations that appear to follow Huntington's formulation of a clear division of responsibilities:

Others will debate the controversial issues, national and international, which divide men's minds; but serene, calm, aloof, you stand as the Nation's war-guardian, as its lifeguard from the raging tides of international conflict, as its gladiator in the arena of battle. . . .

Let civilian voices argue the merits or demerits of our processes of government; whether our strength is being sapped by deficit financing, indulged in too long, by federal paternalism grown too mighty, by power groups grown too arrogant, by politics grown too corrupt, by crime grown too rampant, by morals grown too low, by taxes grown too high, by extremists grown too violent; whether our personal liberties are as thorough and complete as they should be. These great national problems are not for your professional participation or military solution.

These, however, are among the least discussed paragraphs of that speech, nor is any part of the core curriculum dedicated to discussing MacArthur's own problematic relationship with civilian authority. MacArthur, "Address."

porting a political party. Janowitz's assessment of the state of military education in 1960 is directly relevant:

> Military education at all levels fails to give the officer a full understanding of the realities of practical politics as it operates in domestic affairs. Because it is constrained in exploring the strength and weakness of the democratic political process, military education does not necessarily develop realism and respect for the system. Its content is still dominated by moralistic exhortations regarding ideal goals. Equally important, *military education has little interest in discussing the standards that should govern the behavior of officers vis-à-vis civilian appointees and Congress. There is little emphasis on the complex problems of maintaining administrative neutrality.* [Emphasis mine.][89]

While Huntington explicitly recommended against military involvement in partisan politics, curiously he left the door open for political advocacy with his own "moralistic exhortations" at the end of *The Soldier and the State*. In the body of the book, Huntington gives his view of the military ethic, which he contends "holds that the security of the state depends upon the creation and maintenance of strong military forces. It urges the limitation of state action to the direct interests of the state, the restriction of extensive commitments, and the undesirability of bellicose or adventurous policies."[90]

However, a determination of "the direct interests of the state" requires political perspective and judgment, not an apolitical posture. Furthermore, Huntington explicitly states at the end of his book, "The requisite for military security is a shift in basic American values from liberalism to conservatism."[91] He also states that "America can learn more from West Point than West Point from America."[92] And while Huntington tries to make clear that it is not up to the military to bring America to conservatism, and that the military should not seek to promote this change through political advocacy, his approach might encourage military officers to believe that they have a significant political role to play.[93]

---

[89] Janowitz, *Professional Soldier*, 429.

[90] Huntington, *Soldier and the State*, 79.

[91] Ibid., 464.

[92] Ibid., 466.

[93] Although a focus on Huntington's prose at the end of *The Soldier and the State* may be unfair in the context of the rest of his work on civil-military relations, particularly his second book (*The Common Defense: Strategic Programs in National Politics*), it is worth noting that for years *The Soldier and the State* was the only book on the army's professional reading list to address civil-military relations. Anecdotal evidence also suggests that the main idea many officers take away from the book is that civilians would be better off if they modeled their worldviews on Huntington's interpretation of military conservatism. For a more thorough discussion of how Huntington's second book fleshes out his view of civil-military relations, see Betts, "Are Civil-Military Relations Still a Problem?"

Each of these factors combined to create a renewed interest in civil-military relations in the 1990s. Whereas Janowitz and Huntington were motivated by the unique historical position of the military at the height of the Cold War, the post–Cold War environment introduced new challenges to civil-military relationships, inspiring a new interest in the topic.

By the 1990s, the military had been a powerful institution for several decades. Unlike the time of *The Soldier and the State* and *The Professional Soldier,* however, the military of the 1990s was a widely respected institution. It enjoyed a level of prestige that it had not had in the 1950s and 1960s.[94] As David King and Zachary Karabell noted in *The Generation of Trust: How the U.S. Military Has Regained the Public's Confidence since Vietnam,* the military occupied a very respected position in the opinion of the American public.[95] This may have contributed to a feeling among more members of the military that it was acceptable to speak out on political issues normally left to other, less respected, branches of government, and it also heightened the value of military endorsements to political actors.

For some, this may have been a welcome development, particularly those who perceived the newly active and partisan military as supportive of their political views. However, scholars of civil-military relations were unanimous in suggesting that it was not in the military's or the nation's interest for officers to be overtly political. King and Karabell suggested that part of the military's newfound prestige would be lost if the military came to be viewed as politically driven.[96] Marybeth Ulrich called for new norms of "principled officership" that would specifically discourage political activity and encourage avoidance of party affiliation.[97] Herspring suggested that if the military's affiliation with the Republican Party became permanent, this would have serious repercussions for American civil-military relations.[98]

There was even some trepidation among Republicans about the military's newfound political voice. According to Andrew Bacevich, the lesson that Republicans took from the military's performance in the 1990s was that the military was simply incompetent. In this interpretation, the willingness of retired military officers to advocate publicly for political candidates did nothing more for the army than degrade the apolitical reputation and professional autonomy of the institution.[99]

---

[94] Janowitz, *Professional Soldier,* 1.
[95] King and Karabell, *Generation of Trust.*
[96] Ibid., 66.
[97] Ulrich, "Infusing Civil-Military Relations," 258.
[98] Herspring, *The Pentagon and the Presidency,* 425.
[99] Bacevich, *New American Militarism,* 61–62.

Even after the strong endorsements that George W. Bush received from a number of recently retired military officers during the presidential election of 2000, several observers of the presidential transition described the contentious relationship between the military and a new Republican administration intent on asserting control over the military establishment.[100] Whatever capital the military may have felt it had with the Republican Party seemed to evaporate during arguments over the restructuring of the American military.

In short, there was a consensus among military scholars of varying political views that the politicization of the military was a distressing development that should be reversed. Although only a few described the situation as an immediate crisis in civil-military relations, the tone of most discussions revealed the underlying perception of threat. These analyses of the relationship between the military and the state provided no comprehensive assessment of whether the new political activism of the military was a passing phenomenon or a permanent development. As we have seen, a convergence of events and personalities led senior military officers to an overt affiliation with the Republican Party at the beginning of the twenty-first century. Furthermore, the increased prestige of the military, combined with the "careerist" nature of service in the AVF and the historically unique break between civilian elites and military service, left many observers uneasy about the status of American civil-military relations.[101]

We do not, however, know the extent of this affiliation or much about the content of military views beyond snapshots of senior military leaders. This research therefore seeks a clearer picture of the determinants and content of the social and political attitudes of military personnel. The goal of this book is to provide a more nuanced view of the attitudes of this population and a baseline understanding from which to assess future trends and potential conflicts.

---

[100] For a discussion of the new administration's approach, see Feaver, *Armed Servants*, 287–90. Also Cohen, "Rumsfeld's War."

[101] Roth-Douquet and Schaeffer, *AWOL*.

Chapter 3

An Overview of Army Demographics

AS THE UNITED STATES MOVES farther away from the memory of World War II and deeper into the all-volunteer era, fewer people gain exposure to members of the military. Those not in the military are often left with stereotypes to inform their understanding of those who serve. The intent of this chapter is to provide an overview of those aspects of military service relevant to the analysis of military opinion. Here I consider the demographic composition of the army and explain some of the ways in which the military differs from the general population, specifically in the areas of gender, race, education, and income. When discussing the army, I refer specifically to the active-duty army. I do not include members of the reserves or the National Guard.

The Army's Rank Structure

As of February 2004 there were 486,812 active-duty members in the U.S. Army. This population can be split into three primary groups: enlisted soldiers (hereafter referred to simply as soldiers), warrant officers, and regular officers. Soldiers make up the bulk of the army's population—in 2004 about 84%. Soldiers fill the ranks from private (PV1—colloquially known as "buck private") to command sergeant major. These ranks are also often referred to by their corresponding pay grade. For example, the lowest rank of private is also referred to as an E-1, and the highest enlisted rank falls into the pay grade of E-9. The most populated rank in the army is E-4, which includes the ranks of specialist and corporal.[1] About 24% of the army is in this rank, which in 2004 numbered just under 118,000 soldiers. Soldiers will typically achieve this rank by the end of three years of service.

The army's noncommissioned officer (NCO) corps consists of those soldiers in leadership positions with responsibility over other soldiers. The NCO ranks start with corporal and include all higher enlisted ranks up to command sergeant major. In addition to corporals and command

---

[1] The specialist rank is the last vestige of an older dual-track system that was phased out in the 1980s. Both specialists and corporals are E4s, but the rank of corporal is awarded to soldiers in leadership positions. Although both earn the same pay, a corporal is considered a noncommissioned officer (NCO).

sergeants major, the NCO ranks include sergeants (E-5), staff sergeants (E-6), sergeants first class (E-7), and master sergeants or first sergeants (E-8). Warrant officers fall between soldiers and regular commissioned officers. Just over 2% of the army fills the warrant officer ranks. They are "highly specialized, single-track specialty officers" who typically spend several years as soldiers before becoming warrant officers.[2] Jobs for warrant officers include helicopter pilot, maintenance technician, and property book manager (a supply system manager). I include warrant officers to calculate aggregate army attitudes and insert them in the enlisted subsample for comparisons between officers and soldiers.

The army's officer corps consists of the ranks of second lieutenant (O-1) through general (O-10). These ranks make up 14% of the total army population. Officers are required to have a bachelor's degree and go through precommissioning training before beginning service (via the Reserve Officer Training Corps [ROTC], the United States Military Academy, or Officer Candidate School [OCS]), although there are exceptions for those entering into highly specialized fields like medicine.[3] Captains compose the bulk of the officer corps and make up just under 5% of the total army population. There are close to 400 officers in the ranks of brigadier general, major general, lieutenant general, and general. These are the army's most senior leaders. See table 3.1 for a more detailed breakdown of the army's rank structure.

Gender, Race, and Ethnicity

According to the army's capstone doctrinal manual, *Field Manual No. 1: The Army*, "The Army's rich mix of Soldiers' backgrounds and cultures is a natural enabler of cultural awareness."[4] And while the army has had a tumultuous history in terms of racial integration, its efforts in this area have generally been considered a success.[5] As of February 2004, the army was approximately 60% white, 10% Hispanic, 24% black, and 7% "other."[6] Comparably, about 76% of the U.S. population in 2004 classi-

---

[2] See *http://usawocc.army.mil/whatiswo.htm* (accessed March 23, 2009) for more details on the origins and structure of this rank category. Warrant Officer Career Center, "What Is a WO?" United States Army Warrant Officer Career Center.

[3] An officer entering through OCS, which is a common route for soldiers who wish to become officers, can sometimes complete his or her bachelor's degree in the first few years after being commissioned.

[4] U.S. Army, Department of the Army Headquarters, *Field Manual No. 1*, par. 1–19.

[5] Moskos and Butler, *All That We Can Be*.

[6] The U.S. government does not officially recognize this combined racial and ethnic categorization; instead it uses a five-category racial classification in addition to a separate indicator for anyone who is also of Hispanic heritage. As the Hispanic classification is relatively new, many senior officers could be classified as Hispanic but spent the early years of their career classified as white. It is also likely that the army is undercounting Hispanics by as

TABLE 3.1
The Army's Rank Structure

Rank	Pay grade	% of army population	Years of service[a]
Private (PV1)	E1	3.3	0 to 1
Private (PV2)	E2	6.4	0 to 2
Private first class	E3	12.6	0 to 3
Specialist/Corporal	E4	24.2	2 to 4
Sergeant	E5	15.0	3 to 6
Staff sergeant	E6	11.5	5 to 12
Sergeant first class	E7	7.6	7 to 16
First sergeant/Master sergeant	E8	2.2	14 to 20+
Command sergeant major/Sergeant major	E9	0.7	20+
Warrant officers	WO1–WO5	2.5	0 to 20+
Second lieutenant	O1	1.4	0 to 1
First lieutenant	O2	1.9	1 to 3
Captain	O3	4.7	3 to 9
Major	O4	3.0	8 to 17
Lieutenant colonel	O5	1.9	15 to 20
Colonel	O6	0.9	18 to 20+
General officer[b]	O7–O10	0.1	20+

Source: Army Personnel Database, February 2004.

[a] Years of service are approximate and represent only typical career patterns. There are significant variations in career patterns and timelines, particularly at higher ranks and among those who spend time in the enlisted ranks before becoming officers. In recent times the army has also reduced timelines for promotions to make up for shortages in higher ranks.

[b] The general officer category includes officers in the ranks of brigadier general (1 star), major general (2 stars), lieutenant general (3 stars), and general (4 stars).

fied themselves as white, and 12% identified themselves as black and 14% as Hispanic.[7] The distribution of races and ethnicities is uneven across the ranks, however. As shown in figure 3.1, a vast majority of senior officers are white. Minorities are, however, well represented in the senior enlisted ranks, where whites are actually in the minority (see figure 3.1).[8]

---

much as 3–5%. For a more detailed discussion of Hispanics in the army, see Dempsey and Shapiro, "Army's Hispanic Future."

[7] These numbers do not add to 100% due to the fact that the U.S. Census Bureau asks questions about race separately from the question about Hispanic heritage. Many people will classify themselves solely as Hispanic, but a significant number will also identify with another racial category.

[8] The "Jr. Enlisted" category includes all soldiers in grades E-1 through E-3. The "NCO" category includes E-4s through E-6s, and "Sr. NCO" includes E-7s through E-9s. In the

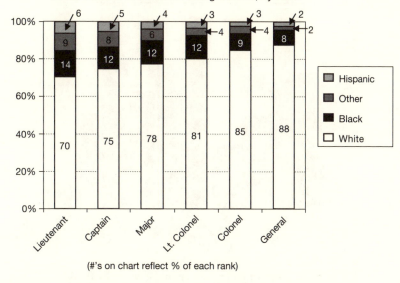

Racial & Ethnic Distribution among Officers, by Rank

(#'s on chart reflect % of each rank)

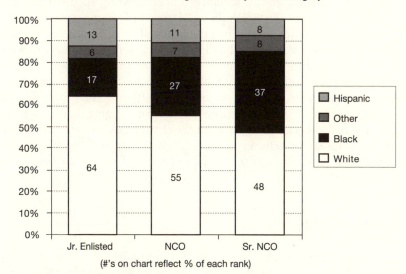

Racial & Ethnic Distribution among Soldiers, by Rank Category

(#'s on chart reflect % of each rank)

Figure 3.1 Racial and Ethnic Composition of the Army
Source: Army Personnel Database, February 2004

officer chart, the "Lieutenant" category includes both second and first lieutenants. The "General" category includes all categories of general officer, from brigadier to four-star general.

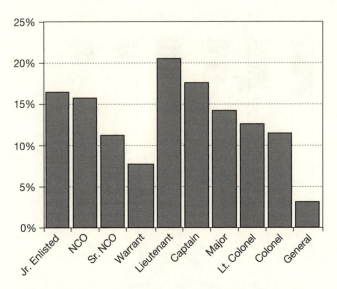

Figure 3.2 Proportion of Women in the Army, by Rank
Source: Army Personnel Database, February 2004

After the advent of the all-volunteer force, the army opened a number of positions to women in which they had previously been unable to serve. Over the years the number of positions available to women has grown, although women are still prohibited by law from serving in positions with a high likelihood of direct ground combat.[9] As of 2004, about 73,000 women were serving in the army, making up 15% of the army population. Approximately 18% of those women were officers. The proportion of women in the army by rank category is shown in figure 3.2. As for the interplay between race and gender in the army, black women have made significant inroads into the institution. Black women make up 40% of the total female population in the army and 63% of women in the senior NCO ranks.

Education and Income

Over the last few decades the military has been fairly successful in maintaining a high school diploma or GED as the baseline standard for entry. Typically only 1% of recruits do not meet this standard, although the proportion of army recruits with high school diplomas has declined since

[9] For an overview of the history and debates surrounding women in the military, readers are encouraged to review the U.S. General Accounting Office's "Gender Issues."

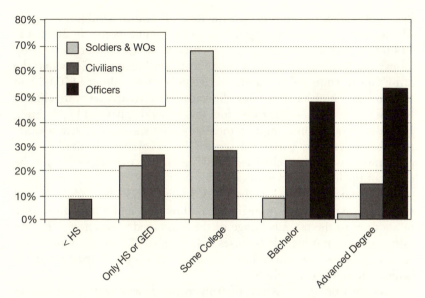

Figure 3.3 Educational Attainment in the Army and Civilian Populations
Source: C&S Survey and 2004 National Annenberg Election Survey

the 1990s and was at 82% in 2005 (compared with 80% for the civilian population).[10] The army also encourages and supports supplemental education during a soldier's service. As a result, proportionally fewer members of the army have only a high school diploma or less compared with the civilian population. The majority of soldiers and warrant officers have an associate's degree or some college credit in addition to a high school diploma. Figure 3.3 shows that a negligible portion of the officer corps has less than a bachelor's degree, and a majority of officers have at least a master's degree.

A similar pattern holds for the distribution of income in the army. As of 2004, the average soldier's pay was just over $37,000.[11] Including base pay and the housing and food allowance that soldiers receive, the lowest salary in the army in 2004 was about $25,000 per year. The housing allowance each soldier receives varies depending upon where the soldier

---

[10] The army average for recruits with high school diplomas was about 60% during the 1970s, before climbing steadily and reaching a high point of 99% in 1992. For statistics over time, see table D-7 in U.S. Department of Defense, "Population Representation: 2005." See also Kane, "Who Are the Recruits?" as well as U.S. Department of Defense, "Population Representation: 2004."

[11] This pay average includes the housing and subsistence allowance soldiers receive in addition to their base pay. Maxfield, "Army Profile."

lives, but neither the housing nor the food allowance is subject to taxes. The absolute lowest *base* pay that a soldier could receive in 2004 was $14,000, which of course does not include the soldier's food or housing allowance. At the other end of the pay scale, the highest base pay that the army's most senior officers could receive in 2004 was about $160,000, in addition to a housing and food allowance (twelve officers were eligible for this pay in 2004—the army's four-star generals). Beyond highlighting basic demographic information, these pay rates should also demonstrate the ethos of equality within the service. In no comparably sized civilian corporation would the chief executives earn just over eleven times the salary of the lowest-paid worker.[12]

The income rates used in the C&S Study include each soldier's and officer's base pay, the average housing allowance, and a food allowance in addition to the tax advantage of these untaxed allowances. The pay rate used does not include bonuses that members of the army may also receive, such as hazardous-duty pay or proficiency pay for specialized skills such as medicine and flying.[13]

A comparison of the income of army members with that of the civilian population shows that soldiers on active duty can be considered neither very poor nor very rich. Figure 3.4 shows that most soldiers and officers earn enough to place them solidly in the middle class. This is also true in the perceptions that soldiers have about their socioeconomic status. When asked to describe their family's socioeconomic class, 57% of soldiers and warrant officers described their family as working class. Twenty-six percent of officers said the same. Forty-two percent of soldiers and warrant officers and 67% of officers described their family as middle class. Only 1% of soldiers and 7% of officers described their families as upper class.

Family and Region

About 51% of army personnel are married, and about 46% of the force has children.[14] While marriage is common in the era of the all-volunteer force, this differs significantly from the draftee army of times past, when typically only senior NCOs and officers had families.

There is also a strong tradition of family service within the military. Eleven percent of soldiers and 21% of officers report having a career-military parent (typically the father). An additional 39% of the army had

---

[12] CEOs and CFOs in the United States now often make four hundred times the salaries of average workers. Hunt, "Letter from Washington."

[13] The source for compiling this consolidated pay scale is Powers's "FY 2004 Average Annual Salary for Military Personnel."

[14] Maxfield, "Army Profile," 5.

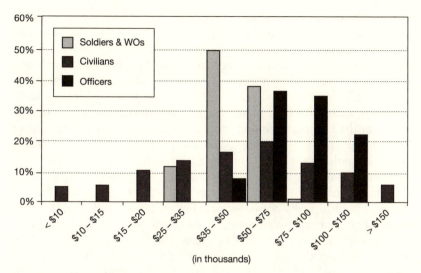

Figure 3.4 Income in the Army and Civilian Populations
Source: C&S Survey and 2004 National Annenberg Election Survey
Note: The army data for soldiers and warrant officers is somewhat skewed due to the exclusion of the 10% of the army in the lowest two ranks, PV1 and PV2, from the dataset. The total salary for soldiers in these two ranks, including housing and subsistence allowance, is typically between $27,000 and $29,000.

a parent who served but did not make a career in the military. There are, however, significant differences in the family history of service among members of the army due to racial and ethnic factors. Whites are more likely to have had a father who served in the military than Hispanics and blacks. Minorities, and particularly blacks, however, are more likely to have a sibling or spouse with some record of military service.[15]

When it comes to place of origin, about 10% of the army reports being born outside the United States, although about one-quarter of these were born in U.S. territories, such as Guam and Puerto Rico. An additional 13% of the army reports that one or both of their parents were born outside the United States.[16]

[15] About 45% of blacks report having a sibling who has also served, compared with only 30% of whites and 35% of Hispanics. The high proportion of blacks with a family history of service is probably driven in part by the high proportion of women among minorities in the army. Women in the army tend to marry other service members at a much higher rate than males. In 2006, 5% of married men in the army were wedded to other service members. The rate among women was 37.3%. Bretschneider, "A Look at Today's Army."

[16] This trend is most likely among Hispanics in the army, a majority of whom (57%) were born either outside the United States (including Puerto Rico) or in the United States to foreign-born parents.

As for the regional distribution of military recruits, most regions in the United States are represented in proportion to their population size. The exception to this is a slight overrepresentation of soldiers from the South and a corresponding underrepresentation of soldiers from the Northeast. The extent of this imbalance in regional representation has often been overstated. In his 1951 study of senior officers in the army between 1898 and 1940, Richard Brown found a significant overrepresentation of officers from the Northeast among those commissioned before 1920. After 1920 this proportion decreased, and the proportion of senior officers from the South grew to 33%, whereas the region made up only 23% of the white population. This overrepresentation is significant but not large enough or consistent enough over time to allow one to declare that the military has historically been dominated by officers from the South.[17] The extent of the current overrepresentation of the South is fairly slight. A look at military recruits in 2004 by region shows that about 43% of recruits came from the South, an area with 38% of the U.S. population. Comparably, 14% of recruits came from the Northeast, a region with about 19% of the total population. In simplified terms, if the population of 2004 military recruits was made up of twenty people, about one extra person would be from the South instead of from the Northeast, with the distribution of the rest almost exactly matching the population distribution across the United States.[18] The same dynamic applies to the proportion of officers from the South, which averaged just under 40% for most of the 1990s.[19]

The Virtual Army and Virtual Officer Corps

Thus far I have briefly highlighted some of the key differences between the army and civilian populations. The most significant of these differences is the proportion of women in the army. There are also significant differences in racial composition, education levels, and income distribution between these two populations. One might reasonably expect these differences to correspond with different views on social and political issues.

But it is not clear that these differences push members of the army in a single direction. The fact that most of the army is male may lead aggregate opinions in one direction, but the education levels of members of the army

[17] Brown, *Social Attitudes*, 3.

[18] This information is from data compiled by Tim Kane from the Census Bureau and the U.S. Department of Defense. Kane, "Who Are the Recruits?" 10.

[19] Data are from the Defense Military Data Center, compiled by Desch; see Desch, "Explaining the Gap."

and the overrepresentation of blacks may lead attitudes in another direction. Throughout this study I control for these demographic differences whenever possible. The best way to do this is through multivariate regression analysis, but this is often cumbersome, and it is not always easy to interpret the cumulative pressure of several demographic variables. In an attempt to succinctly capture the overall effects that these demographic differences may have on attitudes, I augment multivariate regression with the use of a Virtual Army and Virtual Officer Corps when making comparisons with the civilian population.

The Virtual Army and Virtual Officer Corps are groups of civilian respondents weighted to resemble the army or the officer corps on the dimensions of race, gender, income, age, education level, and, in the case of officers, citizenship status. Excluded from each civilian data set are any respondents whose age, income, or education level does not fall within the range of what is found within the active-duty army population.[20] The remaining respondents were tabulated by race, gender, and income and compared with a similar tabulation of the army data set to construct a civilian population resembling the army on these dimensions.

As an example, suppose we wanted to compare the attitudes of the army's officer corps with the attitudes of civilians toward the role that women should have in the workplace. Without accounting for the substantial demographic differences between the two populations, we could not say that any attitudinal differences between the two groups were due solely to army culture. For instance, if we drew a random sample of 100 officers and compared them with a random sample of 100 civilians, we would be comparing a group that was 85% male with a group that was evenly split between men and women. Furthermore, all of the 100 officers would, by definition, be employed in jobs that earned them between about $40,000 and $100,000 per year, including the women. A significant portion of the comparison group of civilians would be unemployed.

Instead, the Virtual Officer Corps offers an opportunity to compare the attitudes of officers with a group of civilians who most closely match the officers on key demographic characteristics. Using this tool allows us to capture the aggregate effect of several variables at once and to isolate the effect that being in the army has on attitudes. Therefore, instead of comparing the overall attitudes of army officers with a group of randomly drawn civilians, the Virtual Officer Corps allows a comparison with a group of civilians that is 85% male, is fully employed and earning solidly middle- to upper-middle-class incomes, is between the ages of twenty-one

---

[20] The primary result of this is the exclusion of the very poor and very rich from the civilian data sets, in addition to the exclusion of the old (those over sixty-five) and those without a high school diploma.

and sixty-five, excludes non-U.S. citizens, matches the racial and ethnic makeup of the officer corps, and meets the minimum standard of education for officers (a bachelor's degree or higher). By using the Virtual Army or Virtual Officer Corps as an initial point of comparison, we can quickly assess if differences between the army and the general civilian population appear to be due to army culture or to the unique demographic composition of the army.[21] These virtual populations are therefore helpful in preliminary analyses of the attitudes explored in the following chapters.

[21] The NAES data set is the primary civilian data set used in constructing these virtual populations. (See Romer, Kenski, Winneg, Adasiewicz, and Jamieson, *Capturing Campaign Dynamics*. Data used for comparison were drawn from the National Rolling Cross Section. See appendix C for information on weighting.) I also use the 2004 National Election Study (NES) and surveys from the Chicago Council on Global Affairs (CCGA) for comparisons with the army population. "The 2004 National Election Study" and "Global Views 2004." However, these are smaller data sets than that of the NAES study, and due to the resulting small sample sizes that remained after deleting respondents who did not fall within the range of ages, education levels, and incomes found within the army, it was not possible to construct a reliable Virtual Officer Corps.

Social and Political Attitudes

HAVING OUTLINED THE DEMOGRAPHIC differences between the members of the U.S. Army and the civilian population in the previous chapter, I now turn to general attitudinal differences between these two populations. In addition to comparisons with the civilian population, I look at key subgroups within the military. Specifically, I look at the army as a whole, soldiers (this category includes the enlisted ranks plus warrant officers), the officer ranks, and senior officers (those in the ranks of major and above). For comparisons with the civilian population, I present data from national surveys of the civilian population conducted in 2004 including the National Election Study, the General Social Survey, the National Annenberg Election Study, and the Chicago Council on Global Affairs survey.[1] I also make use of the Virtual Army and Virtual Officer Corps described in chapter 3 to provide estimates of how demographic differences may explain some of the attitudinal differences between the army and the civilian population.

This chapter provides a broad assessment of the worldview of members of the army. More important, it should help answer some questions that are essential to understanding civil-military relations. Specifically, are the views of members of the army on various social and political issues dramatically different from the views that civilians hold? Also, is the army homogeneous in its views, or are there differences between its various subgroups? As comprehensive data on the social and political views of soldiers are virtually nonexistent, this study can confirm or deny previous speculation suggesting that the military's younger cohorts are more conservative than senior officers.

Reasons for Joining

The end of the draft in 1973 meant that the armed forces had to begin relying on monetary incentives, vice compulsory service, to attract recruits. At the time, observers were concerned that this meant military service would appeal primarily to the lower economic strata of American

[1] See appendix C for a more detailed description of these surveys and how they are used.

society. Even the officer ranks were expected to become less representative of the general population by drawing more heavily from the lower-middle class.[2] However, not everyone in today's army has joined for monetary gain. In 1981 John Faris proposed a useful way of thinking about major recruitment patterns.[3] Faris conceived of splitting the military's manpower streams into two primary groups. The first group responds primarily to "marketplace factors" and can be expected to join for pay, job training, educational benefits, and the like. The second group is driven by more esoteric concerns such as family tradition and service to country. Although not mutually exclusive, in that most soldiers will express a combination of motivations for joining the military, this categorization can help us understand the different perspectives from which various subpopulations in the army approach military service.

A look across the army shows that officers are the most likely to choose the category "Desire to serve my country" as their most important reason for joining. Thirty-four percent of officers list this as their primary motivation compared with 20% of the enlisted and warrant officer ranks. Officers are also most likely to choose "Educational benefits" as their primary reason for joining: 25% of officers listed this as their most important reason for joining compared with only 13% of the rest of the army. At first this percentage might seem counterintuitive, but it is indicative of the power of ROTC scholarships and attendance at the military academies as officer-recruiting tools.[4] On the other hand, enlisted soldiers are most likely to list a reason related to pay and benefits as their primary reason for joining.[5]

Although informative, these figures probably reflect a degree of military indoctrination as well, given that at the time of the survey over 50% of respondents were beyond their tenth year in the army.[6] Limiting the analysis to the 326 respondents with five or fewer years of service shows that this might be the case, as "Educational benefits" is the most popular reason given by young soldiers and officers. Thirty-six percent of new officers

---

[2] Janowitz, "All-Volunteer Military." Also Janowitz and Moskos, "Five Years."

[3] Faris, "All-Volunteer Force."

[4] Students at the United States Military Academy pay no tuition and receive a small monthly stipend during their four years at West Point.

[5] Thirty percent of enlisted soldiers and warrant officers chose one of the six following reasons as their primary motivation for joining, compared with only 12% of officers: (1) earn more money than previous job(s), (2) family support services, (3) lack of civilian employment opportunities, (4) medical care benefits, (5) retirement pay and benefits, (6) security and stability of a job.

[6] This dynamic could work in two ways. People who have served for a long time may increasingly come to view their motivations for joining as primarily altruistic. The other possibility is that those who join for tangible benefits may be more likely to leave the service prior to retirement.

TABLE 4.1
Self-Reported Level of Morale

	High/ Very high	Low/ Very low	High minus low Morale
The army	29%	27%	2%
Soldiers	26	29	−3
Officers	45	12	33
Sr. officers[a]	53	9	44

Source: C&S Survey.
Note: Moderate or neutral responses are excluded from the table. Differences between groups are significant at the 0.001 level.
[a] As represented in the table, "Sr. officers" are a subset of the "Officers" category. However, significance tests are conducted between soldiers, junior officers, and senior officers, which are not overlapping groups.

and 19% of new soldiers and warrant officers list this as their primary motivation for joining the military. Falling to second place, "Desire to serve my country" is listed by 26% of new officers as their primary reason for joining. Seventeen percent of enlisted soldiers and warrant officers picked it as their first choice.[7] The dynamic of pay and benefits as an incentive for joining is the same for this group as it is for the larger army population, with 13% of officers indicating that this was a primary reason for joining compared with 28% of enlisted soldiers and warrant officers.

Views of the Army

Just as soldiers and officers join for different reasons, so they also often have different attitudes toward the army, both in terms of how they evaluate life in the army and army leaders and in their perceptions of the army's mission. This is not unexpected, given the different requirements for entering the army as either an officer or a soldier. A simplistic, but useful, way of looking at the two populations is in terms of blue collar versus white collar, or management versus the workforce.[8]

There is fairly wide variation across the army on one of the most basic questions: "How would you rate your current level of morale?" As we might expect, officers were much more likely than soldiers to answer this

[7] Of the 326 survey respondents who have served less than six years, 211 are enlisted soldiers or warrant officers and 115 are regular officers.
[8] One aspect of army life that makes this division less clear, particularly in combat arms specialties, is the requirement for officers to work directly with and among soldiers on a daily basis as well as share the physical burdens of army life.

question positively, with senior officers reporting the highest level of morale of any subgroup. The reported morale of soldiers and warrant officers is evenly distributed, with a third placing themselves in each category from "high" to "low." The story is dramatically different among officers, with 45% reporting positive morale, and only 12% reporting negative morale. The picture is even more positive among senior officers, over half of whom (53%) report high morale. Only 9% report having low morale.

As to faith in army leadership, soldiers and officers across the army have a generally positive view toward army leaders. Nearly six in ten soldiers agree with the statement "I believe the Army leadership will make the best decisions to maintain a quality Army," and two in ten disagree. Among officers, the proportion who agree with the statement jumps to 73%, and only 10% disagree. This is not entirely unexpected, as officers are leaders themselves.

A similar pattern holds for the proportion of each subpopulation who agree or strongly agree with the statement "I am confident I will be promoted as high as my ability and interest warrant if I stay in the Army." A full 53% of the army agrees with this statement, indicating that a majority are optimistic about their careers and view the army as a meritocracy. Soldiers are most likely to disagree with the statement, with one third saying that they disagree or strongly disagree. Officers in general are the most optimistic, with 61% optimistic about their promotion prospects, but fewer senior officers (51%) share this sentiment. This probably reflects the fact that senior officers are, by definition, near the end of their careers and understand that they probably will not be promoted as high as they would like.

Use of Military Force

Although perceptions of general morale and optimism about the army are interesting starting points for assessing attitudinal differences within the army, responses to questions about proposed uses of the army may better highlight key differences in outlook between the various subgroups. Gaining insight into the perceptions of the appropriate use of military force also provides a starting point for assessing attitudinal differences between members of the army and the civilian population. In essence, what does the army think is its purpose, and how might this differ from what civilians think about the army's purpose?

A key point of contention in civil-military relations in the 1990s was the application of the Weinberger-Powell Doctrine in a post–Cold War world. This doctrine was first articulated by Caspar Weinberger and then later promulgated by General Colin Powell as chairman of the Joint Chiefs of Staff. Its essence is that the military should avoid getting into armed conflicts without clear goals and should always be free to utilize overwhelming force against America's adversaries.[9] Answering the question "Whom do we fight, and how?" is about much more than foreign policy, and debates over this doctrine are fundamentally about the relationship between the state and the military apparatus.[10] Differences in military and civilian attitudes over the appropriate use of the army are therefore especially useful for capturing key differences between the two populations.

The TISS study of senior military officers found that in 1998, 99% of senior officers felt that "to fight and win our nation's wars" was a very important potential role for the military. The next highest percentage for the role of the military was "as an instrument of foreign policy, even if that means engaging in operations other than war." Comparably, only 53% of military leaders felt this was a very important potential role.[11] This overwhelming consensus on "fighting and winning the nation's wars" is in keeping with the Weinberger-Powell Doctrine and is not surprising, given the emphasis of military schooling. However, this was not just a military view. The TISS project found that even among civilians, "substantial majorities . . . were generally comfortable with the most traditional use of the military—fighting and winning wars—while also expressing very limited support for using the military to redress social and economic problems, whether at home or abroad."[12]

Five years after the TISS study and three years after September 11, 2001, the C&S Survey reveals very little change in attitudes toward the military's traditional role of fighting and winning our nation's wars. Some differences, however, are worth highlighting. Only 45% of senior army officers in the 2004 survey agree that a very important potential role of the military is as an instrument of foreign policy. This is only a slight decrease from 1999, but it may signal discouragement over the types of missions that the army was conducting in Afghanistan and Iraq in 2004. On the other hand, there is a significant increase in the percentage of senior officers who feel that "to address humanitarian needs abroad" and "to deal with domestic disorder" are very important potential roles, although this is still a small minority of senior officers. Unfortunately, there is no comparable survey of civilian attitudes from 2004, but it is interest-

---

[9] Feaver and Gelpi, *Choosing Your Battles*, 6.
[10] Nielsen, "Civil Military Relations," 220.
[11] Feaver and Kohn, *Soldiers and Civilians*, 56.
[12] Ibid., 47.

TABLE 4.2
Senior Officer and Civilian Elite Attitudes toward Potential Roles of the Military
(Percentage who say the potential mission is "very important")

	Army (2004)[a]	Military (1999)[b]	Civilian (1999)[c]
To fight and win our country's wars	95	99	90
As an instrument of foreign policy	45	53	32
To provide disaster relief within the U.S.	33	26	37
To deal with domestic disorder	24	9	21
To combat drug trafficking	15	11	21
To address humanitarian needs abroad	14	5	18
To intervene in civil wars abroad	4	1	2

Source: C&S Survey (2004) and TISS survey (1999).
[a] Senior army officers only (majors and above).
[b] Senior military officers in the TISS survey (majors and above).
[c] Nonveteran civilian leaders in the TISS survey.

ing that the shift in army attitudes from 1999 to 2004 aligns the army more closely with the attitudes of civilian leaders, circa 1999, on providing humanitarian relief abroad and dealing with domestic disorder in the United States. These findings are shown in table 4.2.[13]

Although there appears to be a degree of continuity in the attitudes of senior officers between the 1999 TISS survey and the 2004 Citizenship and Service survey, there are a few significant differences between the attitudes of army subgroups in the 2004 survey. Among officers of all ranks, there is general consensus on which potential missions should be rated as very important to the U.S. military. There are, however, significant differences between the attitudes of officers and soldiers. A higher proportion of officers say that "to fight and win our nation's wars" is a very important mission for the military. Furthermore, soldiers appear equally likely to rate "to fight terrorism" and "to fight and win our country's wars" as very important, whereas officers are slightly less likely to view the two missions as equally important.

The next potential use of the military that officers are likely to consider very important is "as an instrument of foreign policy, even if that means engaging in operations other than war (such as nation-building or peacekeeping)." Forty-one percent of officers view this as very important, compared with only 32% of soldiers.

The major difference between officers and soldiers, however, is in the propensity of soldiers to list many potential missions as very important.

[13] TISS data from table 1.10 in Holsti, "Of Chasms and Convergences."

TABLE 4.3

Soldier and Officer Attitudes toward Potential Roles of the Military
(Percentage who say the potential mission is "very important")

	Soldiers	Officers	Difference
To fight and win our country's wars	82	92	10
As an instrument of foreign policy	32	41	8
To fight terrorism[a]	78	80	2
To intervene in civil wars abroad[a]	7	5	−2
To address humanitarian needs abroad[b]	25	15	−10
To combat drug trafficking	35	17	−18
To deal with domestic disorder	48	30	−18
Enforcing immigration laws	33	13	−20
To provide disaster relief within the U.S.	60	37	−23

Source: C&S Survey.

Note: Differences between groups are significant at the 0.001 level, except the ones footnoted below.

[a] Differences are not statistically significant.

[b] Significant at the 0.05 level.

As shown in table 4.3, soldiers are significantly more likely to rate providing disaster relief within the United States, dealing with domestic disorder, combating drug trafficking, enforcing immigration laws, and addressing humanitarian needs abroad as very important potential missions. This indicates a more expansive view of the role of the armed forces compared with the more focused, traditional view of the officer corps.

The only two missions that officers and soldiers are equally likely to rate as very important are fighting terrorism, which about four out of five view as very important, and intervening in civil wars abroad, which very few of either rank category view as very important. That so few soldiers and officers think that intervening in civil wars is an important mission for the army highlights the importance of "framing" in foreign policy debates. Although previous research has addressed the importance of purpose and context to the degree of public support for U.S. participation in armed conflict, these findings highlight that framing can also be important for those serving in the military.[14] More specifically, these findings highlight that how the conflict in Iraq was or is viewed has implications for both public and military support for American efforts there: as a fight against Al Qaeda or as an intervention in the struggle between Iraq's various ethnic and religious factions.

[14] Jentleson and Britton, "Still Pretty Prudent." Also Zaller and Chiu, "Government's Little Helper," and Dempsey, "Public Evaluation."

Defense and Foreign Policy Spending

One surprising overall finding about spending on defense and foreign policy programs is that not everyone in the army believes defense spending should be expanded. Only 47% of soldiers and 49% of officers feel this way. In fact, about 8% of army respondents feel that defense spending should be cut back. On this issue army respondents are fairly consistent across ranks. When it comes to spending on homeland security and military and economic aid to foreign countries, however, again there are key differences between officers and soldiers.

In the enlisted ranks, about 3 out of 4 respondents feel that the United States should spend less money on military aid to other nations. About 2 out of 3 officers agree with this sentiment, but when we look specifically at the subset of senior officers, the percentage who feel that military aid to other nations should be cut back drops to 60%. A similar pattern holds for attitudes toward economic aid to other nations. Seventy-percent of soldiers feel it should be cut back, compared with only 63% of the officer corps and 55% of senior officers. These findings imply that those in the army's senior ranks are slightly more in favor of using money as a tool of foreign policy but are still generally against the idea.[15] On the last defense and foreign policy issue examined in the C&S Survey, homeland security, about 2 out of 3 soldiers (67%) feel spending in this area should be expanded, and only 56% of officers feel the same.

Although soldiers tend to favor more spending on homeland security and less spending on foreign economic and military aid than officers, the differences between these army subpopulations pale in comparison with the significant differences between the army and the civilian population. And the most striking differences in attitudes on these issues are those between the military and civilian elites from the Chicago Council on Global Affairs (CCGA) surveys.[16]

---

[15] Since 2004, it is likely that views on the use of economic aid have shifted even further as more officers gain firsthand experience with the interplay between economic development and security in Iraq and Afghanistan. A sure sign that economic development is being integrated into military planning is the use of martial terms to describe the employment of this kind of aid. Just as engagements with local leaders have become part of the "targeting" process, the introduction of economic aid as a consideration in military decision-making has come with the moniker "money as a weapon."

[16] The CCGA elite sample consists of 450 "leaders with foreign policy power, specialization, and expertise." Although these leaders do not necessarily reflect the opinions of key foreign policy leaders and decision makers in the U.S. government, the sample is an attempt to reach those who influence key decision-makers and shape public debates. More details about the CCGA elite sample can be found in appendix C and "Global Views 2004."

On the question of spending on military or economic aid to other nations, there are slight but consistent differences between the army and civilian populations. On balance, a higher proportion of the army would like to see spending in these areas cut back. The civilian population surveyed in the CCGA study is still overwhelmingly against spending in these areas, but not quite to the same degree as army personnel. Army personnel, however, are significantly more likely than civilians to believe that spending on defense and homeland security should at least be maintained if not expanded. The civilian population is almost evenly split between those who would like to see defense spending expanded and those who would like to see it cut back (29% and 25%, respectively), whereas about half of the army wants defense spending increased and fewer than one in ten would like to see it decreased. A similar pattern holds for spending on homeland security, with 51% of civilians wanting spending to be expanded in this area and 11% wanting spending to be cut back, compared with the 65% who are in favor of expansion and only 3% who are for a reduction in spending within the army.

A look at how a Virtual Army might feel on these issues shows only small differences between this group and the general civilian population. The data in table 4.4 show that a group of civilians that matches the army demographically is likely to have views that are only slightly different from those of the larger civilian population. Weighting the civilian group to look like the army shifts aggregate attitudes slightly closer to those of the army, but it is clear that demographics alone do not explain the differences in attitude between the army and civilian populations on these issues.

The differences between civilian elites and senior army officers are much more dramatic than those between the general army and civilian populations. Civilian elites are generally against any expansion of defense spending, with 35% saying that it should be cut back and only 15% saying it should be expanded. Civilian elites generally agree that military aid to other nations should be reduced, but not to the same degree as senior army officers, the general army population, or the civilian population. A similar pattern holds with attitudes toward homeland security, where 39% of civilian elites say the government should expand spending in this area and 15% say spending should be reduced. The most dramatic difference between civilian elites and other groups is in attitudes toward economic aid to other nations. Unlike any of the other three groups, a clear majority (61%) of civilian elites would like to see spending expanded in this area, and only 8% would like to see economic aid to other nations cut back.

TABLE 4.4
Army and Civilian Attitudes toward Defense and Foreign Policy Spending

		Army	Virtual Army	Civilians	Senior officers	Civilian elites
Defense spending	Expand	48%	35%	29%	51%	15%
	Cut back	8	23	25	4	35
	Difference	40	12	4	46	−19
Military aid to other nations	Expand	3	4	4	5	13
	Cut back	74	67	65	60	40
	Difference	−71	−63	−60	−55	−27
Econ. aid to other nations	Expand	3	8	8	7	61
	Cut back	69	66	64	55	8
	Difference	−66	−59	−56	−48	53
Homeland security	Expand	65	53	51	57	39
	Cut back	3	10	11	4	15
	Difference	62	43	40	53	24

Source: C&S Survey and "Global Views 2004," Chicago Council on Foreign Relations (now Chicago Council on Global Affairs).
Note: Differences between "Army" and "Civilians" are significant at the 0.001 level.
Differences between "Senior officers" and "Civilian elites" are significant at the 0.001 level.

These differences between civilian elites and both the general army and civilian populations are striking but not unexpected. Given that the civilian elites the CCGA surveyed are professionals who work on the nonmilitary aspects of foreign policy, it is understandable that they would like to see funding in economic aid expanded, just as military officers are likely to believe that defense spending should be expanded. Interestingly, with the exception of attitudes toward defense spending, the differences in attitudes between senior officers and civilian elites are slightly less dramatic than the differences between the general army population and civilian elites. The differences are still dramatic, but not as large. In fact, senior army officers are less hostile to military and economic aid to other nations than both the general army population and the general civilian population, indicating that something about their military experience may be making them *slightly* less hostile to these levers of foreign policy.

The Economy and Domestic Spending

The C&S Survey included several questions about respondent attitudes toward the national economy and government spending on domestic programs, as well as a question on respondent attitudes toward the role of the government in providing for the economic well-being of individuals. Answers to these questions revealed interesting differences between army and civilian attitudes, in addition to significant differences between army subgroups.

On the broadest question of economic perspective, namely rating the national economy in 2004, key differences observed within the army population are not seen in the civilian population. Asked whether they thought the economy was getting better or worse, army respondents were fairly evenly split, with 32% saying the economy is improving and 35% saying it is deteriorating. In this respect army respondents were much more pessimistic about the economy than their civilian counterparts. When the National Election Study (NES) 2004 survey asked respondents if they expected the economy to get better over the next year, 35% predicted that the economy would improve and only 16% felt it would deteriorate.[17] The army's pessimism toward the economy seemed to be confined to the army's enlisted ranks. Thirty-eight percent of soldiers felt the economy was getting worse compared with only 15% of officers. Fifty-three percent of officers felt the national economy was getting better.

This finding of optimism is possibly an artifact of the personal economic status of officers, as officers are generally paid more than soldiers. Dividing the sample along income lines and assessing attitudes was one way of seeing if the differences in opinions within the army correlate to income. When this was done, 26% of those soldiers whose incomes fell below the mean income indicated that they felt the national economy was improving, compared with 46% of soldiers whose incomes fell above the mean.[18] However, the same pattern did not hold in analysis of the civilian population sample. Whether in the top or bottom half of the economic spectrum, civilian perceptions of the national economy remained relatively constant, with slightly more pessimism among those at the top of the economic spectrum.

This suggests that income does not necessarily drive perceptions of the national economy within the army, but that something about being an

---

[17] Because of the wording of questions, the army responses are not directly comparable with the responses from the NES survey. The question in the army survey read, "Do you think the economy is getting better or worse?" The question in the NES survey read, "What about the next 12 months? Do you expect the economy, in the country as a whole, to get better, stay about the same, or get worse?"

[18] The populations in this table were split using the mean income of C&S Survey respondents as the dividing point. The mean income of C&S Survey respondents (which obviously excludes soldiers in the two lowest ranks and the army's generals) was $53,000. This figure includes average base pay in addition to subsistence and housing allowances. The mean income of individual respondents (not households) in the NES survey was approximately $22,000. There was no substantial change in reported civilian attitudes when split along either the army or civilian median income.

officer influences the outlook of respondents in this area. As discussed previously, several demographic factors are correlated with being an officer, including gender, education, and race. Later chapters will examine which of these, or other factors, are dominant in shaping army attitudes.

Among the other economic issues the C&S Survey covered were questions about spending on domestic programs such as education, Social Security, and health care and a question that asked respondents to prioritize job growth and the environment. On all three spending questions, army attitudes were very similar to civilian attitudes, although again there were significant differences between the attitudes of officers and soldiers. On the question of the trade-off between jobs and environmental protection, army attitudes were roughly comparable with those of the civilian population, although officers were more protective of the environment than were soldiers.[19] Two-thirds of officers opposed relaxing environmental standards to stimulate economic growth. The enlisted ranks generally agreed, but to a lesser extent. Fifty-six percent of soldiers agreed with prioritizing the environment over jobs. A similar question in the NES survey found that 38% of the civilian population placed themselves on the side of "protecting the environment, even if it costs jobs and standard of living."[20] However, it appears that a group of civilians that looked like the army demographically would be more inclined to protecting the environment. Forty-eight percent of the Virtual Army placed environmental concerns before jobs, possibly due to the higher median income of that population.

A significant portion of the army (34% of soldiers and 45% of officers) listed educational benefits as one of its top three reasons for joining the army. Given that this plays such an important role in encouraging people to enter service, it is not surprising that 77% of army personnel would like to see the government expand spending in this area. This exceeds the 69% of civilian respondents who felt the same. Surprisingly, officers support an expansion of spending in this area to a significantly lesser degree than do enlisted personnel. Given the greater propensity of officers to list education as one of their primary reasons for joining, one can reasonably expect this to be reversed. Most officers still support expanded spending in this area, but only 62% felt this way compared with 80% of soldiers. As for the Virtual Army, attitudes among this group fell almost directly between the civilian and the army populations, with 74% stating

[19] This may be due in part to an increased awareness of environmental issues among officers, who can be held liable for any damage their units do to the environment.

[20] The NES 2004 question, V043182, was "Where would you place YOURSELF on this scale, or haven't you thought much about this?" Respondents were then able to place themselves on a seven-point scale ranging from "1. Protect environment, even if it costs jobs & standard of living," to "7. Jobs & standard of living more important than environment."

TABLE 4.5
Attitudes toward Spending on Domestic Programs

	Education						
	Civilians	Virtual Army	Army	Soldiers	Officers	Senior officers	Civilians elites
Expanded	69%	74%	77%	80%	62%	60%	74%
Kept about the same	25	19	20	18	32	33	17
Cut back	5	6	2	2	5	6	6
Don't know	1	1	1	1	1	1	3
	Health Care						
Expanded	79%	82%	74%	77%	58%	59%	70%
Kept about the same	17	14	22	20	35	34	20
Cut back	3	4	3	2	5	4	7
Don't know	1	1	1	1	3	3	3
	Social Security						
Expanded	65%	70%	56%	61%	33%	33%	30%
Kept about the same	30	26	33	30	50	54	56
Cut back	4	4	8	7	14	10	7
Don't know	1	1	2	2	3	3	7

Source: C&S Survey and "Global Views 2004," Chicago Council on Foreign Relations (now Chicago Council on Global Affairs).

Note: Differences between "Soldiers" and "Officers" are significant at the 0.001 level. Differences between "Army" and "Civilians" are significant at the 0.01 level. Differences between "Sr. officers' " and "Civilian elites" are significant at the 0.02 level.

that education spending should be expanded. These results are shown in the first portion of table 4.5.

The same pattern generally holds true for attitudes toward spending on health care. About three out of four members of the army would like to see spending expanded in this area, which is comparable with the 79% of civilians who felt the same way. Officers were substantially less likely than other subgroups to state that spending on health care should be expanded, but few felt it should be cut back. Given that all members of the army receive comprehensive health care from the government, it is difficult to parse out a reason for these differing attitudes between officers and soldiers, although the availability of health care may explain why members of the army were slightly less likely than the general public to think spending should be expanded in this area.[21]

[21] The quality and type of health care the army provides is ostensibly equal across ranks, although it is easier for officers to navigate the bureaucratic hurdles that often make access to health care difficult.

The last program examined as a point of comparison between army and civilian attitudes on government spending was Social Security. And although overall army attitudes are again comparable with those of the general civilian population, officers were much less likely to support an increase in spending in this area. Part of this divergence may be due to the army's retirement plan, which may lead members of the army to find less value in Social Security. However, this does not explain the difference between officer and soldier attitudes. Officers were only about 10% more likely than soldiers to express an intent to stay in the army until retirement (at which point they are eligible to receive pay and health-care benefits), which means that the perceived need for Social Security benefits cannot explain all of the difference between the two populations. It is also interesting that senior officers and civilian elites have roughly comparable attitudes toward Social Security spending in that a majority of each group felt it should either be "kept about the same" or "cut back." As Social Security reform got some attention in the 2004 elections, later chapters will examine the possible role of partisan affiliation in shaping attitudes on this issue. Table 4.5 also shows subgroup attitudes toward spending on health care and Social Security.

The last question on economic or spending-related issues in the C&S Survey is on the government's role in ensuring the economic well-being of individuals. The following question was asked: "Some people feel that the government in Washington should see to it that every person has a job and a good standard of living. . . . Others think the government should just let each person get ahead on his/her own. Where would you place yourself on this scale?" Respondents then had the option of placing themselves on a seven-point scale that ranged from "Govt. Guarantee Job & Standard of Living" on one end to "Everyone on Their Own" on the other. This question is interesting for assessing army attitudes because it is more than a question on economic policy; it alludes to larger questions about the role of government in looking after citizens.

Among civilians, 46% placed themselves on the side of the scale closest to individual responsibility, and 34% chose to place themselves closer to the idea of having the government ensure that every person has a job and a good standard of living. The remaining 20% placed themselves directly in the middle of the scale. Attitudes across the army generally match those of the civilian population, with 42% placing themselves on the side of individual responsibility and 32% on the side of government responsibility. There are, again, dramatic differences between the attitudes of officer and enlisted personnel. Soldiers are about as likely as civilians to place themselves on the side of government responsibility (35% and 34%, respectively). However, they are more likely to choose the neutral option than civilians are and are less likely to place themselves on the side of

TABLE 4.6
Attitudes toward Government's Role in Economic Well-Being

	Civilians	Virtual Army	Army	Soldiers	Officers
Government responsible	34%	29%	32%	35%	16%
Neutral	20	18	26	27	21
Individual responsible	46	53	42	38	64
Individual minus govt.	11	25	10	3	48

Source: C&S Survey and 2004 American National Election Study.
Note: Differences between "Soldiers" and "Officers" and between "Civilians" and "Officers" are significant at the .001 level.

individual responsibility. Also of note is the fact that the Virtual Army in this instance came down on the side of individual responsibility to a greater degree than either the civilian or the army population, with 53% placing themselves on the side of individual responsibility.

As can be seen in table 4.6, the attitudes of the officer corps differed significantly from both the enlisted ranks and the general civilian population. Only 16% agreed with or leaned toward the idea that government should guarantee every person a job and a good standard of living. A full 64% of officers placed themselves on the other side of the spectrum, stating that the government should let each person get ahead on his or her own. This is somewhat counterintuitive, in that over the years the army has gone to great lengths to provide soldiers and officers with a baseline standard of living. Among the services the army provides its members are housing, medical care, legal assistance, child care, and career counseling. The army's attitudes toward the idea of government responsibility for individual welfare clearly deserve more scrutiny than I can provide here.

In this case it is also worth seeing if the differing attitudes between officers and soldiers on this issue are an artifact of their personal economic status. Again, when dividing the civilian and army data sets in half by income level, in both populations we find a correlation between income level and attitudes toward the government's role in ensuring the economic well-being of individuals. Those in the lower half of the army by income level are evenly split, with 36% on the side of government responsibility and another 36% on the side of individual responsibility. There is a significant shift in attitudes when we look at soldiers at the top half of the economic spectrum. Only 22% place themselves on the side of government responsibility, and a majority, 55%, place themselves on the side of individual responsibility.

And unlike perceptions of the national economy, this pattern holds among civilian respondents as well, albeit to a lesser degree. Civilians on the lower half of the economic spectrum are likely to feel that it is the government's responsibility to see to it that everyone has a job and a good standard of living. Only 29% of those at the top half of the economic spectrum agree.

These attitudes toward government spending, the government's role in ensuring a decent standard of living, and perceptions about the state of the national economy highlight the fact that although the army in general holds attitudes similar to those of the civilian population, it is not homogeneous in its outlook. Officers' attitudes often appear to be distinct from the attitudes of those in the enlisted ranks and the civilian population.[22]

Social Issues

Attitudinal differences between the army and the general civilian population are not as pronounced on social issues as they are on matters related to national defense and the economy. However, the attitudes of officers, and particularly senior officers, differ from the attitudes of the general civilian population and the army's enlisted ranks. Officers are slightly more inclined to be against further restrictions on gun ownership, are more favorable toward outlawing abortion entirely, and are more opposed to banning the death penalty than both soldiers and the civilian population. As mentioned before, they also tend to favor environmental standards over job creation to a higher degree than both the civilian population and soldiers. Officers and senior officers are also much more likely than soldiers to state that religion provides "quite a bit" or a "great deal" of guidance in their everyday lives.

On the question of gun control, army attitudes generally reflect those of society. Fifty-seven percent of the army favors more restrictions on gun ownership. This is comparable to the finding of both the NES and NAES surveys. The NES study found that 56% of civilians believe the federal

---

[22] Unfortunately, it is not possible to isolate the effect of being an officer from the income level of a member of the army. As shown in chapter 3, the income of army officers places them solidly in the middle to upper-middle class, which may drive many of their views on economic issues. The correlation between rank and income in the army is 0.75. Only the most senior enlisted ranks and warrant officers earn as much as or more than junior officers. This is where the Virtual Army and Virtual Officer Corps are invaluable, as they are subsets of the civilian population weighted to reflect the income distribution of the army (in addition to the other demographic characteristics discussed in chapter 3).

government should make it more difficult to own a gun.[23] The NAES study found that 58% of respondents felt the federal government should do more to restrict the kinds of guns that people can buy.[24] Likewise, there was very little difference between the general population and the Virtual Army population on this issue. Fifty-four percent of the Virtual Army felt that the government should make it more difficult to own a gun. Within the army ranks, however, slightly fewer officers were inclined to agree. Only 47% of officers favored more restrictions on gun ownership compared with 59% of soldiers.

On the question of the death penalty, 72% of the army opposed a ban. Seventy-one percent of soldiers opposed banning the death penalty compared with 79% of the officer corps and 82% of senior officers. Members of the army appeared to support the death penalty more than their civilian counterparts, although there are no data from 2004 that use the same question as the C&S Survey. The 2004 NES and GSS each asked a question about whether the respondent would favor or oppose the death penalty for someone convicted of a murder, to which about 68% of each sample said they would favor the death penalty in those circumstances.

On the question of abortion, 19% of the army stated that they favor or strongly favor outlawing abortion entirely. Eighteen percent of soldiers felt this way compared with 26% of officers and 31% of senior officers. Comparably, 30% of the civilian population stated that they strongly favor or somewhat favor a federal government ban on all abortions.[25] This is in keeping with the trend of the officer corps being more conservative than the enlisted ranks; it also provides a unique example of the attitudes of officers closely aligning themselves with civilian opinion on a social issue.[26]

This greater opposition to abortion among officers appears to be due to the religiosity of the officer corps compared with the rest of the army.[27]

---

[23] The NES question, V043188, was "Should the Federal government make it more difficult to buy a gun?"

[24] The NAES question, CCE31, was "Restricting the kinds of guns that people can buy—should the federal government do more about it, do the same as now, do less about it, or do nothing at all?"

[25] The NAES question, CCE01, was "The federal government banning all abortions—do you favor or oppose the federal government doing this?"

[26] The correlation between religiosity and opposition to abortion in the army is 0.37, which is comparable with the correlation of 0.39 found within the civilian population (NES data).

[27] A regression analysis of attitudes on abortion with both rank and religiosity as independent variables shows that religiosity is a significant predictor of attitudes toward abortion, whereas rank is statistically and substantively insignificant. The preponderance of Catholicism within the officer corps may also drive attitudes toward abortion. Although the C&S Survey does not ask about a specific religious denomination, Catholics in recent years have

When asked about the role of religion in their daily lives, 47% of officers and 58% of senior officers stated that religion provided "quite a bit" or "a great deal" of guidance in their day-to-day living. Only 34% of soldiers stated that religion played an equally important role in their daily lives. Using a slightly different question, the NES survey found that 59% of civilians felt that religion provided "quite a bit" or "a great deal" of guidance in their day-to-day living.[28] Fifty-seven percent of the Virtual Army felt the same. It is therefore not clear if the army is overall less religious than the civilian population, but there are certainly differences on the importance of religion between officers and soldiers.

On the question of prayer, the army is overwhelmingly in favor of allowing prayer in public schools. Seventy percent of soldiers and warrant officers, 72% of officers, and 76% of senior officers favor or strongly favor allowing it. Unfortunately, the wording in the army survey was fairly broad, and there were no questions in civilian surveys in 2004 that would allow for a direct comparison.[29]

Attitudes toward Issues of Gender and Race

Within the civilian population, 60% fully agree with the statement "Women should have an equal role with men in running business, industry and government."[30] Significantly, fewer respondents in the army survey feel the same, with only 49% indicating that they agree fully with that statement. This finding may not be a surprising, given that women comprise only about 15% of the army and the fact that the army has traditionally been viewed as a male-dominated institution. However, it is not clear that these attitudinal differences can be attributed to demographic differences. The overall attitudes of the Virtual Army are identical to the civilian population. What is interesting are the varying differences

---

made up about 30% of the officer corps (31.3% in 2001, the most recent year for which I have seen data on officer religiosity).

[28] The NES variable used here, V043220, combines two questions. The first asks if religion is an important part of life, and the second asks how much guidance religion provides in day-to-day living.

[29] The GSS survey specifically asked about allowing Bible prayer in public schools, which could be expected to decrease levels of support. Only 35% of GSS respondents approved of Bible prayers in public schools.

[30] The NES question, V043196, asks respondents to place themselves on a seven-point scale representing a range of opinions about the role of women in business, industry, and government. A response of "1" indicates full agreement with the statement "Women and men should have equal roles," and a response of "7" indicates agreement with the statement "A woman's place is in the home." Respondents could also place themselves somewhere between these two opinions.

TABLE 4.7
Equal Role for Women

Percentage who believe fully that women should have an equal role with men in running business, industry, and government

Army	49	*Civilians*	60	*Virtual Army*	60
Men	45	Men	57	Men	58
Women	68	Women	63	Women	76
Difference	22	Difference	6	Difference	19

		Enlisted	48	*Officers*	51
		Men	45	Men	46
		Women	65	Women	81
		Difference	19	Difference	36

Source: C&S Survey and 2004 American National Election Study.
Note: Differences between civilian men and women are not significant. Differences between "Army" and "Civilian" populations are significant at the 0.001 level. Differences between "Men" and "Women" in the army, across ranks, are significant at the 0.05 level.

in opinion between the sexes within the army and the relative lack of differences in opinion between men and women in the civilian population.

Rank alone does not explain much of the varying opinions on gender equality within the army. The difference between the opinion of an officer and that of a soldier is only 3% (48% for soldiers and 51% for officers). However, there are significant differences in the opinions of men and women, particularly officers. Within the officer ranks, 46% of male officers agree with the idea of full equality for women in the workplace, and 81% of female officers feel the same. This is a significant difference of 35%. The same pattern exists in the enlisted ranks but not to the same degree. Whereas male soldiers seem to have more or less the same opinion as their officer counterparts (45% believe in full gender equality in the workplace), the percentage of women who agree is 65% in the enlisted ranks, compared with 81% of women officers. This is still a significant difference, but not of the same magnitude as the difference between the sexes in the officer corps.

Across all ranks, the difference between the attitudes of men and women on gender equality is 23% (45% of men and 68% of women agree with full gender equality in the workplace). This pattern differs markedly from the attitudes of civilians. The difference between the attitudes of men and women in the civilian world is only 6%. Fifty-seven percent of male respondents agree with the idea of full equality in the workplace, compared with 63% of women. Overall, then, it is accurate to say that men in the army are slightly less accepting of gender equality than their civilian male counterparts. However, women in the army, and particularly women who are officers, are more likely than civilian women to believe in full gender equality in the workplace. This is not surprising, given that these women have self-selected into a traditionally male-dominated profession. A closer look at the Virtual Army results, however, suggests that this phenomenon may not be specific to the army. Within the Virtual Army, 76% of women agree with the idea of full equality, implying that working women in general are likely to believe in equality to a greater degree than their unemployed counterparts.

On the question of racial and ethnic integration, the C&S Survey asked respondents, "Thinking about society in general: In order to make up for past discrimination, do you favor or oppose programs which make special efforts to help minorities get ahead?" Although the question does not perfectly capture the nuances surrounding the debates on affirmative action, responses to this question, particularly among the racial and ethnic subgroups of the army, reveal strongly divergent attitudes.

Among soldiers, 38% oppose and 22% favor these types of programs. Attitudes among officers are significantly different, with 56% of officers opposing these types of programs and only 18% supporting them. Senior officers are most opposed, with 60% against and 15% in support of such programs.

The category of race and ethnicity also makes a difference in how soldiers and officers perceive these programs. Whites are the most opposed to them, followed by Hispanics and blacks. However, the degree of opposition and support among racial and ethnic groups varies between ranks. White officers are more opposed to such programs than white soldiers, and white senior officers register the largest opposition of any group. Blacks generally favor programs that help minorities, although black soldiers are less supportive of them than are officers, and black senior officers are less supportive than black officers in general. Hispanics overall are generally supportive of such programs, but less so than blacks. These differences between senior officers, who are predominantly white, and the army's minorities have significant implications for army perceptions of discrimination, in addition to being a point of contention in efforts to increase diversity in the army (see table 4.8).

These differences in attitudes between racial and ethnic groups in the army are not unexpected. However, whereas the army overall appears comparatively hostile to these types of efforts, army personnel are somewhat less opposed to these programs than civilians appear to be. The 2004 NES survey asked a similar question but focused specifically on affirmative action in the workplace. Respondents in that survey were asked,

Some people say that because of past discrimination, blacks should be given preference in hiring and promotion. Others say that such preference in hiring and promotion of blacks is wrong because it gives blacks advantages they haven't earned. What about your opinion—are you FOR or AGAINST preferential hiring and promotion of blacks?

Whites and Hispanics were overwhelmingly opposed, and blacks were evenly split, with 46% responding that they favored preferential hiring and promotion and 42% responding that they opposed them.

Trust and Efficacy in Government

One might assume that people who volunteer to serve in a nation's military would have a high degree of trust in public officials and a strong feeling of connection to the government. However, this is not necessarily the case with members of the U.S. Army. Studies in the late 1970s found that the all-volunteer force was recruiting from the most socially alienated portion of American youth.[31] Furthermore, political trust is generally at its lowest point at the age when most recruits enter the army.[32]

The C&S Survey included three questions that are often used to assess a person's sense of connection to government officials as well as the degree to which the respondent feels he or she is able to understand and be a part of governmental processes.[33] Overall, this study confirms previous research that members of the army are slightly more likely than the general public to think that they do not have any say in government and that government officials do not care what they think. On the question of understanding how government works, however, members of the army are less likely to feel that politics or government is too complicated for them.

Members of the army are slightly more likely to agree with the statement "People like me don't have any say about what the government does." Fifty-five percent of army respondents agreed with this statement, compared with only 49% of NES respondents.[34] Within the army, soldiers are much more likely than officers to feel this way, with 58% of soldiers agreeing with the statement compared with only 38% of officers.

---

[31] Wesbrook, "Sociopolitical Alienation."

[32] Moskos, "All-Volunteer Force," 317.

[33] Similar measures of "political efficacy" have been in use since the Michigan Survey Research Center began using them in biennial election surveys in 1952. This concept was first articulated by Campbell, Gurin, and Miller, *The Voter Decides*. See also Almond and Verba, *Civic Culture*, and Lipset and Schneider, "Decline of Confidence."

[34] NES question V045202.

TABLE 4.8
Attitudes toward Affirmative Action

Programs to help minorities in society (army attitudes)

	Favor	Oppose	Favor minus oppose
Army	21%	40%	−19%
Whites	8	63	−55
Hispanics	33	17	16
Blacks	48	4	44
Soldiers	22	38	−16
Whites	7	61	−53
Hispanics	33	16	17
Blacks	46	4	42
Officers	18	56	−38
Whites	9	69	−61
Hispanics	34	29	6
Blacks	68	6	62
Sr. officers	15	60	−46
Whites	8	74	−66
Hispanics	29	17	11
Blacks	62	8	54

Preference in hiring and promotion for blacks (civilian attitudes)

Civilians	For	Against	For minus against
Overall	18	77	−58
White	12	84	−72
Hispanic	16	76	−60
Black	46	41	5
Virtual Army			
Overall	20	72	−52
White	10	87	−76
Hispanic	14	84	−69
Black	52	21	31

Source: C&S Survey and 2004 American National Election Study.

Note: The table excludes neutral responses and "Don't knows." Differences between all army rank and racial/ethnic subgroups are significant at the 0.001 level. Differences between civilian racial/ethnic subgroups are also significant at the 0.001 level.

The same pattern holds when survey respondents are asked whether they agree or disagree with the statement "Public officials don't care much what people like me think." About 58% of the respondents in the NES survey agreed with this statement compared with 69% of army respondents. Officers were again less likely to agree with this statement, with only 49% agreeing compared with 72% of soldiers.[35]

Whereas the responses to these two questions show that members of the army are more likely than civilians to feel they have no say in government and that public officials do not care what they think, members of the army are less likely than civilians to state that they cannot understand politics and government. Only 42% of army respondents agree with the statement "Sometimes politics and government seem so complicated that a person like me can't really understand what's going on." A slight majority of civilians, 53%, agree with this statement.[36] The breakdown between soldiers and officers moves in a familiar direction, with 44% of soldiers agreeing that they cannot understand government compared with only 29% of officers.

Interestingly, a look at these same three questions through the use of the Virtual Army shows that if the civilian population matched the army demographically, it would feel more connected to its government. Only 41% of the Virtual Army agreed that they have no say in what the government does compared with 49% of the general population. Similarly, only 52% agreed with the statement that public officials do not care what they think compared with 58% of the public as measured by NES. There was only a slight drop between the Virtual Army and the general public on the question of whether the government was too complex to understand. Fifty percent of the Virtual Army agreed with this statement compared with 53% of the general population. These differences indicate that by virtue of their income, education levels, age, race, and gender, members of the army should feel more connected with the government. However, these differences are not large, and given the artificiality of the Virtual Army's weighting scheme, should be viewed with a degree of skepticism.

[35] Again, the numbers are not directly comparable, as the NES survey explicitly offered a "neither agree nor disagree" option, whereas the C&S Survey did not. In deriving these numbers, I worked on the assumption that those who chose the middle option would have split evenly among the "agree" and "disagree" options had the "neither" option not been offered. Another possibility for comparison is to leave the middle option out of the analysis. This yields a similar marginal, 59% with a smaller sample (906 versus 1,062).

[36] Part of this difference may be due to the wording of the question. In the NAES survey, the question includes only "politics," not "politics and government." The NAES question, CMB10, reads, "Do you agree or disagree that: sometimes politics seems so complicated that a person like me cannot really understand what is going on?"

They do, however, raise interesting questions that I will examine in more detail in chapter 7.

Overall, these findings are somewhat surprising, as members of the military feel less connected to their government than do their civilian counterparts. However, a majority of officers feel that they understand how government works and that they have a say in what the government does. Only a slight majority of officers feel that public officials care what they think. On all three dimensions of trust and efficacy in government, officers are more positive than the general civilian population (there were no significant differences between senior officers and the broader officer population on these three measures). This is in keeping with the education levels and socioeconomic status of the officer corps. Soldiers, on the other hand, are less likely than civilians to believe that public officials care what they think or that they have any say about what the government does. They are, however, less likely than civilians to feel that government is too complicated to understand.

Conclusion

This chapter shows that across a variety of issues the army, in the aggregate, holds opinions more similar to those of the civilian population than outside observers might expect. There are a few areas of divergence, as in attitudes toward the role of women and toward defense spending, which one would expect from a traditionally male, war-fighting institution. Many would not expect that in areas such as spending on domestic programs army attitudes generally would track those of the civilian population. More surprising are attitudes the army had in 2004 toward traditional "hot-button" social issues. One might expect members of the army to take a more conservative stance. Instead, the army overall appears to track civilian attitudes toward such issues as gun control and the death penalty, and appears to be more liberal than the civilian population on issues like protecting the environment, abortion, and the role of religion in day-to-day life.

Aggregate army attitudes, however, mask two very different subpopulations. Soldiers and warrant officers drive overall attitudes due to their larger numbers. Aggregate attitudes conceal very sharp differences between army officers and soldiers. On issues such as personal morale and faith in the army, officers show attitudes that one would expect from those in an organization's managerial ranks. Similarly, officers are generally more positive in their assessment of how government works and in their perceived connection to government officials. They are also more likely than soldiers to take a narrower view of the army's missions and are slightly more likely to support other tools of international relations, such as military and economic aid to other nations.

There are, however, consistent differences concerning government spending, social issues, and race and gender issues that are not readily explained by the role of officers within the army. These differences between officers and both the enlisted ranks and the civilian population warrant further analysis. In the next chapter I therefore move beyond attitudes toward individual issues and explore how members of the army describe their worldview. Specifically, I assess whether members of the army tend to describe themselves as conservative or liberal and whether these labels reflect their viewpoints on specific social and political issues.

Conservatism

As previously discussed, the army has historically been labeled a conservative institution. It has even at times been viewed as reactionary, although attitudes, as seen in the last chapter, have often been more nuanced.

Self-Identification

The C&S Survey breaks no new ground in its finding that the officer corps largely identifies itself on the conservative end of the liberal-conservative spectrum. However, the army is not as uniformly conservative as conventional wisdom would suggest and in the aggregate more closely resembles the general population than many would believe.

The C&S Survey asked respondents to place themselves on a seven-point scale ranging from extremely liberal to extremely conservative. Table 5.1 shows that 68% of officers in the rank of major and above identify themselves on the conservative side of the liberal-conservative continuum. This finding is largely compatible with previous studies of the ideological self-identification of military officers. These include the data that Morris Janowitz collected from army personnel working in the Pentagon in 1954, the Foreign Policy Leadership Project (FPLP) surveys conducted every four years between 1976 and 1996, and the 1999 TISS study.[1] Although the questions used in Janowitz's study, the FPLP surveys, the TISS survey, and the C&S Survey are not identical, there is a remarkable consistency in conservative self-identification across the last fifty years.[2]

However, these three sets of numbers should be used only as a rough guide for assessing the conservative self-placement of senior army officers

---

[1] Janowitz surveyed navy and air force personnel as well, but only the attitudes of the army officers in the study are included here. Janowitz, *Professional Soldier*, 236. The FPLP data include respondents from all services.

[2] The degree of the apparent shift away from liberal self-identification cannot be proven with these data, as the 1954 survey did not offer the same response categories, but such a shift would fit with the general decline in favorability of the term *liberal* in the late 1960s. See Erikson and Tedin, *American Public Opinion*.

In terms of politics and political beliefs, where would you place yourself?

Extremely Liberal	Liberal	Slightly Liberal	Moderate	Slightly Conservative	Conservative	Extremely Conservative
↓	↓	↓	↓	↓	↓	↓
O	O	O	O	O	O	O

Figure 5.1 C&S Survey Liberal-Conservative Scale

over time. The terms "liberal" and "conservative" have evolved considerably over the last five decades. Indeed, both Janowitz and Huntington argued in the 1950s and 1960s that conservatism was a distinctly nonpartisan identification—in part due to a Democratic coalition that included southern conservatives. In the words of Janowitz in 1960, "Military officers are willing to identify themselves as conservatives, if only because such an identification permits political perspectives *without violation of nonpartisanship*" (emphasis mine). For them, it was a conservatism of form over content. This certainly does not hold in today's political lexicon, as conservatism has essentially become synonymous with Republican Party identification.[3]

The extent of the shift of the definition of "conservatism," both in terms of party alignment and away from a term that describes a pragmatic, cautious worldview, is revealed in a statement Peggy Noonan, a conservative journalist, made in 2006. In reference to the perceived conservatism of members of the military, she observed, "I've never met a career military man who was a conservative on social issues. I think they tend to see questions such as abortion and marriage as essentially uninteresting, private and not subject to the movement of machines."[4] In other words, to be a conservative today is to believe that such issues should be viewed as public concerns that should be regulated by "machines," which one would presume to include political or governmental organizations. She thus distinguished between "social conservatism" and the conservatism of the "military mind."

Noonan's characterization of conservatism highlights another problem in discerning the meaning of conservative identification, namely, the several dimensions upon which one might choose to self-identify as a conservative. In 1962 Clinton Rossiter identified four forms of conservatism in America: temperamental, possessive, practical, and philosophical.[5] Such a range of definitions clearly leaves room for someone to make the claim

---

[3] Abramowitz and Saunders, "Ideological Realignment."

[4] Noonan, "Untangling Webb." Noonan was a speechwriter for President Ronald Reagan.

[5] Rossiter, *Conservatism in America.*

TABLE 5.1
Ideological Identification of Senior Officers

	Liberal	Moderate	Conservative	
1954, Pentagon staff (army only)[a]				
MAJ/LTC	29%		69%	$N = 117$
COL/GEN	24		71	$N = 96$
Overall	27		70	$N = 213$
FPLP surveys (all services)[b]				
1976	16	23	61	$N = 493$
1980	4	24	72	$N = 167$
1984	8	17	76	$N = 122$
1988	4	19	77	$N = 156$
1988—army only	4	27	69	$N = 49$
1992	3	24	73	$N = 151$
1992—army only	4	31	65	$N = 49$
1996	3	25	73	$N = 108$
1998–1999, TISS (army only)[c]				
MAJ/LTC	5	26	68	$N = 190$
COL/GEN	4	32	64	$N = 47$
Overall	5	27	67	$N = 237$
2004, C&S survey[d]				
MAJ/LTC	9	22	69	$N = 208$
COL+	6	29	64	$N = 34$
Overall	9	23	68	$N = 242$

Source: C&S Survey (2004), Triangle Institute for Security Studies Survey of the Military in the Post–Cold War Era (1998–1999), Foreign Policy Leadership Project (1976–1996), and Pentagon Staff Officer Questionnaire (1954).

Note: The 1976 FPLP survey's military sample included a large number of younger officers who were enrolled at the Naval Post-Graduate School (typically majors and senior captains). Unfortunately, the FPLP surveys asked only for a specific branch of service in 1988 and 1992, making assessment of army-specific attitudes for other years impossible. Of interest is the higher proportion of moderates within the army ranks, compared with other services, for each of those years. Reported attitudes for 1988 and 1992 are calculated from the original data sets, and the remainder are from an analysis in Holsti, "Of Chasms and Convergences."

[a] "In domestic politics, do you regard yourself as: conservative, a little on the conservative side, a little on the liberal side, liberal?" (No middle response category.)

[b] Seven-point scale from "Far Left" to "Very liberal" to "Very conservative" to "Far Right."

[c] "How would you describe your views on political matters?"

[d] "In terms of politics and political beliefs, where would you place yourself on the following scale?"

that the "military mind" is conservative without having to defend a specific or agreed-upon definition that can be tested empirically.

Compounding the difficulty of assessing conservative identification in the military are the multiple dimensions with which contemporary survey respondents are likely to frame their worldview. A respondent might believe that having a pragmatic or cautious outlook makes him or her conservative. More commonly, someone might identify as conservative on social issues but be liberal on economic issues, and vice versa. All of these are coherent notions of conservatism, creating difficulties in interpreting the military's "conservatism." Later in this chapter I examine the underlying dimensions of respondent identification and attempt to tease out trends in corollaries of ideological identification among members of the army. I will first, however, examine self-identification across the army to see if common perceptions of uniform ideological self-identification are true.

Unfortunately, the Janowitz and FPLP studies do not contain data on junior officers or the enlisted population. However, we do have observations by Ricks that junior enlisted personnel, particularly in the Marine Corps, were leaving basic training in the 1990s with a more conservative outlook and a strong disdain for the values of civilian society.[6] Similarly, Holsti's analysis of the TISS data suggested that in the late 1990s younger members of the military elite were likely to be more conservative than older members of the military's senior ranks.[7]

These observations represent a deviation from more comprehensive studies of the attitudes of more junior members of the military, particularly soldiers. Probably the most-cited finding of the groundbreaking study of soldier attitudes during World War II, published in *The American Soldier* volumes, was the extent to which American soldiers were "profoundly nonideological."[8] This finding, however, came well before the advent of the all-volunteer force, so it is also useful to look at data from the AVF era, such as that collected in the Monitoring the Future project. After looking at these data, David Segal and his fellow researchers found that between 1976 and 1999 people enlisting in the military generally tracked their nonmilitary peers in their propensity to self-identify as conservative.[9]

---

[6] Ricks, *Making the Corps*.

[7] Holsti, "Of Chasms and Convergences," 32.

[8] See Moskos, "The Military," and Stouffer et al., *American Soldier*.

[9] The findings suggested that between 1976 and 1985 those high school seniors bound for the military were more conservative than their peers who were neither entering the military nor going to college. Those bound for the military were only slightly less conservative than those bound for college during this period. For the period from 1985 to 1999, the military-bound cohort most closely resembled the noncollege bound and was significantly less conservative than those going to college. Segal, Freedman-Doan, Bachman, and O'Malley, "Attitudes of Entry-Level Enlisted Personnel."

TABLE 5.2
Ideological Identification in the Army and American Society, 2004

	Civilians	Army	Difference
Conservative	37%	38%	−1%
Moderate	39	41	−2
Liberal	24	21	3
N =	51933ᵃ	1129	

Source: C&S Survey and 2004 National Annenberg Election Survey.
Note: Differences are significant at the 0.001 level.

ᵃ As discussed in appendix C, the population of the NAES survey used for comparison with the C&S Survey was limited to those surveyed after April 1, 2004, to ensure that respondents were answering their respective surveys during approximately the same time period. Active-duty members of the military are also excluded from the NAES data presented here.

The C&S Survey data correspond more closely with the Monitoring the Future project than with the observations of Ricks or the data on junior military elites in the TISS study.[10] Today's soldiers and junior officers are decidedly not as conservative as senior officers. Similarly, when looking at the army as a whole compared with the general population, as in table 5.2, we find little, if any, divergence in the distribution of liberal-conservative self-identification.

While the similarities between the ideological self-identification of the army and the general public may strike some as unexpected—and they certainly refute the anecdotal evidence gathered in the 1990s—one must remember that conventional wisdom about army attitudes is almost exclusively based on studies of the officer corps. The entire officer corps comprises only 14% of the army. Further, the population typically studied by political scientists, namely majors and above, comprises only 6% of the army. The bulk of the army consists of soldiers, who are younger and more racially and ethnically diverse than the population at large.

When looking at the army by rank category in table 5.3, it is easier to see how the enlisted ranks drive overall army classifications. In sum, the army certainly does not overwhelmingly self-identify as ideologically conservative. The similarity between the general American population and the army population masks two very different populations in the army data set. One is heavily conservative but relatively small (the officer corps), and the other is more moderate and liberal but much larger (the

[10] Of course, junior military elites surveyed in the TISS study in 1999 would have advanced another five years by the time of the C&S Survey, putting them among the most senior group of officers to be surveyed in 2004.

TABLE 5.3
Ideology by Rank

	Enlisted	Warrants	Officers	Army
Conservative	32%	69%	63%	38%
Moderate	45	19	23	41
Liberal	23	12	14	21
N =	525	87	517	1,129

Source: C&S Survey.
Note: Differences are significant at the 0.001 level.

enlisted ranks). Soldiers largely reflect the general population, with a slightly higher number of moderates, fewer conservatives, and approximately the same proportion of liberals. The officer corps, however, looks distinctly different from both the enlisted ranks and the larger American population in the propensity of officers to self-identify as conservative.

Part of this may be due to the different demographic characteristics of the officer and enlisted ranks. Officers are required to have at least a bachelor's degree, are predominantly white, and have incomes that place them in the middle- to upper-middle-class strata. There is a higher proportion of minorities in the enlisted ranks. However, even when controlling for factors like race and gender, officers and soldiers differ significantly in their ideological self-identification. The difference between the conservative identification of officers and soldiers among whites, Hispanics, men, and women is a substantial 30 percentage points. Among blacks, the ideological shift between officers and soldiers moves in a similar direction but is considerably less than among other demographic subgroups (only 24% of black enlisted personnel describe themselves as conservative compared with 30% of black officers).

Moving beyond a bivariate analysis to a multiple regression allows for the simultaneous testing of several demographic factors. By regressing ideological identification on age, gender, income, race, and education, we obtain a fuller picture of the influence of these factors on the self-identification of soldiers and officers. Within the army, being male, having a higher income, and having a bachelor's degree (compared with only a high school diploma or some college) contribute to a conservative ideological outlook. Being nonwhite, and particularly being black, contributes significantly to having a more liberal ideological outlook (see model 1 in table 5.5). Overall, however, these demographic factors do little to explain the ideological attitudes of members of the army.

An estimate of a similar model on a representative sample of the civilian population shows somewhat similar, though less pronounced, results.

TABLE 5.4
Ideological Identification by Subgroup

	Liberal	Moderate (summed by row)	Conservative	
White soldiers & WOs	17%	42%	41%	N = 197
White officers	14	18	69	N = 202
Hispanic soldiers & WOs	29	44	27	N = 211
Hispanic officers	16	27	57	N = 166
Black soldiers & WOs	28	48	24	N = 156
Black officers	17	52	30	N = 122
Male soldiers & WOs	21	43	36	N = 482
Male officers	13	21	66	N = 396
Female soldiers & WOs	33	4	19	N = 130
Female officers	18	34	48	N = 121
Total soldiers & WOs	23	44	33	N = 612
Total officers	14	23	63	N = 517

Source: C&S Survey.

Note: Differences between white and Hispanic officers and soldiers are significant at the 0.001 level. Differences between black soldiers and officers are not significant. Differences between male and female officers and soldiers are significant at the 0.01 level.

Among civilians, these demographic factors explain an even smaller amount of the variance in ideological attitudes than among members of the army. Gender, income, and race all influence ideological outlook in the same direction, although with substantially lesser effect. Education is the only demographic factor that influences ideology differently among civilians. Specifically, a civilian with a bachelor's degree is likely to be less conservative than a civilian with less schooling (see model 2 in table 5.5).[11]

Combining members of the army with civilians in the same regression, with the addition of a dichotomous "Army" identifier variable, results in a model that looks very similar to the model run solely on the civilian population. In this case, the "Army" variable is statistically and substantively significant and indicates that even when controlling for these other demographic factors, being in the army moves a respondent's ideological self-identification in a conservative direction (model 3 in table 5.5). Model 4 demonstrates the interaction effects of the "Army" variable and the

[11] Income typically drives ideology to a larger degree than education, with people who earn higher incomes more likely to self-identify as conservative. As people with higher levels of education typically earn more money, this often masks the "liberalizing" effect of more education.

TABLE 5.5
Demographics and Ideological Identification

Dependent variable[a]

Independent variable	Liberal = 0	Moderate = 1	Conservative = 2	
		Model number		
	1	2	3	4
	Army	NAES	Combined	Combined
Age (in years)	0.001	0.004**	0.004**	0.004**
Gender (1 = male)	0.192**	0.108**	0.110**	0.108**
Income				
(1 = < $10k, 9 = > $150k)	0.096**	0.023**	0.023**	0.023**
Hispanic[b]	−0.157**	−0.061**	−0.062**	−0.061**
Black	−0.373**	−0.130**	−0.141**	−0.130**
Other	−0.230**	−0.099**	−0.103**	−0.099**
No high school diploma[c]	−0.462	0.176**	0.173**	0.176**
High school diploma	−0.196*	0.163**	0.156**	0.163**
Some college or associate's degree	−0.237**	0.108**	0.097**	0.108**
Advanced degree	−0.047	−0.177**	−0.168**	−0.177**
Army			0.196**	0.014
Army* Age				−0.003
Army* Hispanic				−0.097
Army* Black				−0.243**
Army* Other				−0.131
Army* Male				0.084
Army* No high school diploma				−0.638
Army* High school diploma				−0.359**
Army* Some college				−0.344**
Army* Advanced degree				0.130
Army* Income				0.074
Constant	0.764**	0.750**	0.750**	0.750**
Adjusted R-squared	0.114	0.034	0.033	0.036
N =	1,126	46,755	47,881	47,881

* $p < .05$, ** $p < .01$

[a] The dependent variable from the C&S Survey was recoded from a 7-point scale to a 3-point scale to allow for comparison with the NAES data set.

[b] The base category for the race variable is white.

[c] The base category for education is a bachelor's degree.

various demographic variables. The results show that black members of the army are more likely to self-identify as liberal. Similarly, being in the army and having earned less than a bachelor's degree corresponds with greater liberal identification.

These models show that demographic factors alone do not explain the ideological leanings of the army. While some demographic factors correlate with ideological self-identification, as we would expect, education seems to have a markedly different effect within the army and civilian populations. And although demographic factors like race, gender, education, income, and age seem to explain a slightly higher percentage of the variance in army attitudes compared with the civilian population, it is important to recognize that it is not fully possible to isolate the influence of some demographic factors, given the structure of the army's rank system. In other words, although regressions with demographic factors imply that characteristics such as race, gender, education, and income all have some effect on a respondent's reported ideological identification, many of these factors are highly correlated, or "bundled," within the army population. Since officers are required to have a bachelor's degree, they have a higher level of education than soldiers—hence the relationship between increased education and increased conservatism in the army, the opposite of the relationship among civilians. Officers also earn substantially more than soldiers and are predominantly white.[12] Even the rate of liberalism among blacks within the army needs to be seen in context, as the data show that it is not because blacks in the army are more liberal but because they are less likely to be conservative than other demographic groups.

In looking at this question from a different angle, one might ask what the aggregate ideological self-identification of the civilian population would be if the civilian population mirrored the army demographically. In discussions about officer attitudes, it is often asserted that most of the divergence in attitudes and outlook is simply due to the fact that the officer corps is a predominantly white, male, upper-middle- class institution. However, the aggregate ideological self-identification of the Virtual Army shifts negligibly from the aggregate attitudes of the sample weighted to reflect the civilian population (see table 5.6). This was not wholly unexpected, given that the regressions showed that demographic factors have relatively little influence on the ideological identifications of both the civilian and the army population. Similarly, we know that the army al-

---

[12] As discussed in chapter 3, the mean income of officers is significantly higher than that of soldiers and warrant officers (about $83,803 versus $45,974 for the ranks included in the C&S Survey). The typical soldier has a high school diploma and some college credit, and most officers have some form of advanced degree. The officer corps is about 76% white, and the soldier and warrant officer population is about 57% white.

TABLE 5.6
Ideological Identification in the Virtual Army and Officer Corps

	Civilians	NAES Virtual Army	Army
Conservative	37%	36%	38%
Moderate	39	40	41
Liberal	24	24	21
N =	51,933	29,710	1,129

	Civilians	NAES Virtual Officer Corps	Army officers
Conservative	37%	35%	63%
Moderate	39	40	23
Liberal	24	25	14
N =	51,933	18,929	517

Source: C&S Survey and 2004 National Annenberg Election Survey.

Note: Differences between "Civilians" and "Army officers" are significant at the 0.001 level. See chapter 3 and appendix C for a discussion of the Virtual Army and Virtual Officer Corps.

ready looks very similar to the civilian population in terms of aggregate ideological identification, so we would not expect a significant shift in the Virtual Army.

However, the army officer corps does not reflect the civilian population in its self-identified ideology, and we know that officers differ demographically from both soldiers and the general American population. I therefore also looked at the attitudes of the Virtual Officer Corps. The results disprove the idea that the differences between the political ideologies of officers and the larger American population are due simply to demographic factors. In fact, a sample of the civilian population that mirrors the officer corps on these dimensions is likely to be slightly *less conservative* and slightly *more liberal* than a simple representative sample of Americans.[13]

---

[13] Although most researchers focus on the preponderance of white males in the officer corps when making the assertion that demographics explain the conservative self-identification of officers, the correlations between being white or male and ideological self-identification are fairly low (each at about 0.06 among civilians). Furthermore, officers are relatively young due to the fact that most enter the army in their early twenties and are due for retirement after twenty years of service. Likewise, the salaries of officers place them solidly in the middle to upper-middle class, with a relatively small proportion earning over $100,000 a year. Last, officers are typically more educated than their civilian counterparts due to the commissioning and promotion requirements discussed in chapter 3.

Overall, then, it appears that traditional demographic factors do little to explain the ideological self-identification of members of the army officer corps.

Self-selection or the institutional effects of military service are other possible causes. There is something about either choosing to be an army officer or being an army officer, or both, that leads one to self-identify as conservative. Considering the army experience, I wanted to see if any characteristics of military service might contribute to this increase in conservative self-identification among army officers. Specifically, I looked at the following respondent characteristics to see which might correlate with an officer's ideology:

1. *Military occupational specialty.* As the core mission of the army is fighting wars, one might expect officers in combat specialties (infantry, armor, field artillery, and so on) to be more inclined to have a conservative outlook than those involved in support specialties (such as intelligence, quartermaster, and ordnance).

2. *Combat veteran.* This variable includes those who reported being in direct ground combat in the previous two years. The expectation is that those who have had this kind of experience are likely to undergo a transformation in their worldview.

3. *Operationally deployed.* This variable is defined as anyone who has received hazardous fire pay during his or her career, indicating that the person was assigned to a designated combat zone. This does not necessarily mean that the person will have experienced direct ground combat, although 26% of respondents in this category have.

4. *Operation Iraqi Freedom or Operation Enduring Freedom veteran.* This variable includes anyone who has deployed in support of either of these two operations. Given the strong political divisions surrounding interpretations of these conflicts, particularly operations in Iraq, it might be supposed that those who participated in either of these operations may have shifted their political ideology as a result of their experience.

5. *Time in service.* If the army shapes worldviews, then one would expect that the longer a person stays in the army, the more conservative his or her views will be.

6. *Son or daughter of career officer.* Because the army officer corps has appeared to sustain a generally conservative outlook over time, I would expect officers whose parents served in the military to be more likely to share a conservative outlook.

7. *Sibling or spouse in service.* This variable tests whether someone's ideological outlook changed by having immediate family members who have served in the military.

8. *Source of commission.* There are different avenues through which one can become an officer, each correlating with a distinct socialization process. The commissioning sources examined here include the Reserve Officers Training Corps, the Officer Candidate School, the United States Military Academy, and direct commissions.

9. *Type of unit.* This variable indicates whether the respondent was serving in a deployable/operational unit at the time of the survey or whether he or she was assigned to a higher headquarters or institutional/training unit. One might expect that those in deployable units would have a different ideological outlook from those in training and institutional support billets.

10. *Leadership position.* This variable indicates whether the respondent was in a position in which he or she had command or leadership responsibility over other soldiers. For officers this includes positions such as platoon leader, company commander, battalion commander, and brigade commander. This variable also serves as a proxy for potential within the army, as these positions are typically required for further advancement and are highly sought after by officers.

11. *Rank.* An officer's rank is an indicator of his or her success in the army. If the army helps shape ideological attitudes in a conservative direction, then one would suspect that officers of higher rank would be more prone to self-identify as conservative.

A look at the correlation between each of these variables and ideological self-identification shows that none of these variables is significantly correlated with "conservatism" in the officer corps. The two variables with the highest correlations are rank and time in service, 0.14 and 0.13 respectively.[14] The only two variables that are significant as predictors of an officer's ideology are his or her gender (with males more likely to be conservative) and whether the officer is black (with black officers more likely to be liberal).

Similar results hold for soldiers, with slight differences. Being male in the enlisted ranks corresponds with an increase in conservatism, although not to the same degree as being male in the officer ranks. Being black again corresponds with a decrease in conservative self-identification. Unlike in the officer ranks, however, being Hispanic also corresponds with a decrease in conservative self-identification. Also unlike the officer corps, rank is statistically significant as a predictor of ideological self-identification among soldiers.

[14] These are also the only two variables that are statistically significant in bivariate regressions of each of these variables on ideology. However, when placed in a multivariate regression with some of the demographic control variables analyzed earlier (sex, race, and education), the rank variable is shown to be statistically insignificant as a predictor of the ideological attitudes of officers. Income, age, and time in service were left out of the equation due to the fact that all three variables are highly correlated with rank.

These findings raise more questions than they answer. If neither demographics nor elements of the army experience explain the ideological outlook of soldiers and officers, what explanatory possibilities remain?

Opting In and Opting Out?

Another possible explanation for the prevalence of conservative self-identification among officers is self-selection into service and, possibly, self-selection out of service by those who find that their worldview is incompatible with those of their peers. And while it is impossible to fully test either of these hypotheses with the C&S Survey data, we can analyze the implications of peer effects on officer and enlisted attitudes.

In addition to asking respondents to place themselves on a seven-point scale ranging from "extremely liberal" to "extremely conservative," the C&S Survey asked respondents to place "officers in general" and "enlisted soldiers in general" on the same scale. Having responses to these questions allows us to assess the perceived distance between the respondent's ideological self-identification and the ideological self-identification of the rest of the army. A plurality of officers, 44%, place "officers in general" at the same point as themselves on the liberal-conservative scale. Thirty-eight percent place themselves to the left of their peers, and the remaining 19% place themselves to the right of other officers. Excluding those who place themselves to the immediate left or right of their peers, 23% of officers place themselves to the left of "officers in general" compared with only 3% who place themselves more than one category to the right of their peers. Given that 63% of officers identify themselves as conservative, it follows that few officers find themselves to the right of their peers.

Also of interest are the perceptions of enlisted soldiers of the ideologies of fellow soldiers and their officers. Twenty-two percent of soldiers place themselves to the left of their peers, and 33% place themselves to the right. Again excluding those who place themselves to the immediate left or right of "enlisted soldiers in general," 10% place themselves to the left and 15% to the right. These findings are in keeping with the more balanced aggregate self-identification of the enlisted ranks. The views of enlisted soldiers on the ideology of the officer corps are also about what one would expect. Forty-four percent place themselves to the left of the officer corps, and 29% to the right.

It is possible to use a measure of perceived ideological distance from peer groups and leaders to assess any potential institutional effects that the officer corps' aggregate political ideology may have on perceptions of the army and the willingness of soldiers and officers to pursue an army career. If there are pressures within the army to identify with a certain political ideology (if it has become an institutional norm), we would expect those who perceive an ideological distance from those around them to be less inclined to have faith in their leaders or to view the army as a viable career.

Preliminary comparisons between those who place themselves to the right or left and those who believe their political ideologies are in line with "officers in general" suggest some key attitudinal differences between these groups. Officers who align themselves ideologically with the rest of the officer corps are slightly more likely to believe that "Army leadership will make the best decisions to maintain a quality Army." They are much more likely than those officers who do not align themselves ideologically with their peers to express intentions to stay in the army until retirement (at least twenty years).[15] They are also much more likely than those officers who place themselves to the left of their peers to state that they agree with the statement "I am confident I will be promoted as high as my ability and interest warrant if I stay in the Army," although officers who place themselves to the right are equally likely to agree with this statement. In terms of morale, officers who place themselves to the right of their peers express the highest level of morale, followed by those aligned with their peers and those to the left of other officers.

However, only the relationship between self-placement to the left or right of other officers and a respondent's intent to stay in the army for a career is statistically significant in a multivariate regression. Even when controlling for other factors that may influence an officer's decision to pursue a career in the army, officers whose ideological self-placements are not in line with those of their peers are less likely to state they intend to make a career of army service. Table 5.7 shows the relationship between perceptions of being to the left or right of other officers and the intent to stay in the army for twenty years or more.

There also appear to be differences between the attitudes of soldiers and warrant officers who perceive themselves to be ideologically aligned with the officer corps and soldiers and warrant officers who place themselves to the right or left of "officers in general." Those perceiving themselves as ideologically aligned with officers are slightly more likely to agree with the statement "I believe that the Army leadership will make the best decisions to maintain a quality Army." They are also slightly more likely to say that they intend to pursue a career in the army. There are larger differences on questions of personal morale and optimism about achieving success in the army. Soldiers and warrant officers who perceive

---

[15] Analyses of the question of career intent and the question of confidence in being promoted are limited to those with less than fifteen years of service.

TABLE 5.7
Perceived Ideological Distance and Career Intent (Officers)

		No intent	Career intent	Career intent (−) No intent
Perceived position	Left	51%	49%	−1%
compared with	Aligned	36	64	28
officers in general	Right	46	54	8

Source: C&S Survey.

Note: Analysis is limited to officers with fewer than 16 years of service. Differences in career intent between those to the "Left" and those "Aligned" are significant at the .05 level. Differences in career intent between "Left" and "Right" and between "Aligned" and "Right" are not significant.

themselves to be to the left of "officers in general" are especially likely to report having lower morale and less optimism about their army careers than those who perceive themselves to be to the right of, or aligned with, the officer corps.

In a multivariate analysis controlling for demographic factors and other likely explanations for these attitudes, perceived ideological "distance" from officers is statistically significant in predicting the morale and optimism of soldiers and warrant officers. This is different from the findings about officer attitudes, as it appears that among soldiers there is no significant effect on a respondent's desire to pursue a career in the army. Furthermore, only perceived placement to the left of the officer corps is statistically significant in predicting responses to these questions. The effects of this perception of ideological distance from the officer corps are fairly minimal among soldiers and warrant officers, as can be seen in table 5.8, but this variable still explains more than other possible factors such as gender, race, deployment history, occupational specialty, current unit, or leadership position.

In sum, it appears that a perceived distance between one's political ideology and the ideology of "officers in general" has some effect on soldiers' and officers' attitudes. Among soldiers, being to the left of the officer corps correlates with a slight decrease in personal morale and a slight increase in disagreement with the statement "I am confident I will be promoted as high as my ability and interest warrant if I stay in the Army." There does not, however, appear to be any effect on soldiers' overall faith in army leadership or their desire to pursue a career in the army. Among officers, perceived ideological distance from other officers has a different effect. Officers who do not believe their political ideology is aligned with that of other officers are less likely to state that they desire to pursue a career in the army. This finding hints at a self-selection effect, in that

TABLE 5.8
Perceived Ideological Distance and Morale/Optimism (Soldiers)

"I am confident I will be promoted as high as my ability and interest warrant if I stay in the Army"

		Agree	Neither	Disagree	Agree (−) Disagree*
Perceived position	Left	48%	15%	37%	10%
compared with	Aligned	61	13	26	36
officers in general	Right	51	19	30	21

"How would you rate your current level of morale?"

		High	Moderate	Low	High (−) Low
Perceived position	Left	21%	47%	32%	−11%
compared with	Aligned	25	46	28	−3
officers in general	Right	30	40	29	1

Source: C&S Survey.

Note: Numbers in the first half of the table reflect soldiers and warrant officers with less than 16 years of service. Numbers in the second half reflect all soldiers and warrant officers. In terms of confidence in being promoted, only the differences between those who perceive themselves to the "Left" of the officer corps and those "Aligned" are statistically significant at the .05 level. In terms of current level of morale, only the differences between "Left" and "Right" are statistically significant at the .05 level. Only placement to the left of the officer corps is statistically significant in multivariate regression.

officers who feel that their outlook is in line with the majority of their peers are more likely to remain in the army and pursue a career.

Of course, it is also possible that the causal mechanism works in the opposite direction, that soldiers with lower morale or faith in army leaders extrapolate from these feelings of dissatisfaction a sense that they have a different worldview than what is common in the army. Similarly, officers who are less likely to pursue a career in the military may have a perception of "thinking differently" from those officers willing to express a long-term commitment. Either way, the findings imply the perception of an institutional norm in ideological identification on a liberal-conservative scale.

Social and Economic Dimensions of Conservatism

A preliminary analysis of attitudes on social and economic issues in chapter 3 shows that officers in general are prone to taking more conservative positions on these questions than are soldiers and warrant officers. This section will assess whether ideological self-identification correlates with positions on these issues.

A look at simple correlations between liberal-conservative self-placement and specific questions on social and economic issues yields interesting results. First, the correlations between attitudes on specific issues and a respondent's self-reported political ideology are uniformly higher for officers than they are for soldiers and warrant officers. For example, among officers the correlation between attitudes toward "outlawing abortion entirely" and ideological self-identification is 0.41. Among soldiers and warrant officers, the correlation drops to 0.18. Likewise, the correlation between attitudes toward efforts to help minorities and ideological self-identification among officers is 0.36, whereas it is only 0.20 among soldiers. This pattern holds for every social and economic attitude assessed in the C&S Survey and suggests that the political ideologies of soldiers are somewhat less coherent than those of officers. In other words, if an officer states that he or she is conservative or liberal, this should make it easier to predict his or her opinion on these issues than it would be to predict the position of a soldier.[16]

Another interesting finding is the role of religion, or the absence of religion, in predicting ideological self-identification. As reported in chapter 4, 47% of officers and 58% of senior officers state that religion provides "quite a bit" or "a great deal" of guidance in their day-to-day living. Thirty-four percent of soldiers state that religion plays an equally important role. This finding might lead one to suspect that a primary source of the overwhelming conservative self-identification among officers is their religiosity. However, that is not the case. The correlation between the reported role of religion in the daily lives of officers and their political ideologies is only 0.16. Among soldiers and warrant officers, the correlation drops to 0.08.

A closer look at the relationships between social and economic issues and liberal-conservative self-identification reveals that these issues are fairly significant in predicting an officer's political ideology. Every question on social issues in the C&S Survey is statistically significant as a predictor of an officer's position on the liberal-conservative scale. The most significant questions address women's equality, abortion, gun control, and government programs to help minorities. The two most significant questions, on women's equality and abortion, can explain shifts of 1.75 and 1.41 points, respectively, on the seven-point liberal-conservative

---

[16] This is in keeping with several studies of public opinion research that suggest that those with more information, or education, are more likely to have more stable political views. By extension, these people are also more likely to place their worldview accurately within a commonly accepted framework such as a liberal-conservative self-identification. See Converse, "Information Flow." See also Zaller, *Nature and Origins of Mass Opinion*.

TABLE 5.9
Correlations between Social and Political Attitudes and Ideology

Issue	Correlations[a]			Officers only[b]		
	Army	Officers	Enl + WO[c]	Coefficient	Adjusted R²	t
Govt. and indiv. welfare	0.25	0.38	0.11	0.29	0.14	9.21
Education spending	0.25	0.26	0.19	0.60	0.07	6.08
Health-care spending	0.23	0.24	0.18	0.55	0.06	5.57
Economy over environment	−0.09	−0.26	0.02	−0.36	0.06	−5.75
Social Security spending	0.21	0.17	0.16	0.32	0.03	3.95
Violence/Crime spending	0.09	0.12	0.02	0.26	0.01	2.74
Women's role	0.21	0.33	0.16	0.29	0.11	7.90
Outlawing all abortion	−0.29	−0.41	−0.18	−0.47	0.17	−9.61
Tighter gun control	0.28	0.32	0.23	0.36	0.10	7.52
Efforts to help minorities	0.27	0.36	0.20	0.51	0.13	8.58
Allowing prayer in schools	−0.14	−0.24	−0.07	−0.32	0.06	−5.33
Banning death penalty	0.19	0.22	0.15	0.29	0.05	4.86
Religion in daily life	0.14	0.16	0.08	0.16	0.02	3.60

Source: C&S Survey.

[a] The first three columns represent simple correlations between ideology and attitudes on each specific social or economic issue.

[b] The last three columns reflect the results of a bivariate regression of ideology of officers on each social or economic issue.

[c] Enlisted soldiers and warrant officers.

scale.[17] Among these questions, the least significant predictor of a respondent's political ideology is the reported role of religion in day-to-day life, which accounts for a maximum shift of only 0.65 points on the ideological scale (see table 5.9).

Attitudes about economic issues appear to play an equally important role in determining an officer's conservatism. Whether an officer feels that the "government should see to it that every person has a job and a good standard of living" or agrees more with the statement that "the government should just let each person get ahead on his/her own" can explain a shift of 1.75 points on the liberal-conservative scale. Attitudes toward

[17] Here is an example of how these numbers were calculated: The coefficient for a respondent's attitude toward the role of women in the workplace is 0.292. As respondents could place themselves on a scale of one to seven in response to this question, there is a difference of 1.75, or 6 times 0.292, in the predicted ideology of someone who fully agreed with the statement "Women should have an equal role" compared with someone who stated that "a woman's place is in the home."

government spending on education and health care also explain shifts of over 1 point.[18]

While these data show that these social and economic attitudes do play a role in determining an officer's political ideology, they are clearly not the sole determinants of an officer's self-placement. And while these calculations help us predict an individual's ideology, they do not provide a comprehensive picture of attitudes across the army. In an attempt to present a broader view of how members of the army respond across a range of social and economic issues, and how those responses align with ideological self-placement, I constructed two separate scales. The first was an economic-attitudes scale consisting of four questions related to government spending and the economy. The scale was constructed by assigning a score of -1 for each response that would generally be considered liberal. A score of 1 was given for each response considered conservative, and a score of 0 was given for moderate responses. The second scale was similarly constructed using attitudes toward social issues. The choice of questions used in constructing the scales was somewhat arbitrary, and the indexes should in no way be considered as comprehensive measures of a respondent's social or economic philosophy.[19] However, the questions do provide a broad enough range of topics to make them useful for obtaining a more nuanced perspective on the political ideologies of soldiers and officers than what is provided by the liberal-conservative self-identification question alone. The eight questions used in constructing the two scales are shown in figure 5.2.[20]

The distribution of members of the army on these scales solidly refutes the idea that they are uniformly conservative in their social or economic outlook. The same can be said even of officers, despite their overwhelming self-identification as conservative.

As seen in table 5.10, a plurality of soldiers and officers, 48%, score as moderates (overall scores between -1 and 1) on the social-issues scale.[21] On the economic-attitudes scale, a majority of soldiers, 67%, end

---

[18] In a multivariate analysis with demographic controls, most of these variables remain statistically significant, with the exception of attitudes toward education and health-care spending. The remaining six variables include four on social attitudes and two on economic attitudes. Together, these variables explain about 37% of the variance in the ideological self-placement of army officers.

[19] A factor analysis was performed on the various subsets of social and economic questions to identify the underlying themes that these questions address. The questions on both the economic scale and the social-issues scale load on a single factor. Cronbach's alpha is 0.72 for the economic scale and 0.56 for the social-issues scale.

[20] Someone who gave "liberal" responses to all four questions on the social-attitudes scale would score a –4. Giving "conservative" responses would result in a score of +4. The same holds for the economic-issues scale.

[21] To calculate 48%, total the three numbers for "Army" in the "Moderate" column under "Social Issues" (32% + 15% + 1%).

Economic Issue Scale Questions

1. Some people feel that the government in Washington should see to it that every person has a job and a good standard of living...Others think the government should just let each person get ahead on his/her own. Where would you place yourself on this scale?

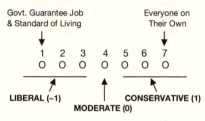

Govt. Guarantee Job & Standard of Living — Everyone on Their Own

1 2 3 4 5 6 7

LIBERAL (−1)   MODERATE (0)   CONSERVATIVE (1)

For each of the following government programs, indicate whether you feel it should be expanded, kept about the same, or cut back.

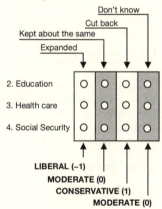

Expanded / Kept about the same / Cut back / Don't know

2. Education
3. Health care
4. Social Security

LIBERAL (−1)
MODERATE (0)
CONSERVATIVE (1)
MODERATE (0)

Social Issue Scale Questions

Please indicate your position on the following domestic issues

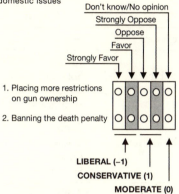

Strongly Favor / Favor / Oppose / Strongly Oppose / Don't know/No opinion

1. Placing more restrictions on gun ownership
2. Banning the death penalty

LIBERAL (−1)
CONSERVATIVE (1)
MODERATE (0)

3. Some people feel that women should have an equal role with men in running business, industry, and government. Others feel that women's place is in the home. Where would you place yourself on this scale?

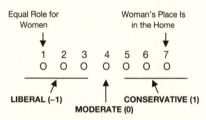

Equal Role for Women — Woman's Place Is in the Home

1 2 3 4 5 6 7

LIBERAL (−1)   MODERATE (0)   CONSERVATIVE (1)

4. Thinking about society in general: In order to make up for past discrimination, do you favor or oppose programs which make special efforts to help minorities get ahead?

O Favor —LIBERAL (−1)
O Neither favor or oppose —MODERATE (0)
O Oppose —CONSERVATIVE (1)
O Don't know / no opinion —MODERATE (0)

Figure 5.2 Social Issue and Economic Attitudes Scales

Table 5.10
Distribution of Social and Economic Attitudes

Economic issues		Social issues Liberal −4 −3 −2		Moderate −1 0 1		Conservative 2 3 4	
Liberal	−4	Army	21%	Army	**32%**	Army	10%
	−3	Soldiers	23	Soldiers	**34**	Soldiers	10
	−2	Officers	12	Officers	18	Officers	8
		Sr. officers[a]	10	Sr. officer	20	Sr. officer	7
Moderate	−1	Army	5	Army	15	Army	14
	0	Soldiers	6	Soldiers	13	Soldiers	12
	1	Officers	5	Officers	**27**	Officers	21
		Sr. officers	3	Sr. officers	**28**	Sr. officers	22
Conservative	2	Army	0	Army	1	Army	2
	3	Soldiers	0	Soldiers	1	Soldiers	1
	4	Officers	1	Officers	3	Officers	6
		Sr. officers	1	Sr. officers	2	Sr. officers	7

BOLD = modal cells

Source: C&S Survey.

Note: The idea for this table came from a similar table constructed by Holsti in "Of Chasms and Convergences." Holsti's scale reflected the attitudes of senior leaders across all of the armed forces. A solid majority of his sample of military leaders, 77%, placed themselves on the side of social conservatism. A slight majority, 51%, placed themselves on the liberal side of economic issues. In addition to significant differences in the two samples, Holsti used different questions to construct his scale, although many cover the same issues included here.

[a] The senior officers category includes officers in the rank of major and above.

up on the liberal side of the scale (overall scores of -2 or less), and a majority of officers, 53%, could again be classified as moderates. What is remarkable is how few soldiers and officers answered the social- or economic-issue questions in a consistently conservative manner (overall scores of 2 or more). Only 2% of the enlisted and warrant-officer ranks score a 2 or greater on the economic-attitudes scale, and 23% score 2 or greater on the social-issues scale. Among officers, only 10% answered the economic-issue questions and 35% answered the social-issue questions in a consistently conservative manner. Furthermore, only 6% of the officer corps, and only 7% of senior officers, gave consistently conservative responses to both the social- and economic-issue questions.

Most remarkable is the fact that the cell containing officers who gave consistently moderate responses to questions on social and economic issues is the most populated cell in the table for the officer subgroup (the modal category for soldiers was "moderate" on social issues and "liberal" on economic issues).

Since the bulk of officers will answer questions about social and economic issues in a consistently moderate to liberal manner, what does this say about the overwhelming conservative self-identification of the officer corps? As expected, almost all, 93%, of those whose answers placed them in the lower-right quadrant on the table of social and economic attitudes also identified themselves on the conservative side of the liberal-conservative spectrum. However, the question of ideological self-placement becomes more interesting as we move up and to the left. Among officers whose responses placed them directly in the middle of the table (moderates on both social and economic issues), only 20% identified themselves as moderate in their political beliefs. A full 64% still identified themselves on the conservative side of the political spectrum. Among those officers whose answers placed them solidly in the liberal quadrant (liberal on both social and economic issues), only 31% also identified themselves as liberal. Most officers in this quadrant, 39%, identified themselves as moderates, and 30% still identified themselves as conservatives, despite their liberal leanings on social and economic issues. In sum, there is a significant disconnect between the self-identified political ideologies of officers and their positions on social and economic issues, at least as represented by this scale.

One explanation for this disconnect may have to do with the salience of defense issues for members of the military. In a population that has joined an organization whose purpose is to fight, it seems plausible that many soldiers and officers would identify themselves as conservative because the word often corresponds with a worldview that emphasizes security and armed might over other means of maintaining peace or asserting national interests. We might therefore expect members of the military to consider issues of military strength the most salient determinants of their ideological outlook, but in fact this is not the case.

There is a lower correlation between self-identified political ideology and attitudes toward defense policy than there is with social or economic attitudes. Part of this is probably due to the fact that it is difficult to articulate what a conservative or liberal approach to foreign policy might be. These labels typically are not used in foreign policy debates.

In looking at the correlations between political ideology and aspects of foreign policy and potential uses of the military in the C&S Survey, as shown in table 5.11, we find that these questions correlate with ideological self-identification to a much lesser degree than questions on economic or social policy. The question relevant to military and national security policy that had the highest correlation with liberal-conservative self-identification (0.25) was the one asking if the government should expand or cut back on defense spending. This was also the only question that achieved statistical significance when placed in a multivariate regression

TABLE 5.11
Correlations between Foreign Policy Issues and Ideology

Issue	Correlations[a]			Officers only[b]		
	Army	Officers	Enl + WO[c]	Coefficient	Adjusted R²	t
Defense spending	−0.18	−0.25	−0.12	−0.49	0.06	−5.71
Fight and win wars	−0.12	−0.16	−0.06	−0.51	0.02	−3.65
Fight terrorism	−0.09	−0.15	−0.05	−0.36	0.02	−3.31
Disaster relief in U.S.	0.16	0.12	0.13	0.18	0.01	2.79
Intervene in civil wars	−0.08	−0.11	−0.06	−0.14	0.01	−2.41
Combat drug trafficking	−0.01	−0.08	−0.01	−0.10	0.00	−1.81
Mil. aid to other nations	−0.07	−0.07	−0.06	−0.16	0.00	−1.55
Humanitarian needs abroad	0.05	0.06	0.03	0.08	0.00	1.41
Instrument of foreign policy	−0.08	−0.04	−0.06	−0.06	0.00	−0.97
Homeland security	−0.01	−0.03	−0.01	−0.08	0.00	−0.78
Econ. aid to other nations	−0.01	0.03	−0.01	0.07	0.00	0.76
Enforcing immigration law	0.02	−0.03	−0.04	−0.03	0.00	−0.66
Deal with domestic disorder	0.06	−0.01	0.06	−0.01	0.00	−0.27

Source: C&S Survey.

[a] The first three columns represent simple correlations between ideology and attitudes on each specific foreign policy or defense issue.

[b] The last three columns reflect the results of bivariate regression of ideology of officers on each policy or defense issue.

[c] Enlisted soldiers and warrant officers.

with questions on social and economic issues. Even then, in terms of substantive effect, it ranked behind questions on the role of women in the workplace, programs to help minorities, the government's role in ensuring an individual's economic well-being, and abortion in its power to predict an officer's ideological self-identification.

Conclusion

The army has historically been viewed as a conservative institution. In this chapter I have shown that this is still the case, at least among the small segment of the army population that political scientists and sociologists usually study, namely senior officers. However, the bulk of the army consists of soldiers, who are much less conservative, much more moderate, and more liberal than their officer counterparts in their ideological self-identification. In fact, the enlisted ranks generally reflect the American population in their propensity toward liberal self-identification. It is when you put officers and enlisted soldiers together that you get an organization that is surprisingly similar to the American population in terms of self-identification on a liberal-conservative scale. However, this should not be taken to mean that the aggregate conservative identification of the officer corps corresponds with a coherent outlook in regards to questions of social or economic policy. Very few officers can be described as being consistently conservative on a range of economic and social issues.

These findings are probably surprising to some observers. However, they are in keeping with most studies of the military and ideology. Indeed, as one reviews studies of the American military, one finds that the idea that service members have a distinctly different worldview (that is, a "military mind")—conservative and dramatically out of step with the rest of society—is a myth that must be continually debunked. Richard Brown, in his overview of American generals at the beginning of the twentieth century, found a few high-profile examples of radical conservatives in the ranks but observed the population overall to be moderate in its worldview. S. A. Stouffer, in his study of soldiers from World War II, likewise found the common soldier to be profoundly nonideological in his outlook. In a panel study of youth who served in the military between 1965 and 1973, M. Kent Jennings and Gregory Markus discovered that military service did not appear to have a significant effect on the attitudes of soldiers.[22] These findings were confirmed by David Segal and his colleagues in the Monitoring the Future project; they found that the attitudes of soldiers typically tracked those of their civilian peers. Most recently, Darrell Driver conducted a thorough investigation of military conservatism among officers and found that "there appears to be nothing inherent in the nature of military service or the military experience that leads to a basic public philosophical conservatism."[23]

In sum, research on the military's role in the formation of ideological attitudes, including this study, shows that the military does not appear significantly to shape the beliefs of those who serve. Likewise, the incoherence in the worldviews of soldiers, especially the apparent mismatch between conservative self-identification and opinions on specific issues, is in keeping with decades of social science research indicating that individuals rarely possess a coherent ideology that might fit into a preexisting label such as liberal or conservative.[24] It would be surprising to find that soldiers have a more coherent worldview than those who have not served in the military.

[22] Jennings and Markus, "Effect of Military Service."
[23] Driver, "Sparta in Bablyon," 265.
[24] Campbell, Converse, Miller, and Stokes, *American Voter*.

However, and sometimes despite their underlying views, the conservative label still clearly appeals to senior members of the military. And although the conservative label, as used by soldiers, may not always correspond with prevailing perceptions of what is conservative and what is not, this preponderance of conservative self-identification probably informs how soldiers approach the political process.

I have shown in this chapter that officers who perceive an ideological distance between themselves and officers in general are less likely to express the intent to pursue a career in the army. Therefore, those who perceive themselves to be ideologically out of step with the rest of the officer corps may be more likely to opt out of the army, leaving a higher proportion of self-identified conservatives behind. This would be one way in which the "team identification" phenomenon of conservative self-identification might influence the actions of service members. In the next chapter I will pursue this concept further, but will also move beyond the realm of generalized perspectives and ideological labels and into a more concrete form of thinking about politics—partisan identification.

Party Affiliation in the Army

THE QUESTION OF THE PARTISAN political identification of members of the army has served as a lightning rod for public debates over the Iraq War, has been a central focus of the last two presidential campaigns, and has generated volumes of discussion among students of civil-military relations. Unlike the question of ideological self-identification, the question of party affiliation has direct implications for perceptions of the military among the American public, for the role of active and retired members of the military in political campaigns, and for the interactions between senior military officers and civilian political elites. In this chapter I attempt to separate the substance from the noise that has surrounded debates over the army and partisan politics.

Deriving Party Affiliation

According to the TISS data set, 67% of army officers in the ranks of major and above identified with the Republican Party in 1998. Within those same ranks, the C&S Survey found that in 2004, 51% identified themselves as Republican, with an additional 15% leaning toward a Republican identification. However, one must use caution in making direct comparisons between the two data sets.

Whereas the TISS survey explicitly asked respondents whether they thought of themselves as Republicans or Democrats, the C&S Survey did not ask respondents directly about which party they affiliated themselves with. The survey did ask about party affiliation in general and strength of attachment to a political party. Using this information, along with the respondent's ideological self-placement relative to his or her placement of the Republican and Democratic Parties along the same ideological scale, it was possible to create a simple algorithm to predict each respondent's party affiliation.

Respondents were asked to place themselves, the Democratic Party, and the Republican Party on the same seven-point liberal-to-conservative scale. Respondents who placed themselves between the two parties were classified as neutral or independent. When respondents placed themselves closer to one of the two parties *and* stated that they thought of themselves as "someone who identifies with one of the major political parties (i.e.

Republican or Democratic Party)," they were classified as either a Republican or a Democratic Party identifier. One advantage of this method is that it does not depend on a "correct" ideological identification of either party. For instance, a respondent could claim that Republicans are liberal and Democrats are conservative, but the only relevant information drawn from the scales to impute the respondent's self-identification was the absolute distance between the respondent's self-placement and his or her placement of the two parties. Figure 6.1 shows the questions used in the algorithm and examples of how they were coded.

The one shortcoming of the algorithm is that it is possible for respondents to place themselves directly between the two parties but still claim to belong to one of the two parties. This applied to sixty-five survey respondents, whom I categorized as "Unknown Partisans." To find out how this group might split between the two parties and to test the overall accuracy of the algorithm, I applied the same predictive method to two sets of data that asked the same questions used in the C&S Survey in addition to a question that asked directly about the respondent's party affiliation.

The first comparison data set was the NES 2004 data set. By using this data set, the algorithm correctly predicted Republican Party identifiers 85% of the time, and Democratic Party identifiers 90% of the time. When analyzing the parties chosen by those the algorithm classified as "Unknown Partisans," we find that 37% actually identified with the Republican Party, and the majority, 63%, identified with the Democratic Party.[1]

The other data set used to evaluate the algorithm was the West Point cadet preelection survey administered in the fall of 2004. This was an especially interesting test case, as it is likely that the party affiliation of cadets is more comparable with members of the army, and with junior officers in particular, than with the general civilian population. In contrast with the results from the NES data set, the algorithm correctly predicted Republican identification among cadets in 99% of cases. Further, 82% of those cadets the algorithm classified as "Unknown Partisans" actually identified with the Republican Party. Continuing with this trend, a full 29% of cadets that the algorithm predicted would identify with the Democratic Party instead chose to affiliate themselves with the Republican Party.[2]

---

[1] The correlation between this derived party identification measure and liberal-conservative ideological self-placement is 0.56. The correlation between party identification and ideological self-placement in the NES 2004 data set is 0.60.

[2] Only 93 of 885 cadets self-identified with the Democratic Party, and 543 identified themselves as Republicans. The algorithm predicted that 112 cadets would identify as Democrats because they placed themselves closer to the Democratic Party on the ideological scale. However, 36 of those 112 who more closely aligned themselves with the Democratic Party actually identified themselves as Republicans. Of the cadets who placed themselves closest to the Republican Party on the ideological scale, only 5 identified themselves as Democrats.

Example #1

In terms of politics and political beliefs, we hear a lot of talk these days about liberals and conservatives. Where would you place the Republican Party on the following scale?

Extremely Liberal	Liberal	Slightly Liberal	Moderate	Slightly Conservative	Conservative	Extremely Conservative
↓	↓	↓	↓	↓	↓	↓
O	O	O	O	O	⊗	O

In terms of politics and political beliefs, where would you place the Democratic Party?

Extremely Liberal	Liberal	Slightly Liberal	Moderate	Slightly Conservative	Conservative	Extremely Conservative
↓	↓	↓	↓	↓	↓	↓
O	⊗	O	O	O	O	O

In terms of politics and political beliefs, where would you place yourself?

Extremely Liberal	Liberal	Slightly Liberal	Moderate	Slightly Conservative	Conservative	Extremely Conservative
↓	↓	↓	↓	↓	↓	↓
O	O	⊗	O	O	O	O

Do you think of yourself as someone who identifies with one of the major political parties (i.e., Republican or Democratic Party)?

O Yes   ⊗ No   O Don't Know

= Lean Democratic

Example #2

In terms of politics and political beliefs, we hear a lot of talk these days about liberals and conservatives. Where would you place the Republican Party on the following scale?

Extremely Liberal	Liberal	Slightly Liberal	Moderate	Slightly Conservative	Conservative	Extremely Conservative
↓	↓	↓	↓	↓	↓	↓
O	O	O	O	⊗	O	O

In terms of politics and political beliefs, where would you place the Democratic Party?

Extremely Liberal	Liberal	Slightly Liberal	Moderate	Slightly Conservative	Conservative	Extremely Conservative
↓	↓	↓	↓	↓	↓	↓
⊗	O	O	O	O	O	O

In terms of politics and political beliefs, where would you place yourself?

Extremely Liberal	Liberal	Slightly Liberal	Moderate	Slightly Conservative	Conservative	Extremely Conservative
↓	↓	↓	↓	↓	↓	↓
O	O	O	O	O	⊗	O

Do you think of yourself as someone who identifies with one of the major political parties (i.e., Republican or Democratic Party)?

⊗ Yes   O No   O Don't Know

= ID as Republican

Figure 6.1 Party Affiliation Algorithm

Whereas the "errors" in predicting party affiliation seem to move in both directions with the NES data, with a slight bias toward the Democratic Party, the errors in the cadet predictions move uniformly in the direction of underestimating Republicans and overestimating Democrats. Although this trend is probably not applicable to the entire army population, it is safe to assume that the algorithm underestimates the proportion of junior officers who identify themselves as Republicans and overestimates the number who identify themselves as Democrats. (This finding may also hint at institutional pressures or a "team identification" that trumps ideology as a determinant of party affiliation, which I will discuss later in this chapter.)

The category of "Unknown Partisans" is excluded from the analysis for the rest of this chapter. And although I use the terms "Republican" and "Democrat" to describe the political affiliations of members of the army, those not comfortable with this algorithm can substitute "Someone who is aligned with the Republican (or Democratic) Party and also states that he or she belongs to one of the two major parties" in their place.

Generic Party Identification

Before examining the results of the party-identification algorithm in more detail, it is worth looking at responses to the generic question "Do you think of yourself as someone who identifies with one of the major political parties (i.e. Republican or Democratic Party)?" and comparing the overall level of political party affiliation in the army with rates found in the civilian population. According to the NAES survey, 65% of Americans in 2004 thought of themselves as either Republicans or Democrats. Additionally, 39% of Americans identified strongly with one of these two parties. These figures provide a baseline for assessing the propensity of members of the army to identify with a political party. If members of the army are still nonpartisan, as Janowitz found in 1956, then the proportion of partisans and strong partisans should be significantly less within the army population.

After first looking at the Virtual Army to see what role demographic differences might play in explaining any differences between the army and the civilian population, I found that demographic factors play a minor role in determining whether civilians think of themselves as Republican or Democrat. This is reflected in the fact that the proportion of partisans in the Virtual Army population was 60%, a small drop from the 65% found in the general population. Among the Virtual Officer Corps, the proportion thinking of themselves as either Republican or Democrat was 62%. Similarly, 36% of the Virtual Army considered itself strong Republicans or Democrats, and 38% of the Virtual Officer Corps felt the same, compared with 39% of the civilian population. These numbers suggest there should be only slightly fewer partisans in the army than in the civilian population. They also suggest that any significant differences between the two populations cannot be attributed solely to demographic factors such as gender, race, age, income, or education.

Among respondents to the C&S Survey, slightly fewer than half, 43%, answered that they thought of themselves as identified with one of the two major political parties. The fact that members of the army are significantly less likely than civilians to identify with one of the two major political parties indicates that some vestige of the nonpartisan outlook shown in 1956 may still exist. If it does, however, it does not reside in today's officer corps.

A look at party affiliation by rank category reveals that two out of three officers, or 67%, identified themselves as either Republicans or Democrats in 2004. As with self-identified political ideology, soldiers were more likely to be moderate or, in this case, apolitical: Only 37% of soldiers said that they identified with one of the two major political parties on the C&S Survey.[3] This places the officer corps on a par with the civilian population, whereas the enlisted ranks lag significantly in their propensity to identify as Republican or Democrat. Similarly, 37% of officers said that they identified strongly with one of the two major political parties—nearly equal to the 39% of civilians who said the same, while the rate in the army overall was only 24%.

Unlike the civilian population, the propensity to identify with a major political party does correlate with certain demographic factors among members of the army. However, the two demographic factors with the highest correlation to partisanship in the army are income and education, which are again merely proxies for being an officer.[4] When looking more closely at the interplay between rank and partisanship, one sees that the proportion of respondents who identify with one of the two major political parties increases steadily with rank. Only 31% of junior enlisted soldiers identify as Republican or Democrat. Among senior officers, lieutenant colonels and colonels, the proportion increases to 79% and 81%, respectively. A different pattern holds for the proportion who identify *strongly* as Republican or Democrat. In this case the newest soldiers and officers (junior soldiers and lieutenants) are less likely than their higher-ranking counterparts to strongly identify with a political party.[5]

---

[3] In the case of party identification, warrant officers' appear to reflect the outlook of officers, with 61% reporting that they identified themselves as Republican or Democrat.

[4] Both education and income show a correlation with partisanship of 0.26. The next-highest correlation is between age and partisanship, at 0.18.

[5] The pattern is fairly consistent, although there is a drop from lieutenant colonel to colonel. This may be an artifact of the relatively small size of the population of colonels in the survey.

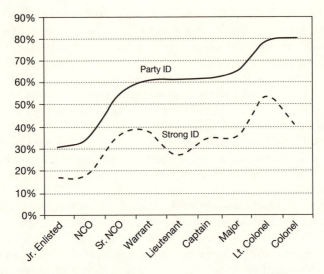

Figure 6.2 Party Affiliation by Rank
Source: C&S Survey
Note: Differences among ranks significant at .001 level.

A regression of partisanship on demographic factors and elements of the army experience reveals that among officers, being black decreases the odds of a respondent's identifying with one of the two major parties, whereas having one or more parents who served in the army is likely to increase the odds.[6] Among soldiers, those with only a high school education are less likely to be partisans, whereas a move up in rank increases the odds of identifying with one of the two major political parties. A further analysis of these influences on partisanship will be addressed in more detail in the next section, which moves beyond analyzing generic party affiliation and focuses on specific identification with either the Republican or the Democratic Party.

The fact that members of the army are generally less likely to identify with a political party than their civilian counterparts is probably surprising to many observers of current American civil-military relations, although it is in keeping with previous scholarly research. The TISS project seemed to confirm anecdotal evidence and conventional wisdom in suggesting that the American military had become strongly identified with the Republican Party. Again, however, it must be noted that the TISS

---

[6] Among officers, being black decreases the odds of identifying with one of the two major political parties by 54%. Having one or more parents who served increases the odds by 76%. Among soldiers, having only a high school education (as opposed to some college or more) decreases the odds of belonging to a party by 58%.

TABLE 6.1
Party Identification in the Army and Civilian Populations

	C&S	NAES	Difference
Republican ID	29%	31%	2%
Lean Rep.	15	12	−3
Neutral	26	9	−17
Lean Dem.	15	15	0
Democratic ID	11	33	22
Unknown partisans	4		
N =	1,114	51,867	

Source: C&S Survey and 2004 National Annenberg Election Survey.
Note: Differences between army and civilian populations are significant at the 0.001 level.

project drew primarily from the attitudes of senior officers attending advanced military schooling. And while the C&S Survey reveals an army that, overall, is less likely to identify with a political party than conventional wisdom would suggest, the C&S Survey does confirm the findings of the TISS project among army officers of comparable rank. It is among the enlisted ranks that political engagement is depressed in comparison with the civilian population, but this is in keeping with the sociopolitical detachment that scholars such as Moskos and Wesbrook documented among enlistees and recruiting-age youth.[7]

Identification with the Republican and Democratic Parties

Moving beyond generic party affiliation and using the previously explained algorithm to predict the party affiliation of members of the army resulted in the distribution shown in table 6.1.

There are some clear and substantial differences between the army and the American public in terms of party affiliation. While the two groups are comparable in terms of the proportion who identify with the Republican Party, a greater proportion of the army does not identify with or lean toward either party, and a much greater proportion of the general public identifies with the Democratic Party.

Although this comparatively low overall identification with the Republican Party may be surprising to some, it is important to account for the fact that conventional wisdom regarding the army's party affiliations generally rests on studies of senior officers. Broken down by rank in

[7] Wesbrook, "Sociopolitical Alienation," and Moskos, "All-Volunteer Force."

TABLE 6.2
Party Identification by Rank

Rank	Republican ID	Democratic ID	Avg. yrs. service	Modal yrs. service
Junior enlisted	18%	9%	3.1	2
NCOs	21	12	9.6	8
Senior NCOs	36	8	17.5	17
Warrants	54	7	17.2	17
Lieutenants	44	19	4.9	1
Captains	48	9	8.7	5
Majors	50	13	15.1	14
Lt. colonels	64	12	19.8	18
Colonels	65	11	23.5	23.5

Source: C&S Survey.

Note: Those who only lean toward a party, are independent, or belong to another party are excluded from this table. Differences among ranks are significant at the 0.001 level. The high average years of service among lieutenants is due to the presence of those who have spent time in the enlisted ranks prior to becoming officers. Officers typically spend a maximum of four years in the lieutenant ranks (second and first lieutenant).

table 6.2, the C&S Survey data reveal a population where rank is strongly correlated with increasing Republican Party identification.

When writing about rank in the army, it is important to control for race and gender, given that the officer corps in general, and the senior officer ranks in particular, are predominantly white and male.[8] Here it is helpful to again see what the Virtual Army and Virtual Officer Corps look like in terms of party affiliation. As can be seen in figure 6.3, a group of civilians that correlated with the army on the dimensions of gender, race, income, age, and education would differ only slightly from the general population in its party affiliation. Demographics clearly do not account for the higher proportion of moderates and the significantly lower proportion of Democratic Party identifiers within the army. Similarly, a Virtual Officer Corps would contain a slightly higher proportion of Republican Party identifiers and fewer Democratic Party identifiers than the general public, but not enough to account for the large differences between the actual officer corps and the American population (see figure 6.4).

If we look more closely at party affiliation within racial/ethnic and gender groups in table 6.3, we find significant differences between the enlisted

[8] Only 17% of officers are women, and 76% of officers are white. Among the ranks of lieutenant colonels and above, 82% are white and 88% are male.

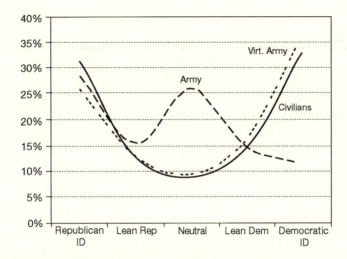

Figure 6.3 Party Affiliation (Army vs. Civilians)
Source: C&S Survey and 2004 National Annenberg Election Survey
Note: Differences between army and civilian populations significant at the .001 level.

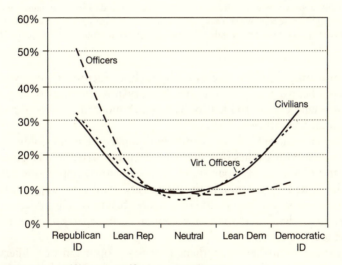

Figure 6.4 Party Affiliation (Officers vs. Civilians)
Source: C&S Survey and 2004 National Annenberg Election Survey
Note: Differences between officers and civilians significant at the .001 level.

TABLE 6.3
Party Identification by Demographic Subgroup

	Republican identifiers	Democratic identifiers
White soldiers & WOs	32%	5%
White officers	58	9
Hispanic soldiers & WOs	14	17
Hispanic officers	34	17
Black soldiers & WOs	11	18
Black officers	17	33
Male soldiers & WOs	26	10
Male officers	52	12
Female soldiers & WOs	11	14
Female officers	46	13
Total soldiers & WOs	24	11
Total officers	51	13

Source: C&S Survey.

Note: Differences between white and Hispanic soldiers and officers are significant at the 0.001 level. Differences between black soldiers and officers are significant at the 0.01 level. Differences between male and female soldiers and officers are significant at the 0.001 level.

ranks and officers, with officers more likely to identify themselves with the Republican Party. Of note are the very few numbers of any army subgroup who choose to identify with the Democratic Party—the exception being black officers.

Officers are more likely to identify with a party than are soldiers. This is in keeping with studies that find a correlation between socioeconomic status and political participation. However, the army population deviates from the general population in the propensity of all subgroups to identify with the Democratic Party. Whether white, black, or Hispanic, male or female, all are less likely than their civilian counterparts to identify with the Democratic Party.

This trend is further strengthened by the proportion of soldiers and officers who are willing to identify strongly with the Republican or Democratic Party. Among civilians in the NAES data set, approximately 60% of those who say they identify with a party also say that they identify strongly with that party. The same holds true in the army, but only with Republican Party identifiers. Fifty-eight percent of those who identify with the Republican Party indicate that their attachment to the party is strong. However, only 47% of the few soldiers and officers who identify with the Democratic Party also say that their attachment is strong. This trend is even more pronounced among officers. Sixty-one percent of Republican Party identifiers in the officer corps say their attachment to the party is strong compared with only 35% of Democratic Party identifiers.

In terms of simple ratios, the ratio of partisans to nonpartisans in the army is 3 to 4. Among officers, the ratio jumps to 2 to 1. The ratio of Republicans to Democrats in the army is approximately 2.6 to 1. Among officers, the ratio increases to 4.1 to 1. Even more striking is the ratio of "strong" Republicans to "strong" Democrats in the officer corps. Almost one in three officers, or 31%, considers him or herself a strong Republican compared with only 4% who consider themselves strong Democrats. This means that strong Republicans in the officer corps outnumber Democrats by a ratio of 7.1 to 1 (although, to keep this in perspective, 65% of army officers do not identify themselves strongly with either party).

Determinants of Republican Identification

What drives this preponderance of Republican identifiers and the virtual absence of Democrats in the army, as well as the overwhelming number of Republicans in the officer corps? As shown earlier, the demographic differences between the army and the civilian society have little to do with aggregate differences in partisan affiliation. A Virtual Army would have slightly fewer Republican Party identifiers and more respondents who would lean toward a Democratic affiliation, but it would still largely track the general American population in the overall distribution of party affiliation. Similarly, a Virtual Officer Corps would have fewer Democratic Party identifiers and a slightly higher proportion of Republicans than exist in the civilian population, but it would still not come close to matching the partisan distribution of the actual officer corps.

A multivariate regression analysis provides a more nuanced picture of how demographics influence party affiliation in the army and in the civilian population. Similar to the findings on ideological self-identification, being white, being male, and having a higher income lead to a greater likelihood of a Republican Party affiliation. Blacks and Hispanics are more likely to identify themselves as Democrats. Compared with the civilian population, income and gender appear to play a greater role in determining party affiliation, whereas the category of race and ethnicity seems to have less of an impact. Combining the NAES and C&S Survey data in a single regression with an army dummy variable reveals that being in the army is second only to race as a predictor of party affiliation.[9]

A combined regression with interaction variables shows that blacks in the army are less likely to lean toward a Democratic Party affiliation than their civilian counterparts. Similarly, a soldier with an advanced degree (master's or above) is more likely to identify with the Republican Party than a civilian with an advanced degree (which is associated with a greater chance of identifying as a Democrat in the civilian population). In sum, race and ethnicity influence party affiliation in the army in the same manner as in the civilian population, but the differences between the races in the army are somewhat muted. As for the influence of education on party affiliation, having an advanced degree in the army appears to correlate with a greater tendency to identify with the Republican Party. One must remember, however, that in the army having an advanced degree is nearly synonymous with being an officer.

A closer look at the determinants of party affiliation within the army reveals that factors related to military service such as occupational specialty, type of unit, and combat experience are largely irrelevant in determining partisan affiliation. Race, again, is a demographic factor predictive of partisan affiliation, but education disappears as a significant influence when controlling for rank. Even when controlling for factors related to military service, Hispanics and blacks are more likely to identify with the Democratic Party, whereas whites lean toward the Republican Party. Higher rank is also associated with an increase in Republican Party affiliation. These findings hold for both the officer and the enlisted ranks.

These results indicate that greater racial and ethnic diversity in the army would also correlate with a greater diversity of political thought. However, the finding of increased Republican Party affiliation with higher rank requires a more nuanced interpretation. There are three possible explanations for this finding, each with different implications for our understanding of internal army culture.

The first possible explanation is that this is simply a generational or cohort effect. Although impossible to test without panel data, this explanation is entirely plausible. The current generation of lieutenant colonels and colonels entered the army between 1980 and 1984—the height of the Reagan buildup of the military. One might expect those who joined the army in that era to form a fairly strong bond with the Republican Party, which persisted throughout their careers. Similarly, there are quite a few

---

[9] Party identification was predicted as both a continuous variable (from strong Republican to strong Democrat) and a dichotomous variable (Republican or non-Republican, for example). Substantive results between the various models were similar. This discussion refers to the model with party identification as a continuous variable.

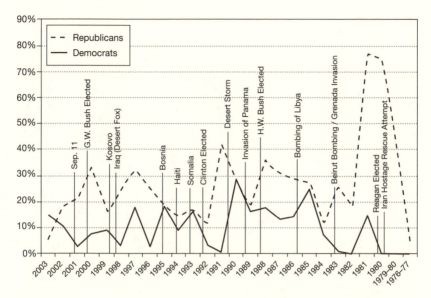

Figure 6.5 Year of Entry and Party Affiliation in 2004 (Soldiers and Warrant Officers)
Source: C&S Survey

Republicans and virtually no Democrats among the cohort of officers who joined the army immediately before and after Operations Desert Spring and Desert Storm. The variations between cohorts shown in figures 6.5 and 6.6 indicate that there may be some validity to the idea that members of the army retain the attitudes with which they enter the army, and that variations in party affiliation reflect early formative experiences.[10] If this is the case, the implication of these figures is that the military will swing back to a distribution of party affiliation that is more balanced between the two parties as the latest cohort advances through the ranks.[11]

One must use caution, however, in taking too much from figures 6.5 and 6.6. The use of these charts alone to assess influences on partisan attitudes excludes a possible socialization effect from being in the army or from changes in respondent attitudes over time. Furthermore, these charts cannot account for the possibility that an equal number of Democratic Party identifiers joined the army in the early 1980s, but left the service at a higher rate than their Republican counterparts. These alter-

[10] For more discussion about how the military may or may not influence political socialization, see Moskos, "The Military," and Lovell and Stiehm, "Military Service." See also Leal, "It's Not Just a Job."

[11] Officers who entered in 2002–3 would have started the commissioning process in 1999–2000. Enlisted soldiers in this category would have joined after September 11, 2001.

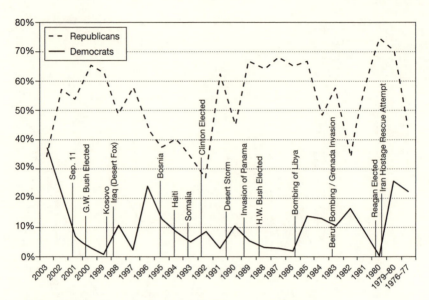

Figure 6.6 Year of Entry and Party Affiliation in 2004 (Officers)
Source: C&S Survey

nate hypotheses are also impossible to test without panel data, but it is possible to indirectly assess if the current army culture may lead non–Republican Party identifiers to opt out of military service at a greater rate than those who identify themselves with the Republican Party.

To start with, in an organization where the proportion of Republican Party identifiers increases with rank, one would expect a young soldier or officer to conflate Republican Party affiliation with success in the army. Similarly, a soldier who perceives that his or her political views are out of step with those of senior leaders may have less faith in the leadership and the vision of senior leaders. Fortunately for the army, the regression analysis does not support the idea that the army's internal culture might lead a soldier or officer who does not identify with the Republican Party to have a lower self-reported level of morale than his or her Republican counterparts. Likewise, party affiliation approaches statistical significance in predicting an officer's degree of faith in senior army leaders, but the substantive effect is negligible. In the enlisted ranks, party affiliation is neither substantively nor statistically significant in predicting faith in army leadership.

However, there is a relationship between party affiliation and an officer's intent to make a career of the army. Even when controlling for demographic factors and characteristics of service, officers who identify with the Democratic Party are about 10% less likely than Republican Party identifiers to state that they intend to make a career of the army. There is no relationship between partisanship and career intent among soldiers.

The Meaning of Party Affiliation in the Army

Given the overwhelming affiliation with the Republican Party among officers, it is worth deciphering what it means to be a Republican in the army. As shown when looking at the West Point cadet data, it appears that many future officers would align themselves ideologically with the Democratic Party but still self-identify as Republican. It is also clear that a majority of officers are moderate to liberal on many social and economic issues. This alludes to institutional influences on party affiliation. In other words, members of the military may think like Democrats on specific issues but still see themselves as Republicans. Given that the army has been viewed as an institution dominated by Republican Party affiliation for some time, we may be noticing the phenomenon of "team identification." In other words, officers may conflate Republican Party affiliation, or at least an aversion to the Democratic Party, with being in the army. The existence of such a phenomenon would inflate the number of Republican Party identifiers in the army and depress the number willing to identify themselves as Democrats. Those officers who were truly apolitical would easily default to Republican Party identification when asked, despite not having any inclination to do so. Likewise, officers who lean toward the Democratic Party may be less likely to state their true views and default to a neutral or even pro—Republican Party stance. Finally, the idea of team identification may also explain why proportionally fewer Democratic Party identifiers are willing to identify strongly with the party than their Republican counterparts.

Here I assess whether a Republican Party affiliation in the army correlates with specific positions on commonly debated issues. If we look at simple correlations between party affiliation and attitudes toward specific issues, we see that the correlations are again higher among officers than among soldiers and warrant officers.[12] This means that if an officer states he or she affiliates with the Republican or Democratic Party, it should be easier to predict his or her opinion on these issues than it would be to predict the position of a soldier.

Another interesting finding is the complete absence of religiosity in predicting party affiliation. As mentioned in chapter 5, the correlation between the reported role of religion in the daily lives of officers and their

---

[12] Correlations were run on a simple seven-point scale from strong Republican to strong Democrat.

TABLE 6.4
Social and Political Attitudes and Party Identification

Issue	Correlations	
	Officers	Enl. + WOs[a]
Efforts to help minorities	0.44	0.30
Gun control	0.38	0.22
Govt.'s role in individual welfare	0.34	0.23
Abortion	0.33	0.14
Death penalty	0.30	0.20
Women's role	0.30	0.16
Education spending	0.28	0.19
Economy vs. the environment	0.26	0.08
Health-care spending	0.25	0.17
Prayer in public schools	0.21	0.05
Social Security spending	0.17	0.15
Violence/Crime spending	0.13	0.03
Religion in daily life	0.04	0.03

Source: C&S Survey.
[a] Enlisted soldiers and warrant officers.

political ideologies was only 0.16. Among soldiers and warrant officers, the correlation dropped to 0.08. Religiosity plays an even smaller role in determining whether someone in the army identifies as a Republican or a Democrat. Among officers, the correlation between the reported role of religion and party affiliation is only 0.04. Among soldiers and warrant officers, it is only 0.03. Most social and economic issues, however, show a reasonably high correlation with party affiliation (see table 6.4).[13]

Although these data show that these social and economic attitudes do play a role in determining an officer's party affiliation, it is worth looking at attitudes on specific issues to assess the meaning of party affiliation within the army. Republican officers have fairly uniform views on a number of social and economic issues. For simplicity's sake, I have taken the views of Republican identifiers on each issue and simplified them to one number that reflects the lopsidedness of opinion on that issue. For example, on the question of banning the death penalty, a full 86% of Republi-

[13] In a multivariate analysis with demographic controls, 8 of the 13 questions on economic and social issues remained statistically significant as predictors of the party identification of officers. Together, these 8 variables explain about 44% of the variance in the party identification of army officers.

can officers are opposed or strongly opposed, compared with only 12% who would support the ban. Subtracting the percentage of Republican officers who support the ban from those who oppose it leaves 74%. A look at all of the social-issue and economic-issue questions on the C&S Survey in this manner reveals fairly uniform opinions across a host of topics. The lone exception relates to attitudes toward Social Security spending, where 27.8% of Republican officers favor expanded spending and 18.4% favor reduced spending, resulting in a difference of only 9.4% (the other 53.8% either have no opinion or say it should remain the same).

Soldier and Officer Differences

As shown in table 6.5, soldiers and warrant officers who identify themselves as Republican also have fairly uniform views across issues, although significant differences between this population and officers exist. As outlined in chapter 5, the propensity of soldiers and warrant officers to generally favor increased government spending is shown here within the ranks of Republican identifiers. They are also less likely than officers who are Republicans to report getting a lot of guidance from religion in daily life. Their aggregate attitudes, however, are similar to those of officers on issues like the death penalty, prayer in schools, abortion, and the environment.

A similar pattern exists between officers and soldiers who identify with the Democratic Party, although the subpopulations are too small to obtain statistically significant differences. The only statistically significant differences are in the greater rates at which soldiers and warrant officers favor allowing prayer in public schools, increased Social Security spending, and further restrictions on gun ownership (see table 6.6).

Military and Civilian Differences

As seen in table 6.7, there are significant differences between Republican Party identifiers in the civilian population and those in the army. Republicans across the army are less supportive of spending on Social Security than their Republican counterparts in the civilian population and are more opposed to gun control. Republicans in the army are also more inclined to protect the environment and to tolerate some forms of abortion, and they are less likely to state that religion provides a lot of guidance in their day-to-day lives. Officers are more libertarian than civilians in their view of the government's role in ensuring an individual's economic well-being. Officers are also less supportive than civilians of spending on health care, although that may be due to the extensive health care coverage the army provides through retirement.

TABLE 6.5
Aggregate Attitudes of Army Republicans

Members of the army who identify with the Republican Party

Issue	Officers	Soldiers & warrant officers	
Condition of the national economy**	78%	48%	(Good–bad)
Banning the death penalty	74	74	(Oppose–favor)
Govt. role in ensuring a good standard of living*	70	31	(Individual–govt. responsibility)
Equal role for women	67	54	(Equal role–place is in the home)
Favor programs to help minorities	62	4	(Oppose–favor)
Allow prayer in school	59	57	(Favor–oppose)
Education spending**	45	72	(Expand–cut back)
Religious guidance in daily life**	39	18	(Quite a bit/A great deal–none)
Health-care spending*	39	58	(Expand–cut back)
Further restricting gun ownership	32	19	(Oppose–favor)
Spending on antiviolence and crime programs***	27	55	(Expand–cut back)
Outlawing abortion entirely*	26	29	(Oppose–favor)
Relaxing environmental regs. to stimulate economy*	26	22	(Oppose–favor)
Social Security spending**	9	28	(Expand–cut back)

(N = 218 Republican identifiers in the officer corps)
(N = 133 Republican identifiers among warrant officers and enlisted soldiers)
* $p < .05$,   ** $p < .01$,   *** $p < .001$
Source: C&S Survey.
Note: Significance tests are for differences in means between the two populations, with "don't know" responses excluded from analysis.

Overall, Republican officers appear to take more libertarian or conservative stances on economic issues than do their civilian Republican counterparts, with the exception of protecting the environment. On social issues the results are mixed, with officers more opposed to gun control but more accepting of abortion than their civilian counterparts. Soldier and warrant officer Republicans are not quite as libertarian when it comes to economic issues but otherwise differ similarly from civilians who identify themselves as Republican. These differences highlight the fact that while the officer corps is dominated by those who identify themselves as Repub-

TABLE 6.6
Aggregate Attitudes of Army Democrats

Members of the army who identify with the Democratic Party

Issue	Officers	Soldiers & warrant officers	
Equal role for women	97%	83%	(Equal role–place is in the home)
Relaxing environmental regs. to stimulate economy	79	60	(Oppose–favor)
Outlawing abortion entirely	74	54	(Oppose–favor)
Health-care spending	72	90	(Expand–cut back)
Education spending	63	87	(Expand–cut back)
Spending on antiviolence and crime programs	37	39	(Expand–cut back)
Allowing prayer in school*	36	60	(Favor–oppose)
Banning the death penalty	34	43	(Oppose–favor)
Social Security spending**	25	70	(Expand–cut back)
Religious guidance in daily life	16	34	(Quite a bit/A great deal–none)
Condition of the national economy	16	−33	(Good–bad)
Govt. role in ensuring a good standard of living	4	−20	(Individual–govt. responsibility)
Favoring programs to help minorities	−13	−31	(Oppose–favor)
Further restricting gun ownership**	−68	−43	(Oppose–favor)

(N = 73 Democratic identifiers in the officer corps)
(N = 66 Democratic identifiers among warrant officers and enlisted soldiers)
* $p < .05$, ** $p < .01$
Source: C&S Survey.
Note: Significance tests are for differences in means between the two populations, with "don't know" responses excluded from analysis.

lican, the views of these officers do not necessarily match the views of Republicans in the civilian population. Similarly, the 24% of soldiers and warrant officers who identify themselves as Republican may not hold views on social and economic issues that one would normally expect from them (particularly on economic issues).

Compared with Democrats in the civilian population, the views of Democratic soldiers and warrant officers are more in line with the views of Democratic civilians than are the views of officers, with the exception of gun control. Officers who are Democrats have more libertarian views on economic issues and are less supportive of government spending on

TABLE 6.7

Republicans in the Army and Civilian Republicans

Aggregate attitudes among members of the army and civilians who identify Republican

Issue	Civilians	Officers	Soldiers & warrant officers	
Condition of the national economy	43%	78%***	48%	(Good–bad)
Govt. role in ensuring a good standard of living	54	70***	31**	(Individual–govt. responsibility)
Equal role for women	65	67	54*	(Equal role–place is in the home)
Education spending	41	45	72***	(Expand–cut back)
Religious guidance in daily life	45	39	18***	(Quite a bit/A great deal–none)
Health-care spending	55	39***	58	(Expand–cut back)
Further restricting gun ownership[a]	–14	32***	19***	(Oppose–favor)
Outlawing abortion entirely	3	26***	29***	(Oppose–favor)
Relaxing environmental regs. to stimulate economy[a]	8	26***	22***	(Oppose–favor)
Social Security spending	44	9***	28**	(Expand–cut back)

$* p < .05$, $** p < .01$, $*** p < .001$

Source: C&S Survey, 2004 National Annenberg Election Survey, "Global Views 2004," Chicago Council on Foreign Relations (now Chicago Council on Global Affairs), and 2004 American National Election Study.

Note: The asterisks apply to differences between civilians and each military subgroup.

[a] Response categories between NES and the C&S Survey are not exact on the questions of gun control and environmental regulations versus the economy, which makes the comparisons approximate.

health care, Social Security, and education. Officers are also less likely to state that religion plays a significant role in their daily lives. They are more opposed to banning abortion entirely and more supportive of an equal role for women than either soldiers or civilians who also identify with the Democratic Party (see table 6.8).[14]

[14] Caution should be used in assessing aggregate views in these subsamples. In the C&S Survey sample, only 73 officers and 66 soldiers and warrant officers identify with the Democratic Party. The sample of Republican Party identifiers is significantly larger: 218 officers and 133 soldiers and warrant officers.

TABLE 6.8
Democrats in the Army and Civilian Democrats

Aggregate attitudes among members of the army and civilians who identify themselves as Democrats

Issue	Civilians	Officers	Soldiers & warrant officers	
Condition of national economy	−35%	16%***	−33%	(Good–bad)
Govt. role in ensuring a good standard of living	−23	4***	−20	(Individual–govt. responsibility)
Equal role for women	78	97***	83	(Equal role–place is in the home)
Education spending	76	63*	87*	(Expand–cut back)
Religious guidance in daily life	44	16***	34	(Quite a bit/A great deal–none)
Health-care spending	85	72*	90	(Expand–cut back)
Further restricting gun ownership[a]	−63	−68	−43*	(Oppose–favor)
Outlawing abortion entirely	57	74**	54	(Oppose–favor)
Relaxing environmental regs. to stimulate economy[a]	−37	79***	60***	(Oppose–favor)
Social Security spending	72	25***	70	(Expand–cut back)

* $p < .05$,   ** $p < .01$, *** $p < .001$

Source: C&S Survey, 2004 National Annenberg Election Survey, "Global Views 2004," Chicago Council on Foreign Relations (now Chicago Council on Global Affairs), and 2004 American National Election Study.

Note: The asterisks apply to differences between civilians and each military subgroup.

[a] Response categories between NES and the C&S Survey are not exact on the questions of gun control and environmental regulations versus the economy, which makes the comparisons approximate.

Republican-Democratic Differences

In this section I discuss the gap between Republicans and Democrats. I first examine differences within the army before comparing those differences with what we find in the civilian population.

Partisans in the officer ranks have the most divergent views on the question of gun control. A solid majority of Democratic officers favor further restricting gun ownership, while a plurality of Republican officers oppose such measures. The next most contentious issue is whether society should embrace programs to help minorities get ahead in order to make up for past discrimination (see table 6.9). Republican officers overwhelmingly oppose such programs, whereas Democratic officers, in the aggregate, slightly favor them. This is followed by attitudes toward the government's role in guaranteeing a good standard of living. Democratic officers are fairly evenly split on the question, whereas Republican officers overwhelmingly come down on the side of individual responsibility.

The three issues that generate the least disagreement along party lines in the officer corps are questions on government spending. Both Republicans and Democrats support the expansion of government spending in education, Social Security, and antiviolence and crime programs more or less to the same degree.

The differences between Republicans and Democrats in the enlisted and warrant officer ranks on these fourteen issues are generally less than the differences between officers. Aggregate opinions of Republican and Democratic officers on these issues differ by an average of 43 percentage points. Among soldiers and officers, the average partisan differences are only 37 percentage points. The top four divisive issues are the same for nonofficers as for the officer corps, although within the enlisted and warrant officer ranks perceptions of the state of the national economy differ most along partisan lines, and the question of support for programs to help minorities is the second most divisive issue (see table 6.9). This is followed by the questions of gun control and the government's role in guaranteeing an individual's standard of living. Unlike officers, soldiers and warrant officers who identify themselves as Republican or Democrat are least split on the issue of allowing prayer in public schools. However, the other issues on which they are least divided are related to government spending on education and antiviolence and crime programs. There are also relatively few differences between party identifiers in the enlisted and warrant officer ranks on the reported role of religion in their daily lives.

Overall, these differences show that party affiliation in the army correlates with real differences in opinion on issues of social and economic policy. Particularly among officers, social issues are generally more divisive than questions of economic policy.

Having identified some of the attitudinal differences between Republican and Democratic Party identifiers within the army, I now turn to the question of whether comparable differences are found between partisans in the civilian population. A look at the relative differences in opinion between the army and civilian populations shows that while Republicans and Democrats in the army disagree with each other on many of the same issues as Republicans and Democrats in the civilian population, there are some differences in patterns of disagreement.

TABLE 6.9
Party Disagreement Index (Army, Internal)

Issue	Officers			Soldiers & warrant officers		
	Dems	Reps	Diff	Dems	Reps	Diff
Further restricting gun ownership	−68%	32%	100%***	−43%	19%	62%***
Oppose programs to help minorities	−13	62	75***	−31	44	74***
Govt. role in guaranteeing a good standard of living	4	70	66***	−20	31	52***
Condition of national economy	16	78	62***	−33	48	82***
Relaxing environmental regs. to stimulate economy	79	26	53***	60	22	38*
Outlawing abortion entirely	74	26	47***	54	29	25**
Banning the death penalty	34	74	41***	43	74	31**
Health-care spending	72	39	34***	90	58	33***
Equal role for women	97	67	30***	83	54	29**
Allowing prayer in school	36	59	23**	60	57	3
Religious guidance in daily life	16	39	23	34	18	16
Education spending	63	45	18***	87	72	15***
Social Security spending	25	9	15**	70	28	43**
Spending on antiviolence and crime programs	37	27	11*	39	55	16

* $p < .05$,   ** $p < .01$,   *** $p < .001$
Source: C&S Survey.
Note: The asterisks apply to the relationship between Democrats and Republicans in each subpopulation (among officers or among soldiers and warrant officers). Also, differences might not sum correctly due to rounding.

Using the index shown in table 6.10 to present a simplified picture of differences, we see that social issues such as gun control and the role of women are more divisive within the army officer corps than they are in the civilian world. Greater disagreement in the army on these issues is to be expected. A large portion of the army is drawn from a population that is comfortable with weapons and gun ownership. Another segment of the army is drawn from urban areas where violence and crime are serious concerns and gun ownership is rare. The former group is more likely to be Republican and the latter Democratic, so greater disagreement in this regard is natural. On the issue of the role of women in the workplace, Republicans in the army and civilian Republicans generally hold the same view. However, Democrats in the army are more likely to believe in full

TABLE 6.10
Party Disagreement Index (Officers vs. Civilians)

Issue	Republican vs. Democrat disagreement		Officers minus civilians	
	Officers	Civilians		
Further restricting gun ownership	100%	48%	52%	More disagreement in the army
Equal role for women	30	13	17	
Relaxing environmental regs. to stimulate economy	53	46	7	
Health-care spending	34	29	5	
Outlawing abortion entirely	47	52	–5	
Govt. role in guaranteeing a good standard of living	66	77	–11	
Social Security spending	15	28	–13	
Banning the death penalty	41	56	–16	
Condition of the national economy	62	78	–16	Less disagreement in the army
Education spending	18	35	–17	

Note: The first two data columns of tables 6.10 and 6.11 show the aggregate differences between Republican and Democratic identifiers in each population. The last column reflects the difference in difference" between the two populations. A simple way of thinking about what this table means is to imagine putting a Republican and a Democrat in a room and asking them to discuss a certain topic. The positive numbers in the last column reflect issues where you are more likely to get an argument between a Republican member of the army and a Democratic member of the army than between a Democratic civilian and a Republican civilian. On these issues, the difference in attitude between a Republican and a Democrat in the army is likely to be greater than the difference in opinion between a civilian Republican and Democrat. The negative numbers reflect topics that members of the army that identify with different parties are less likely to argue over than their civilian counterparts.

equality than their civilian counterparts. In chapter 3 I showed that women in the officer corps are more likely to believe in full equality than civilian women. If we combine this with the fact that a greater portion of Democrats are women in the officer ranks compared with the proportion of Republicans who are women, the increased disagreement over this issue along party lines becomes understandable.

On the other hand, there seems to be more agreement among officers of different parties on the question of the death penalty (see table 6.10) and issues related to government spending. On the question of the death penalty, officers who are Democrats are more likely to support it than their civilian counterparts, whereas Republicans in and out of the army generally share the same outlook on this issue. This means that while there is disagreement on the issue along party lines, partisans in the army are closer to each other on this than their civilian counterparts. In terms of

TABLE 6.11
Party Disagreement Index (Soldiers vs. Civilians)

Issue	Republican vs. Democrat disagreement		Enl. & WO minus civilians	
	Enl. & WO	civilians		
Equal role for women	29%	13%	16%	More disagreement in the army
Social Security spending	43	28	15	
Further restricting gun ownership	62	48	14	
Condition of the national economy	82	78	4	
Health-care spending	33	29	3	
Relaxing environmental regs. to stimulate economy	38	46	−8	
Education spending	15	35	−20	
Banning the death penalty	31	56	−25	
Govt. role in guaranteeing a good standard of living	52	77	−25	
				Less disagreement
Outlawing abortion entirely	25	52	−27	in the army

economic issues, more officers of both parties are against expansion of government spending in these areas than their civilian counterparts.

The situation is largely the same with soldiers and warrant officers, although there is more agreement between Republicans and Democrats in these ranks on social issues. This is primarily because Democratic identifiers among the enlisted and warrant officer ranks tend to take more conservative positions on these issues than their civilian counterparts.

When assessing the potential for disagreement along party lines, it becomes clear that there are real differences between Republican and Democratic Party identifiers in the army. These differences are predominantly centered on social issues, and there is a greater degree of agreement on economic issues. And aside from two demographically driven social issues (gun ownership and the role of women in the workplace), it appears that the divide between Republicans and Democrats in the army is not as great as the divide between Republicans and Democrats in the civilian population.

Party Affiliation and Foreign Policy

Although these differences on social and economic issues are interesting when examining how partisanship in the army can shape interarmy relations, the more important question is whether partisan differences of opinion carry over to questions of foreign policy and national security.

The C&S Survey replicated a series of questions asked by the Chicago Council on Global Affairs on foreign policy and defense expenditures. One might expect members of the army to be less split on these issues, given that their profession is focused specifically on national security. One might also assume that on these topics officers would adopt an institutionally defined worldview and rely less on external partisan cues. A look at how Republican and Democratic Party identifiers differ on these issues reveals that partisanship still matters in shaping the opinions of members of the army, but that there are key differences between civilians and members of the army independent of party affiliation.

For instance, on the question of whether a respondent favors expanded defense spending, members of the army, regardless of their party affiliation, are more likely to support expanded spending than their civilian counterparts. However, there are differences in support for expanded defense spending between Republican and Democratic Party identifiers within the army. In fact, the degree of difference is the same as the degree of difference between partisans in the civilian population. This pattern generally holds across all four issues related to defense and foreign policy expenditures which can be directly compared with attitudes in the civilian population, including spending on homeland security and providing military aid to other nations. The only exception among officers is that Democratic Party identifiers are less hostile to the idea of expanding economic aid to other nations than either their Republican peers or their civilian counterparts; as a result, there is a greater chance of potential conflict between party identifiers in the army than in civilian society. Overall, these findings suggest that party affiliation still correlates strongly with attitudes within the army, even on questions of defense and foreign policy.

When we look at questions about the potential uses of the army, we note the possible limits of partisanship to shape attitudes within the army. Among officers responding to the C&S Survey, there is very little disagreement along party lines about the relative importance of seven of the nine potential missions of the U.S. military. Both Republican and Democratic Party identifiers are nearly unanimous in believing that "to fight and win our nation's wars" and "to fight terrorism" are important missions for the military. Similar proportions from each party are also likely to believe that "to intervene in civil wars abroad" is not an important mission. The only two potential missions where the opinions of Republican and Democratic Party identifiers in the officer corps diverge are "to address humanitarian needs abroad" and "to provide disaster relief within the U.S." Democratic Party identifiers are slightly more likely than Republican Party identifiers to believe that addressing humanitarian needs abroad is an im-

TABLE 6.12
Party Identification and Potential Army Missions (Officers)

Potential use of military	Important minus unimportant		Absolute difference
	Reps	Dems	
To fight and win our nation's wars	100%	99%	1%*
To deal with domestic disorder	30	27	2
To fight terrorism	97	94	3
To intervene in civil wars abroad	−31	−36	5
As an instrument of foreign policy, including nation building & peacekeeping	76	70	6
Enforcing immigration laws	−11	−18	7
To combat drug trafficking	17	25	8
To address humanitarian needs abroad	11	32	21
To provide disaster relief within U.S.	51	93	42*

* $p < .05$
Source: C&S Survey.
Note: Asterisks reflect significance from difference of means tests between groups. The difference in "To fight and win our nation's wars" comes from the relative importance that Republican and Democratic officers place on the mission. Among officers, 99% who identify as Republican say it is very important compared with 85% of officers who identify as Democratic. Another 15% of Democratic officers say it is somewhat important.

portant potential mission and are nearly unanimous in believing that providing disaster relief in the United States is an important mission. By contrast, only a slight majority of Republican Party identifiers believe that providing disaster relief is an important potential mission.

There appear to be greater levels of disagreement along party lines among soldiers and warrant officers. Within these ranks, Republican Party identifiers are more likely to believe in the importance of the more traditional missions of the military such as fighting wars and terrorism, whereas Democratic Party identifiers are more likely to believe in the importance of nontraditional missions such as providing disaster relief in the United States and humanitarian assistance abroad (see tables 6.12 and 6.13).

After examining the nature of party affiliation in the army across a range of social, economic, defense, and foreign policy issues, it becomes clear that there are real and substantial differences between Republican and Democratic Party identifiers in the army. In many ways these differences are similar to attitudinal differences between Republican and Demo-

TABLE 6.13
Party Identification and Potential Army Missions (Soldiers and Warrant Officers)

	Important minus unimportant		
Potential use of military	Reps	Dems	Absolute difference
Enforcing immigration laws	30%	33%	3%
As an instrument of foreign policy, including nation building & peacekeeping	38	34	3
To fight and win our nation's wars	97	87	9
To combat drug trafficking	31	42	11
To fight terrorism	96	82	13
To address humanitarian needs abroad	20	39	20*
To provide disaster relief within U.S.	66	86	20
To intervene in civil wars abroad	−40	−64	2
To deal with domestic disorder	40	64	25

* $p < .05$
Source: C&S Survey.
Note: Asterisks reflect significance from difference of means tests between groups.

cratic Party identifiers in the civilian population. However, the major points of possible contention within the army center on issues of social and economic policy.

Among officers there is general agreement across party lines on the relative importance of potential missions for the American military. This suggests that partisanship does not shape the thinking of army officers to the extent that partisan affiliations influence attitudes toward the organization's basic roles and missions. Table 6.14 presents all twenty-seven issues addressed in this chapter. The issues are ordered from those with the smallest disagreement along partisan lines to those where party affiliation correlates with strong differences in opinion.

Of note is that the bottom half of the table is populated primarily with social and economic issues. The good news is that it appears the attitudes of members of the army toward the potential uses of the military are formed independent of partisan affiliation. Furthermore, most issues on which the attitudes of officers are split along partisan lines are on topics that are tangential to military service and should not be an issue in the internal operations of the army. However, there is cause for concern on issues related to the army's manpower policies and on questions of national defense policy.

TABLE 6.14
Partisan Differences among Officers across 27 Issues

Type	Specific issue	Reps	Others	Dems	Abs diff
MIL	To fight and win our nation's wars	100%	95%	99%	1%*
MIL	To deal with domestic disorder	30	39	27	2
MIL	To fight terrorism	97	97	94	3
Foreign pol.	Military aid to other nations	−60	−70	−64	4
MIL	To intervene in civil wars abroad	−31	−33	−36	5
MIL	As an instrument of foreign policy, including nation building & peacekeeping	76	76	70	6
MIL	Enforcing immigration laws	−11	−8	−18	7
MIL	To combat drug trafficking	17	11	25	8
Economic	Spending on antiviolence and crime programs	27	35	37	11*
Economic	Social Security spending	9	27	25	15**
Economic	Education spending	45	71	63	18***
Foreign pol.	Spending on homeland security	52	58	34	19
Foreign pol.	Economic aid to other nations	−59	−66	−38	21
MIL	To address humanitarian needs abroad	11	30	32	21
Social	Religious guidance in daily life	−39	−17	−16	23
Social	Allowing prayer in school	59	45	36	23**
Social	Equal role for women	67	82	97	30***
Economic	Health-care spending	39	65	72	34***
Social	Banning the death penalty	−74	−60	−34	41***
MIL	To provide disaster relief within U.S.	51	70	93	42*
Social	Outlawing abortion entirely	−26	−44	−74	47***
Foreign pol.	Spending on defense	57	41	8	49***
Economic	Relaxing environmental regs. to stimulate economy	−26	−44	−79	53***
Economic	Condition of the national economy	78	48	16	62***
Economic	Govt. role in ensuring a good standard of living	−70	−38	−4	66***
Social	Programs to help minorities	−62	−22	13	75***
Social	Further restricting gun ownership	−32	8	68	100***

* $p < .05$,   ** $p < .01$,   *** $p < .001$
Source: C&S Survey.
Note: Asterisks reflect significance from difference of means tests between groups, with the difference in "To fight our nation's wars" coming from the proportion who rate it as "very important" versus "somewhat important" between the two groups.

The attitudes of army officers on the role of women in the workplace and the appeal of programs designed to help minorities make up for past discrimination correlate strongly with party affiliation. This suggests that when the army leadership makes decisions on topics related to the integration of women and minorities, conflicts may erupt, with officers taking sides along partisan political lines.

Army officers are also significantly split along partisan lines in their perceptions of the condition of the national economy. In 2004 Republicans overwhelmingly thought that the economy was sound, whereas Democrats were more evenly split on the question. Likewise, Republican officers in 2004 predominantly felt that spending on defense should be expanded, whereas Democratic officers were again somewhat split on the issue. Officers were also split along partisan lines on attitudes toward spending on homeland security and economic aid to other nations, though not to the same degree as on the economy and defense spending.[15] These findings suggest that officers do not necessarily approach questions of national military strategy from a unified and internally developed perspective, but default to partisan cues when thinking about these issues.

Conclusion

The data presented in this chapter show that members of the army are less likely to identify with one of the two major political parties than their civilian counterparts. At first glance this would appear to confirm the idea of a relatively apolitical army. However, when we look at the data by rank, it becomes clear that army officers think of themselves as Republicans or Democrats at a rate roughly equal to their civilian counterparts. This implies that being apolitical is not at all a part of army culture, as least as defined by the officer corps. The army's low overall rates of party affiliation are driven by the low numbers of party identifiers in the enlisted ranks.

The idea of a Republican "team identification" phenomenon among members of the army is reinforced by the finding that differences in party affiliation between the army and the civilian population are not entirely attributable to demographics. The Virtual Army and Virtual Officer Corps analysis of partisanship showed that a group of civilians who matched the army on the dimensions of gender, race/ethnicity, age, education, and income would correlate closely with the general civilian popula-

---

[15] Soldiers and warrant officers generally showed the same differences, although soldiers were more likely to disagree on economic issues along partisan lines and slightly less likely to disagree on social issues.

tion in the proportion who identified as Republicans or Democrats. However, it is also clear that increased rank is associated with greater Republican Party affiliation, which raises several other questions about the relationship between the army and partisan politics.

There are several possible explanations for this correlation of rank and Republican Party affiliation in the army. Unfortunately, it is impossible to conclusively determine the cause of this correlation without panel data, which the C&S Survey does not provide. We can therefore only speculate as to the reason why Republican Party identification increases with rank. One possible explanation is that over time the army experience leads soldiers and officers to identify with the Republican Party. However, the data in the C&S Survey do not support such a hypothesis. Variables relating to the army experience, such as combat deployments, occupational specialty, family history of service, and type of unit, were statistically and substantively insignificant in predicting party affiliation.

Similarly, if the army culture played a role in shaping party affiliations, then one might expect that those who did not identify with the Republican Party might have a lower level of morale than their Republican counterparts. This was not the case. Likewise, there is no evidence that partisan politics plays a role in the judgments soldiers make about army leadership. The fact that party affiliation does not appear to influence soldier or officer morale or faith in the army's leaders indicates that the officer corps' overwhelming identification with the Republican Party does not significantly affect working relationships among officers or between soldiers and officers. This is good news because it indicates that members of the army maintain a degree of professionalism whereby partisan attitudes do not appear to directly affect the work environment.

However, there is evidence that in 2004 non–Republican Party identifiers were less likely to express a desire to make a career in the army than their Republican counterparts. Without panel data it is impossible to assert that this pattern persists over time. Nor does it prove that there may be internal pressures to leave the army if one does not identify as a Republican. The fact that party affiliation corresponds with career intent and not morale or faith in the army's leaders suggests that such decisions are shaped by factors external to the army. These findings indicate that the external political environment of 2004, and most likely the war in Iraq, played a significant role in shaping the career intentions of officers, an environment that army leaders have little ability to influence. Specifically, perceptions of the war in Iraq in 2004 were already split significantly along party lines. It is entirely plausible that some non–Republican Party identifiers in the army were merely expressing a lack of desire to serve a specific foreign policy agenda.

As in the civilian population, there are significant attitudinal differences between Republican and Democratic Party identifiers in the army. As for the question of how these differences may affect internal army relations, the possibility does exist that differences of opinion on gender equality and racial integration may cause conflict along party lines. However, most of the significant differences are on issues that are tangential to service in the army, such as gun control and abortion.

Furthermore, when it comes to opinions on the potential uses of the military, army officers show little disagreement along party lines. This suggests that partisan disagreements among officers do not extend to views on which missions are most important for the army. However, there is evidence that the views of army officers on questions of national defense policy may split along party lines.

The C&S Survey also found that the opinions of soldiers and officers on the state of the national economy strongly correlated with party affiliation.[16] Taken together, these findings imply that military recommendations to policy makers on the potential uses of the military will not be influenced by party affiliation. However, differences along party lines in opinions on the state of the national economy and on the necessity of expanding or cutting back defense spending implies that army officers rely on political cues to form opinions on national policy and overall defense strategies.

One weakness of the analysis presented here is the general nature of the issues examined. Questions for the C&S Survey were chosen to reflect a range of issues that have been salient to national politics over an extended period of time. This means that while these questions are useful for assessing the outlook of members of the military and comparing them with the civilian population broadly, they were not necessarily the most salient to the 2004 election. Furthermore, the general consensus on the importance to the army of various missions probably masks significant divisions in opinion on the war in Iraq. Members of the army are overwhelmingly opposed to intervening in the civil wars of other countries. Conversely, they are uniformly supportive of the mission "to fight and win our country's wars." An interesting area for further inquiry would be whether members of the army viewed efforts in Iraq as central to the broader struggle against Al Qaeda or whether this was viewed as a diversion of resources from the primary conflict against Al Qaeda in Afghanistan. It is very likely that, as with the civilian population, army perceptions of the purposes of the war in Iraq correlate strongly with party identification.

---

[16] Party identification was significant even in regression models that controlled for income and rank.

Chapter 7

Political Participation

THIS CHAPTER EXAMINES how the attitudes of members of the army translate into political activity. This is an important topic for two reasons. First, news reports in recent years have cited extraordinary voting rates among members of the military, based primarily on claims by the Federal Voting Assistance Program about military voting rates in the 2000 and 2004 elections. In its 2005 report, the Federal Voting Assistance Program reported voting participation rates of 69% and 79% for 2000 and 2004, respectively (including those who reported attempting to vote and failing to do so—12% and 6% in 2000 and 2004, respectively).[1] The belief that soldiers vote in extraordinary numbers (paired with their perceived Republican inclinations) significantly shaped the strategies of the two presidential candidates during the Florida recount in 2000. Was this a valid assumption to make? Second, the types and prevalence of political activity can indicate the strength of a group's engagement with the political process. If members of the army are more likely than civilians to donate money or display signs in support of political candidates, this might indicate that the army has become less apolitical and more like traditional interest groups. The concern that many have expressed over the civil-military gap in recent years has been driven by an impression of the military as a monolithic and active voting bloc. As previous chapters have shown, the army is much less monolithic in its political views than conventional wisdom suggests; it is also likely that the army is not as politically active as many believe it to be.

The political activities I examine in this chapter are voting, donating money to political campaigns, and displaying support for political candidates in the form of buttons, bumper stickers, and signs. These three actions do not represent the full array of partisan activity open to civilians but do cover most of what service members are allowed to do under Department of Defense regulations.[2] These actions also cover several dimen-

---

[1] Brunelli, "Federal Voting Assistance Program."

[2] Political bumper stickers are common among members of the military, but other types of signs are much rarer, if not nonexistent. Wearing a campaign button would be allowed only when a service member is off duty and out of uniform. Similarly, I have never seen a campaign sign on the lawn or in the window of government housing, and I could not conceive of this happening on an army post. However, a member of the military could place a campaign sign on his or her lawn if this service member lived off post. See the text of enclo-

sions of political participation. The act of voting, the iconic political act in a democracy, is the most private means of expressing a political opinion. It is also, however, the most encouraged act and is generally portrayed as a civic duty. Displaying a political sign or bumper sticker is clearly a more public expression of one's opinion, albeit easier to do than voting and less costly than donating money. And while the act of donating money to a candidate or campaign is a semiprivate affair, it probably signals a stronger and more explicit commitment to a political cause than either displaying a bumper sticker or voting.

Given what we know of the party affiliations and reported strength of attachment that soldiers and officers have to the two major political parties, it is possible to predict the nature and extent of the political activity of members of the army. Overall, we would expect the army to vote, display political signs, and donate money at lower rates than the civilian population. This would not be due to any cultural norm of refraining from political participation in the army but be driven by the general lack of political engagement among soldiers.[3] We should, however, expect the officer corps to vote at least at rates equal to the civilian population. Whether or not officers donate money and publicly display support for specific parties or candidates are the more interesting questions for civil-military relations.

Department of Defense regulations strictly prohibit members of the army from using their military position to endorse political candidates. This is not an especially onerous restriction, but it does prevent members of the army from offering the kind of endorsement that the CEO of a civilian company might make. Similarly, most military officers understand that they must refrain from giving endorsements that might be construed in any way as an official endorsement by the army (making an endorsement in uniform, for example). These restrictions should limit public expressions of support for political parties or candidates. We would therefore expect all members of the army, including officers, to be less likely to report displaying political buttons, stickers, or signs.

The question of monetary donations to political parties or candidates is less straightforward. On the one hand, we might expect members of the army to be less inclined to donate money than their civilian counterparts. This would reflect a hesitancy to engage in the political process beyond the act of voting, which is often viewed as simply a civic duty. On the other hand, the restrictions on public endorsements or direct participation in political campaigns might frustrate the desire of some to

---

sure 3, DOD Directive 1344.10, in appendix E for specific limitations on political activity by members of the military.

[3] Moskos, "All-Volunteer Force," 316.

be politically involved. In this case donating money might be viewed as an alternative means of expressing strong political opinions among those who are otherwise limited in their participation in the political process.[4] Strong partisans in the army might therefore be more inclined to donate money than their civilian counterparts. The next section takes a summary look at participation rates and why they might differ between the two populations.

Voting

Administered in the summer and early fall of 2004, the C&S Survey asked respondents if they had voted in 2000. Within the army, only 43% of soldiers and officers reported having voted in that election.[5] This lags significantly behind the reported civilian rate. A strong majority, 80%, of NAES respondents in 2004 reported that they voted in the 2000 election. There are two possible explanations for this discrepancy. The first is that members of the military simply do not vote at the same rate as their civilian counterparts. The second is that this discrepancy is largely due to the dynamic of voters reporting that they voted even when they did not (known as overreporting).

The actual voting rate in 2000 was about 50.5%.[6] This means that the army's reported rate of 43% was less than the civilian rate, regardless of any overreporting effect. The only remaining question is whether civilians and members of the military overreport to the same degree. About three in ten NAES survey respondents in 2004 stated that they voted in 2000 when they actually did not. If army voters overreported at the same rate as their civilian counterparts, the actual overall army voting rate would be about 27%.[7]

This is unlikely for several reasons. Studies of voting overreporting show that this phenomenon is due primarily to the "social desirability"

[4] Discussions of donations by military members during the 2008 presidential election often focused on the fact that many service members appeared to be donating to Ron Paul and Barack Obama, candidates who had expressed opposition to the Iraq War. See Rosiak, "Troops Deployed Abroad."

[5] The analysis of this question was limited to respondents who turned at least eighteen years old in 2000 and were citizens of the United States.

[6] Leip, "Atlas of U.S. Presidential Elections." Turnout is based on the percentage of those voting among the total voting-age population. The Census Bureau reports a voting rate of 55% among the voting-age population, but of course this is based on answers given by survey respondents. Jamieson, Shin, and Day, "Voting and Registration."

[7] This was calculated simply by using the ratio of actual votes (50.5%) to reported votes (80%) in the civilian population and applying it to the reported voting rate (43%) in the military.

of the act of voting.[8] In this case, those asked whether they had performed what many see as a civic duty would be inclined to avoid embarrassment and say that they did vote even if they had not. These studies also show that overreporting is most often done by those who would vote anyway, specifically the highly educated and strong partisans. While the army has fewer people who did not graduate from high school than the civilian population and a slightly higher proportion of members with some college education, there are fewer college graduates in the army than in the civilian population (25% versus 38%). Similarly, fewer people in the army state that they identify strongly with a political party (25% versus 39%). This indicates that fewer people in the army are likely to overreport voting, but also fewer are likely to vote in the first place.

Also, the social-desirability factor is likely to play a greater role in the NAES survey than in the C&S Survey due to the fact that the C&S Survey was conducted via mail, whereas the NAES survey was conducted over the phone. Talking to another human being is apt to induce a desire to please or impress by giving a socially desirable answer.

Another reason that members of the army may not overreport to the same degree as civilians is that they may be less susceptible to feeling awkward for not voting. Members of the army generally feel that they are serving the country and that their very career choice is a real and extended form of civic duty. People who feel they are performing a valuable civic duty on a daily basis would therefore be less embarrassed to admit that they had not voted. In sum, it is likely that overreporting in the army occurs at a lesser rate than in the civilian population. Regardless of exact overreporting rates, the data show that members of the army voted at lower rates than their civilian counterparts in the 2000 election.

Although it is impossible to predict with any certainty what military voting rates were in 2004 from how respondents said they voted in 2000, the C&S Survey did ask respondents in 2004 whether they were currently registered to vote. On this question, 68% of the army answered in the

---

[8] Abramson, Anderson, and Silver, "Who Overreports Voting?" Evidence for how social desirability may influence voter overreporting is seen by comparing the NAES responses to the "did you vote in 2000?" question with a similar question from the NES 2004 surveys. The NES study asked a similar question as the NAES study but offered an "out," whereby respondents could answer no without embarrassing themselves. The NES survey specifically asked, "In 2000 Al Gore ran on the Democratic ticket against George W. Bush for the Republicans and Ralph Nader as the Reform party candidate. Do you *remember for sure* whether or not you voted in that election?" (emphasis mine). This question format changes the question from a straightforward "did you vote?" to one that allows people to answer that they do not remember. In this case, the social-desirability factor may be muted, making the 65% reported voting rate in the NES study more accurate than rates reported in the NAES study. The C&S Survey and NAES study used the more straightforward question form.

affirmative compared with 86% of civilian respondents in the NAES survey.[9] This again signals a lower rate of political participation among members of the army than in the civilian population. And lest one may think
that this difference is due solely to a greater rate of overreporting among
civilians, the NAES question explicitly offered respondents a way to save
face yet still state that they were not registered to vote.[10] From these findings it is probably safe to say that not only did members of the army vote
at lower rates than the civilian population in 2000 but that they voted at
a lower rate in the 2004 election as well.

Displaying Support

In addition to investigating voting patterns, the C&S Survey asked respondents whether during an election or campaign they had ever "worn
a campaign button, put a campaign sticker on your car, or placed a sign
in your window." Nine percent of the army answered yes. Although this
means that one in ten members of the army is open enough about his or
her political preferences to display them publicly, people in the army are
still significantly less likely to openly advertise their feelings on political
issues than their civilian counterparts. In the 2004 NAES study, 21% of
respondents answered yes to the question "During this presidential campaign, have you worn a presidential campaign button, put a campaign
sticker on your car, or placed a sign in your window or in front of your
house?" This difference between the general population and the army is
probably more significant than reflected here due to the fact that the
C&S survey asked about activity during *any* election or campaign
whereas the NAES survey asked specifically about the 2004 election. One
can assume that a greater proportion of civilians would have answered
yes had the question included past campaigns.

Donating Money

Reported rates of donations to political campaigns and candidates follow
the same pattern as voting and displaying support, but differences between the army and civilian populations on this question are somewhat
more difficult to discern. As one would expect, people generally give

[9] Noncitizens were excluded from analysis in both data sets.

[10] The NAES survey asked, "These days, many people are so busy they cannot find time
to register to vote, or they move around so often they do not get a chance to re-register. Are
you currently registered to vote in your precinct or election district, or haven't you been
able to register so far?" In comparison, the C&S Survey was more direct and simply asked,
"Are you currently registered to vote?"

TABLE 7.1
Political Activity

Single acts	Civilians	Army
Displayed button, sticker, or sign	21%	9%
Donated money	14	10
Registered to vote in 2004	86	68
Voted in 2000	80	43
Multiple acts Voted +	Civilians	Army
Displayed button, sticker, or sign	19%	7%
Donated money	14	7
Voted + donated $ + sign	8	4

Source: C&S Survey and 2004 National Annenberg Election Survey.
Note: All differences are significant at the 0.001 level.

money to political campaigns and candidates to a lesser degree than they vote or display signs. In 2004 the NAES survey found that about 14% of Americans reported giving money to a presidential candidate during the 2004 campaign. Comparably, only 10% of the army reported *ever* giving money to a political organization, party, or committee favoring a particular candidate or slate of candidates. This demonstrates that once again members of the army are less likely to engage in political activity than their civilian counterparts.

As for how many members of the army engage in multiple forms of political expression, the C&S Survey reveals that they are less likely than civilians to vote *and* display buttons, stickers, or signs in support of political campaigns or candidates. This is expected, given that the army trails the civilian population in the proportion of those who do either of these things independently. Likewise, the army trails the civilian population in the proportion of the population who both votes and donates money. In terms of people who are fully engaged politically (that is, people who vote, donate money, and display political buttons, stickers, or signs), only about 1 in 28 members of the army reports having done all three acts compared with about 1 in 13 civilians (see table 7.1).

Determinants of Political Activity

I now turn to determinants of political activity and examine what might explain the differences between the army and civilian populations. As a

TABLE 7.2
Rates of Political Participation

	Civilians	Army	Virtual Army	Officers	Virtual Officer Corps
Displayed button, sticker, or sign**	21%	9%	22%	16%	25%
Donated money*	14	10	13	18	21
Registered to vote in 2004	86	68	85	83	94
Voted in 2000***	80	43	79	68	90

Civilians	Civilians	Army	Virtual Army	Officers	Virtual Officer Corps
Displayed button, sticker, or sign**	19%	7%	20%	14%	23%
Donated money	14	7	13	16	20
Voted + donated $ + sign	8	4	7	7	11

$* p < .05$, $** p < .01$, $*** p < .001$
Source: C&S Survey and 2004 National Annenberg Election Survey.
Note: Sigificance tests apply to comparisons between civilians and officers.

starting point, it must be noted that there are significant differences in the participation rates of officers and soldiers and warrant officers. Only 38% of soldiers and warrant officers report voting in the 2000 election compared with 68% of officers. Officers are also almost twice as likely as the rest of the army to report donating money or displaying a political sign or bumper sticker.

Likewise, it appears that the proportion of officers who engage in all three political acts measured in the C&S Survey matches the proportion of civilians who vote, donate money, and display signs, stickers, or buttons. That the army's officer corps contains as many people who engage in public, private, and monetary forms of political expression may come as a surprise to those who remember that the army used to frown upon even voting. These findings imply that the primary cause of depressed rates of political participation is not army culture. As the institution's leaders, army officers determine the culture of the organization. And clearly among officers political participation is at least implicitly accepted.

However, table 7.2 shows that demographic factors do not fully explain the differences between the army and the civilian population or between officers and the rest of the army. Another look at the Virtual Army reveals that a group of civilians that matched the army on age, race, income, education, and gender would have higher rates of political participation than the actual army population. Similarly, a look at the Virtual Officer Corps reveals that such a group would have higher rates of participation than the general population. On the one hand this reinforces the finding of depressed participation in the enlisted and warrant officer ranks compared with the officer population. On the other hand it indicates that officers may participate largely to the same degree as the general population, but less so than a comparable group of civilians.

Another way of isolating the effect that being in the army may have on the propensity to participate in the political process is shown in figure 7.1. This figure shows the proportion of the army who voted in the 2000 election, by time in service. Of note is the fact that participation rates start relatively high but appear to drop among those who have been in the army for three to five years, before climbing steadily back among respondents who have been in even longer. While the differences between cohorts are not statistically significant, this is an interesting chart because those who had been in the army for less than three years in 2004 were civilians during the 2000 election. This raises two possibilities. The first is that even among those who join the military, there is a greater propensity to vote before one puts on the uniform. The second possibility, which will be discussed in more detail later in this chapter, is that attitudes toward participation are shaped before a person joins the army and that the army has little effect on participation rates. If this is the case, then variations in participation rates within the army may primarily be due to cohort effects.

A further look at demographics and political participation rates reveals that within the civilian population, education, income, and age are correlated with voting (0.22, 0.20, and 0.20, respectively). Correlations between voting and these characteristics in the army are slightly higher, but again one must remember that education and income correlate closely with being an officer. The correlations between voting and education, voting and income, and voting and age in the army are 0.31, 0.29, and 0.19, respectively. As for the correlations between these demographic characteristics and donations or the display of signs, buttons, or stickers, similar patterns hold for the two populations, although the correlations are much lower.

Predicting each of these political activities (voting, displaying signs, and donating) in the army through a multivariate regression controlling for age, sex, race, education, and income reveals that for voting, each of these demographic factors is significant with the exception of age. Males and those with higher incomes are more likely to vote, whereas members of the army with less education than a bachelor's degree are less likely to vote than their more educated counterparts. As for race, Hispanics are significantly less likely to vote than whites. The same patterns hold for

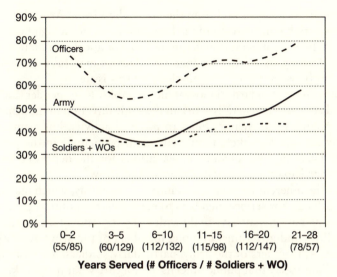

Figure 7.1 Voting Rates by Time in Service
Source: C&S Survey
Note: Differences between cohorts (year groups) are not statistically significant, with the exception of the difference between officers with 3–5 years of service and those with greater than 21 years of service. Differences between officers and soldiers are significant at .001 level.

the display of signs, except that all nonwhites are less likely to wear a button or display a bumper sticker or sign in support of a political campaign or candidate. The only significant factor in determining the likelihood of a soldier's or officer's donating money is whether he or she is black or Hispanic; these two groups are less likely to donate money than their white counterparts.

An analysis of these activities in the civilian population with the same models reveals a few key differences. Advanced age is associated with a slight increase in the likelihood of voting, whereas being male decreases the likelihood of voting. Higher income is associated with an increased likelihood of voting, as in the army population, and Hispanics are less likely to vote than their white counterparts. Higher education levels are also associated with a greater propensity to vote. When it comes to donating money, however, the civilian population differs from the army in that race does not appear to be a factor, and greater income and education increase the likelihood of donations.

An analysis of the combined civilian and army data sets reveals that being in the army is associated with a significant decrease in the likelihood of voting or displaying a sign, button, or sticker, even when controlling for the other demographic factors. This confirms the findings derived from a simple bivariate analysis and from the use of the Virtual Army. However, the army variable in these combined regressions is not a significant predictor of whether someone donates money to a political candidate or campaign, indicating that other demographic factors may fully account for differences between the two populations on this issue.

In sum, these standard demographic variables (age, gender, income, race, and education) generally work in the same direction in the army and civilian populations when it comes to political activity, but members of the army are still less likely than civilians to participate in the political process. There are five possible explanations for the depressed rate of political participation among members of the army.

One is the inherent mobility of members of the army, which may make it more difficult for service members to engage in the political process. A second explanation may have to do with a greater sense of disengagement from politics and government among members of the army. As outlined in chapter 4, members of the army, particularly soldiers, are more likely than civilians to say that public officials do not care what people like them think and that they do not have any say in what the government does. One would expect a person who feels this way to be less likely to take the time to vote or otherwise participate in the political process. To test whether this is the cause of decreased political participation among members of the army, these variables will be incorporated into models of political participation later in the chapter.

Another explanation for this overall depressed rate of political participation may be the underlying partisan attitudes and strength of political affiliation among members of the army. One key difference between the army and civilian populations is that blacks in the army are less likely than their civilian counterparts to display buttons, stickers, or signs. Part of this may be due to the political affiliations of those involved. As we saw in chapter 6, blacks in the army are more likely than their white or Hispanic counterparts to identify with the Democratic Party. Because conventional wisdom asserts that the army is a predominantly Republican institution, Democratic Party identifiers in the army may be less likely to advertise political disagreements with their peers. We also know that fewer members of the army identify strongly with one of the two major political parties (39% of civilians identify strongly with the Republican or Democratic Party compared with only 24% of the army population). We can look at models that include party affiliation and strength of partisanship to assess whether these factors influenced reported political activity in 2004.

The fourth explanation is a legacy of the army ethic that once actively discouraged political participation. Although officers are as likely to participate as their civilian counterparts, they lag slightly behind civilians with comparable levels of education and income. It is possible to look at army-specific experiences to assess whether there are core elements that correlate with decreased participation rates.

The final possible explanation is that the army experience does not depress participation rates and that the disposition of individuals to participate in the political process is established by the time they enter the army. In this explanation, the army's rate of political participation is not due to any cultural or demographic differences but can be explained by the type of people who join the military at any given time.

Mobility and Ease of Voting

As discussed previously, members of the army are highly mobile and typically move every two to four years. Therefore they face additional hurdles to voting, specifically in applying for absentee ballots or registering to vote in a new area. Among voters in the C&S Survey who were in the army during the 2000 election, 68% reported voting via absentee ballot for that election.

The government attempts to help soldiers overcome these obstacles through the Federal Voting Assistance Program and the designation of unit voting officers. Twenty-six percent of those who were in the army and eligible to vote in the 2000 election reported being briefed by their voting officers on procedures for registering to vote. Having received this brief apparently made some difference in reported voting rates. Of all the soldiers and officers who were briefed, 52% reported voting in the 2000 election compared with only 39% of those who were not briefed. This effect was most pronounced among soldiers and warrant officers, with 48% of those who received the brief reporting voting compared with only 35% of those who did not receive a briefing. Among officers the difference was 6% (72% versus 66%).[11] All told, efforts to educate and train members of the army on procedures for registering to vote and voting (typically by absentee ballot) appear to make a difference in facilitating participation in the army.

This relationship between receiving a briefing from a unit voting officer and actually voting holds up in a multivariate regression controlling for other influences on voting. However, it is possible that some of this finding is due to a muddled recall effect. Someone who voted would have probably picked up the necessary registration forms from his or her voting officer and is therefore more likely to remember receiving a briefing or having contact with the voting officer. Evidence that this may have occurred can be seen in the proportion of voters, broken down by method of voting,

---

[11] This lesser effect among officers makes sense given their high propensity to vote.

who reported receiving the briefing from their voting officer. Among those who reported voting by absentee ballot, 37% reported receiving a briefing from their voting officer prior to the election. Comparably, only 23% of those who voted in person reported receiving the briefing. The likely reason for this discrepancy is that those who voted via absentee ballot probably got the appropriate paperwork from their voting officer and are therefore much more likely to remember the interaction than those who were able to vote locally.

It is also likely that a greater percentage than 26 actually received some form of briefing from their unit's voting officer. Briefings from unit voting officers are typically done in mass formations in conjunction with announcements about the unit's upcoming training, safety issues, and other administrative topics. Soldiers and officers who typically do not vote are likely to catalogue these briefings with the hundreds of others they have received in the army and are therefore less likely to recall having contact with the voting officer. Also of note is that these briefings are not comparable to the mobilization efforts that a civilian will usually encounter before an election. Whereas civilian mobilization efforts are typically for a specific candidate or slate of candidates, the briefing that unit voting officers give is typically a neutral and straightforward affair that announces the upcoming election, relevant deadlines, and resources available for registration and voting. It is therefore less likely to involve any of the vested interests or interpersonal dynamics that are inherent in mobilization efforts by civilian organizations.

Among civilians, 51% of respondents to the NES survey report being contacted by a political party or other organization that tried to get them to support specific candidates prior to the 2004 election. Of those who reported being contacted, 89% reported voting compared with only 64% among those who were not similarly contacted. This implies that these types of mobilization efforts may be more effective in encouraging voting than a simple briefing on registration or voting procedures. Unfortunately, the C&S Survey did not collect data on civilian mobilization efforts that may have reached soldiers, although it can be assumed that soldiers are less likely to be exposed to such efforts. This is due to both their mobility and the fact that many live on inaccessible federal installations. So although this study does not have the data to fully evaluate the difference in mobilization rates between the army and civilian populations, these differing types of mobilization efforts may help explain some of the army's lower reported voting rates.[12]

---

[12] On the other hand, there is evidence that in recent years campaigns have been more likely to target habitual voters, which means that the civilians contacted prior to the election may have been more likely to vote anyway. Goldstein and Ridout, "Politics of Participation."

Efficacy and Political Participation

To test the second possible explanation for the army's decreased voting rate, I will look at the correlations between feelings of connection and trust toward the government and political participation in both the army and civilian populations. I will then look at how various measures of efficacy hold up in models that control for the previously assessed demographic variables. Finally, I will assess these factors in models that combine the civilian (NAES or NES) and army data sets.

The specific variables I assess are:

1. *Complexity:* This variable is defined as measuring those who agree with the statement "Sometimes politics and government seem so complicated that a person like me can't really understand what's going on." I would expect a person who agrees with this statement to be less likely to participate in the political process. The NAES asked this question in 2004 in addition to the C&S Survey. As noted in chapter 4, members of the army are slightly less likely to agree with this statement than their civilian counterparts.

2. *Voice:* This variable captures those respondents who agree with the statement "People like me don't have any say about what the government does." The comparison civilian data set for this question will be the 2004 NES.[13] Someone who agrees with this statement should be less likely to vote or otherwise participate in the political process. The proportion of respondents who agree with this statement is greater in the army than it is in the civilian population.

3. *Govt. cares:* This variable captures those who agree with the statement "Public officials don't care much what people like me think." The comparison data set for this variable is again the 2004 NES data set. Someone who agrees with this statement would also be less likely to participate in the political process. The proportion of respondents who agree with this statement is also greater in the army than it is in the civilian population.

Starting with the concept of complexity and inability to understand the workings of government, both the NAES and army data sets included questions that asked respondents whether they felt government was too complex for them. The correlation between this variable and voting is roughly the same for both populations (0.12 for the army and 0.10 for the civilian population). In a bivariate regression, the concept is also statis-

---

[13] This question was included in the NAES but was asked only through the beginning of April 2004. It would be preferable to use this question due to the NAES's sample size, but the time period does not overlap with the C&S Survey, and, more important, it cannot be used in regressions with questions about participation in 2004, as most respondents had not yet engaged in the presidential campaign by April.

tically and substantively significant for predicting voting, although it does appear to have a greater effect among civilians. The same pattern holds for the correlations between complexity and the political actions analyzed here (registering to vote, donating money, and displaying buttons, stickers, or signs).

In a multivariate regression on the civilian population controlling for age, gender, race, education, and income, a person who thinks that "politics seems so complicated that a person like me cannot really understand what is going on" is less likely participate in the political process. But unlike in the civilian population, among members of the army the complexity variable was not significant in predicting voting rates, registering to vote, donating money, or displaying a sign, sticker, or button in support of a campaign or candidate. This means that even though members of the army are less likely than civilians to believe that government is too complicated, their greater sense of understanding does not translate into political activity. This further confuses the question of why members of the army participate at rates lower than their civilian counterparts.

The second and third questions in the C&S Survey, which asked about the connection respondents felt with the government, namely "voice" and "govt. cares," are taken from the NES survey. Because a greater proportion of the army feels they have no say in what the government does (voice) and that public officials do not care much what people like them think (govt. cares), these variables could help explain the participation gap between the army and the general public. In a multivariate regression controlling for demographic factors, among members of the army only "voice" is significant for predicting the likelihood of a respondent's wearing a button or displaying a bumper sticker or sign.[14] Overall, these findings indicate that the army's lower rates of political participation are not primarily due to more widespread feelings of having no say in the government or that public officials do not care what they think.

Partisanship and Political Participation

People who identify with political parties are more likely to participate in the political process than those who do not identify with any party. Furthermore, those who say they have a strong attachment to a party are more likely to participate than both those who do not identify with a party and those who identify with one, but not strongly. Given that there are fewer people who identify with a political party in the army than in

---

[14] The category of "voice" approaches statistical significance in models on voting and being registered to vote, but is not quite significant at the 0.05 level.

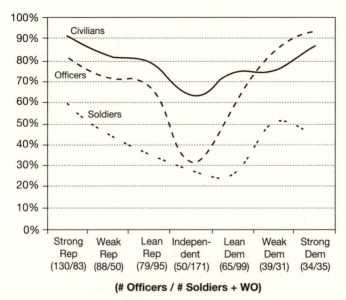

(# Officers / # Soldiers + WO)

Figure 7.2 Voting Rates by Party Identification
Source: C&S Survey and 2004 National Annenberg Election Survey
Note: Voting rate differences by party affiliation significant for all groups at the .001 level.

the civilian population, we would expect this partly to explain the army's lower rates of political participation.

In a multivariate regression, partisanship does indeed correlate with increased rates of participation, both in the army and in civilian populations. This effect is larger in the army. Figure 7.2 displays reported voting rates by party affiliation for the civilian population, officers, and soldiers and warrant officers. The chart shows that across the political spectrum, members of the army vote at lower rates than their civilian counterparts. The exceptions to this are officers who identify with the Democratic Party. This group appears to vote at slightly higher rates than their civilian counterparts, although the population in the army sample is very small (73 officers identify with the Democratic Party, and 34 of those identify strongly with the party).

Also of note in figure 7.2 is that civilian voting rates are relatively consistent across the partisan political spectrum, with the voting rate of independents only 25% less than strong Democrats and 29% less than strong Republicans. The differences within the officer corps are much more dramatic, with neutral or independent officers voting at a rate of 50–60% less than their counterparts who identify strongly with the Republican or

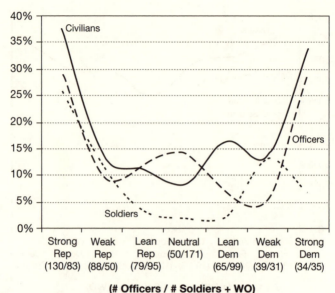

(# Officers / # Soldiers + WO)

Figure 7.3 Buttons, Stickers, and Signs by Party Identification
Source: C&S Survey and 2004 National Annenberg Election Survey
Note: Differences in rates of displaying signs by party affiliation significant for
civilians and soldiers at .001 level. Significant for officers at the .01 level.

Democratic Parties. Among soldiers and warrant officers, the same general pattern holds, although voting rates are less across the spectrum and strong Democrats are less likely to vote than their counterparts who identify strongly as Republicans.

The same holds for rates in the display of buttons, bumper stickers, or signs in support of campaigns and candidates. Figure 7.3 highlights how members of the army are typically less likely than their civilian counterparts to display their political views openly. Soldiers and officers on the Republican side of the spectrum are more likely to display such signs than soldiers and officers on the Democratic side, but officers who identify strongly with a political party are equally likely to show signs of support regardless of party affiliation. Democrats in the enlisted and warrant officer ranks are again the least likely to participate in this kind of political activity.

The last form of political participation that the C&S Survey asked about, donating money to political campaigns or candidates, reveals a slightly different relationship between party affiliation and participation. In the case of donating money, figure 7.4 shows that Republicans in the army are more likely to report having donated money to a campaign or

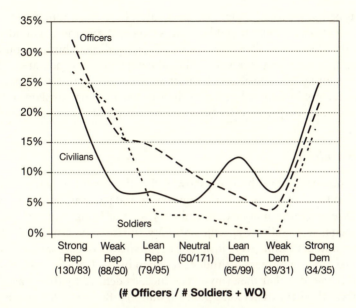

Figure 7.4 Donating Money by Party Identification
Source: C&S Survey and 2004 National Annenberg Election Survey
Note: Differences in rates of displaying signs by party affiliation significant for civilians and soldiers at .001 level. Significant for officers at the .01 level.

candidate than either their Democratic counterparts in the army or their Republican counterparts in the civilian population. However, part of the difference with the civilian population may be the time frame (the NAES asked specifically about donations during the 2004 campaign, whereas the C&S Survey asked about *ever* giving money to a campaign or candidate).

These charts of party affiliation and political participation confirm earlier findings that fewer members of the army vote and display support for political campaigns and candidates than their civilian counterparts. However, the charts also show key differences in rates of participation in the army that depend upon an identification with either the Republican or the Democratic Party. Those who identify strongly with either party are more likely to participate than those who are independent or neutral. And the difference between the rate of participation between partisans and nonpartisans in the army is typically larger than the differences between partisans and nonpartisans in the civilian population. As for differences between parties, Republicans in the army are more likely to display signs in support of campaigns or candidates than either independents or those who identify with the Democratic Party. The same holds true for donating money to campaigns or candidates. In an institution that is typically viewed as heavily Republican, it is expected that those who identify with the Democratic Party will be less likely to display buttons, bumper stickers, or signs in support of political campaigns or candidates. These soldiers and officers probably hesitate to demonstrate that their political views are not in line with those of their peers. This may explain some of the gap in participation rates between the army and civilian populations.

Army Culture

The data analyzed in chapter 6 showed that there was no significant relationship between the nature of army service and party affiliation. In other words, experiences unique to the military, such as being deployed to combat, being in a military-specific specialty (infantry or armor), or being from a military family were insignificant predictors of partisan affiliation. The snapshot of military attitudes presented by the C&S Survey does not support the idea that the army experience, as defined by these variables, significantly shapes a person's political outlook. But it is still possible that some aspects of military service promote or discourage political participation. As members of the army work directly for the government, they may be especially attuned to government actions, particularly in the realm of foreign policy. One might then presume that members of the army would actively seek to promote specific agendas through political activity.

On the other hand, if the army's culture specifically discouraged political activity, we would expect someone who has gone through what can be considered core military experiences to have a lesser propensity to vote or otherwise engage in the political process. As Van Riper and Unwalla noted in their study about military voting between 1944 and 1956, the evidence they collected indicated that the military tradition worked to inhibit voting among senior officers. Specifically, the two researchers found that coming from a military family, graduating from a military academy, making a career out of the military, and serving in a military-specific specialty all correlated with decreased voting rates among senior military officers. Although the Van Riper and Unwalla study is not directly comparable with the C&S Survey because their study focused specifically on generals and colonels, it is still worthwhile to see if the political behavior of the senior officers in the C&S Survey mimics that of officers in the aftermath of World War II.

Among majors and colonels in the army in 2004, it did not appear that military tradition, as defined by Van Riper and Unwalla, worked to inhibit voting. The intention to stay in the army and pursue a career correlated with a slight increase in voting among officers (71% versus 61% for noncareerists).[15] Likewise, having a parent who served in the military correlated with a slight increase (4% to 5%) in voting among officers, particularly those in the rank of major and above. This is distinct from Van Riper and Unwalla's finding of a negative correlation between voting rates and having a parent who served in the military. The correlation between an academy education and voting rates was unclear in the C&S Survey, although fewer academy graduates appeared to vote than officers commissioned through Officer Candidate School or via direct appointment. Finally, in 2004 it appeared that being in the army's core operational branches, such as infantry and armor, correlated with a slight decrease in voting (70% compared with 64%)—the only factor that remained consistent between the two studies.

In sum, it does not appear that military culture or tradition correlates uniformly with a decrease in political participation. In fact, in a multivariate regression controlling for party affiliation, a sense of connectedness to government (the variables *complexity, voice,* and *gov. cares*), and demographic factors, elements of military service were largely irrelevant in predicting political participation. Among the few exceptions were the following:

1. Among officers, being a veteran of Operation Iraqi Freedom or Operation Enduring Freedom increased the likelihood that a respondent would report voting *in the 2000 election.* This is an interesting finding in that it relies on overreporting to make any sense. These events took place after 2001 and so could not have influenced a person's decision to vote in 2000, but this may highlight the idea that officers who have gone through this experience are more likely to feel that they *should have voted* in 2000, even if they did not. This finding also highlights how the core military experience of going to war may promote political activity.[16]

2. Officers who intend to stay in the army for a career are less likely to have donated money in support of a political campaign or candidate.

3. Officers who belong to an operational unit (one that is deployable and not part of the military education system or institutional support) are more likely

---

[15] Van Riper used the type of commission that officers held as an indicator of career intentions in his study. The criteria for awarding commissions and the meaning of those commissions have changed significantly in the interim; this means that they are no longer a valid proxy for career intentions. For comparison purposes I therefore asked respondents specifically about their career intentions as a means of replicating Van Riper's analysis.

[16] Studies of war veterans have sometimes shown an increase in faith in government and slightly lower levels of political cynicism (see Laufer, "Aftermath of War"). In a preliminary analysis of the effects of combat experience in the C&S Survey, it appears that combat veterans report having slightly higher confidence in understanding government but are also slightly less likely to believe that they can influence the political process.

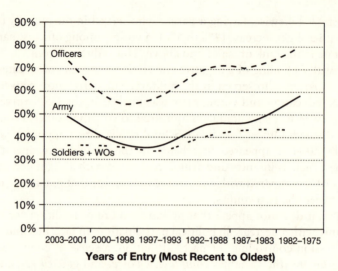

Figure 7.5 Voting Rates by Year of Entry
Source: C&S Survey
Note: Differences between cohorts (year groups) are not statistically significant, with the exception of the difference between officers with 3–5 years of service and those with greater than 21 years of service. Differences between officers and soldiers are significant at the .001 level.

to have posted a sign, bumper sticker, or button in support of a political campaign or candidate.

4. Soldiers and warrant officers who had a parent serve in the military were also more likely to have posted a sign, bumper sticker, or button in support of a political campaign or candidate.

Clearly these findings are not enough to support the general hypothesis that military culture inhibits political activity. The absence of any significant relationships between experiences unique to the military and political participation reinforces the idea that soldiers develop their propensity to be politically active independent of the army. If this were not the case, we would see more of these factors playing a role in discouraging political participation.

Self-Selection Effect

An earlier analysis of party affiliation and of reported voting rates by year of entry into service raised the possibility that the outlook soldiers and officers have toward the political process is largely shaped prior to entry into the army. Figure 7.1, reprinted above as figure 7.5, shows that the

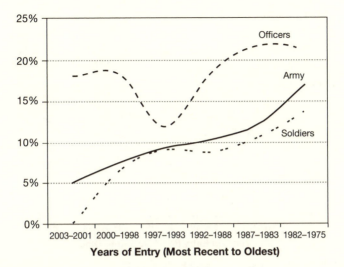

Figure 7.6 Donations by Year of Entry
Source: C&S Survey
Note: Differences between cohorts (year groups) are not statistically significant.

cohort of soldiers who entered the military after 2000 were much more likely to vote in the 2000 election than their counterparts who were already in the army during the 2000 election. On the one hand, this could mean that being in the army depresses voting rates. Given that members of the army must typically register by mail and vote via absentee ballot, and that only 26% of them remember having received a briefing from their unit voting officer on the procedures for this prior to the 2000 election, it is likely that this explains some of the depressed participation rates. On the other hand, it is also likely that a large portion of this voting pattern is due to a cohort effect whereby those who joined the army between 2001 and 2003 are simply more politically active.

A look at the rates of voting, monetary donations, and display of signs, stickers, or buttons by year of entry into the army lends credence to the second hypothesis, although the differences are small and do not achieve statistical significance due to the small subgroup sizes. The chart on voting rates by year of entry shows that 74% of the army's newest officers report voting in 2000. This drops to 55% among those who have been in the army from three to five years, before steadily climbing to 80% among officers who joined the army between 1975 and 1982. If we omit the voting rates of the newest officers, this chart *could* reflect steadily increasing voting rates as the population advances in age.

The rate of political donations among officers, shown in figure 7.6, follows the same pattern, with the army's newest officers reporting a rela-

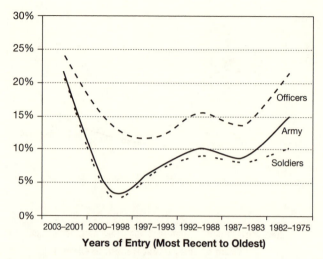

Figure 7.7 Displaying Signs/Stickers by Year of Entry
Source: C&S Survey
Note: Differences between cohorts statistically significant only for the army overall at .05 level.

tively high rate (18%); the rate drops to 12% for officers who joined the army between 1993 and 1997. It then steadily climbs to about 22% for the army's senior officers. The pattern for displaying signs, stickers, or buttons in support of political campaigns or candidates looks similar, although in this respect the army's newest cohort, including officers and warrant officers and soldiers, is more likely to have made some public display of political attitudes than any other group in the army. Twenty-two percent of those who joined the army between 2001 and 2003 report doing this compared with only 15% of those who have been in the army for over twenty years (see figure 7.7).

This book cannot definitively address why this new generation of soldiers and officers appears more politically active than those already in the army before 2001, but such a change could be attributed to the events of September 11, 2001. It is possible that these events attracted a cohort that was more prone to political activity.[17] A more in-depth analysis of the differences between these cohorts is beyond the scope of this study, but regardless of cause, the C&S data suggest that the next generation of officers and soldiers is likely to be much more politically active than their more senior counterparts.

[17] This cohort reported joining the army for educational and job-training benefits at a rate similar to those who joined the army between 1998 and 2000, although they were slightly more likely to list "Desire to serve my country" as their primary reason for joining.

Conclusion

Members of the army participate in the political process to a lesser degree than their civilian counterparts. The findings of this chapter shed serious doubts on the reported voting rate of 79% among members of the military in 2004. The idea that a population composed primarily of eighteen- to twenty-four-year-old males would be more politically active than practically every other segment of the American public should have been questioned immediately upon the release of the FVAP report in 2005. That it was not questioned is indicative of the distance, and lack of understanding, between the military and the public. The findings presented here are more in keeping with previous studies of political engagement among members of the military.

They are also in keeping with previous findings that members of the army are less likely to identify with a political party. Once again, however, aggregate participation rates mask two very different subpopulations within the army. While the army overall reports voting rates that are significantly lower than the civilian population's, officers are again the exception. Officers appear to vote at rates approaching those of their civilian counterparts. Members of the army are also less likely to display a button, bumper sticker, or sign in support of political campaigns or candidates, although officers are about twice as likely to engage in this type of political activity than the rest of the army. Finally, the army overall appears to donate money at a lower rate than the civilian population, although army officers seem to donate at a higher rate than either soldiers or civilians. However, this increased rate of donation among officers appears to be due to socioeconomic factors and is not necessarily a function of hyperpoliticization. As shown by the Virtual Officer Corps, a group of civilians that was similar to the officer corps demographically would in fact participate at rates greater than either the rest of the civilian population or the actual officer corps.

The cohort of officers who entered the army in the late 1970s and early 1980s is simultaneously the most politically active and most Republican of any group in the army. Although the cause of this cannot be tested here, it is entirely plausible that this cohort of officers' propensity toward political activity and political affiliations were directly shaped by the external political environment of that era. In the wake of the tumultuous Carter years and Reagan's open embrace of the military, these officers might have formed lasting loyalties and habits of political participation in their formative years immediately before and after joining the army as commissioned officers. There is also a spike in both the participation rates and Republican identification of those officers who entered the service around the time of the first Gulf War. It is possible that this also served as a shaping experience for young officers and those about to enter the army at that time.

Following from this, it is possible to state that the depressed participation rates (as compared with their civilian counterparts) of officers between their fifth and tenth year of service, those who joined between 1994 and 1999, is a function of a more muddled domestic political environment and the lack of any distinct military threat against the United States. For this cohort, soldiering could simply be a profession, distinct and separate from any ideological or political cause. Finally, if we believe that the preceding explanations have any merit, then the army's newest cohort presents a new dynamic for the military. The cohort of officers who joined the army between 2001 and 2003 is almost as likely as the most senior cohort to vote and donate money to political campaigns or candidates. More interesting, they are also more likely than any other cohort to have publicly displayed their political attitudes through signs, buttons, or bumper stickers. Unlike the previously mentioned cohorts, however, this new cohort appears to be almost evenly split between Republican and Democratic Party identifiers.[18] That junior officers and soldiers seem to be making political choices independent of the views of their seniors is another indicator that the army culture does little to directly affect participation rates or political attitudes.[19]

In sum, the evidence presented in this chapter does not support the idea that the army's culture explicitly discourages political participation. Instead, it is more likely that depressed participation rates are primarily a function of two factors. The first is that it is more difficult for a mobile population to participate. Such a population is also likely to have less contact with local politics and the type of mobilization efforts that reach the civilian population, although this is untested in this study.

The second factor may be a form of self-selection. People who join the military are perhaps less likely to engage in the political process. This is partly manifest in the tendency of members of the military to feel they have less connection with the government or that they do not have any say in the political process. Members of the military are also less likely to identify with a political party, which again may, in part, be an artifact of mobility and the lack of exposure to civilian mobilization efforts.

[18] Although in keeping with the findings of chapter 6 that the algorithm probably underestimates the number of Republican identifiers in the junior officer ranks, the parity is probably not as close as these numbers suggest.

[19] More important for domestic politics, these findings may reflect a fundamental shift in how the public, and a specific section of the public especially attuned to foreign policy and defense, may be shifting away from the Republican Party on these issues. These larger implications will be discussed in more detail in chapter 9.

Finally, differing participation rates of various military cohorts suggest that attitudes toward politics and political participation may be shaped by the domestic political environment and significant events related to defense and foreign policy during their formative years, which typically coincide with the age at which most people join the army. If true, this has broad implications for our understanding of internal army affairs and civil-military relations.

Chapter 8

The Army's Next Generation

THE FINDINGS OF THE PREVIOUS chapters suggest that the political attitudes and propensity toward political activity of members of the army may be shaped prior to their entry into military service. It also appears that officers are quite different from enlisted personnel, both in their rates of political participation and in their ideology and political affiliations. To explore the reason for the differences between officers and soldiers, and to more closely examine how the military may or may not socialize new members, in this chapter I depart from an analysis of the active-duty army to take a closer look at future officers in precommissioning training.

Cadets at the United States Military Academy (West Point) provide an interesting group to study. West Point has often been viewed as the birthplace and home of the army's professional ethic.[1] Furthermore, from an individual perspective, choosing to go to West Point is not like choosing to go to any other college. A person who decides to go to West Point is making a commitment to eight years of military service, in addition to the four years spent at the academy.[2] The mission of West Point is "to educate, train, and inspire the Corps of Cadets so that each graduate is a commissioned leader of character committed to the values of Duty, Honor, Country and prepared for a career of professional excellence and service to the Nation as an officer in the United States Army."[3] This focus on preparation for an army career means that cadets are immersed in military culture from the day they arrive at the academy and spend the next four years surrounded by current and future army officers. They are largely isolated from the civilian world and even spend most of their summers in military training.[4] The immersion of cadets in this environment and the fairly rigid

[1] Watson, "How the Army Became Accepted."

[2] The current obligation for attending West Point is five years of active-duty military service immediately after graduation, followed by three years on reserve status. This obligation is officially incurred at the beginning of a cadet's third year at West Point.

[3] United States Military Academy, "USMA Mission."

[4] Cadets spend a significant part of every summer at West Point conducting military training. During their third and fourth summers, they are also required to attend military-skills training provided by the army (such as the airborne school) and spend one summer training with a regular army unit.

and hierarchical control that West Point exerts over the lives of cadets is so great that apart from prisons and mental institutions, the military academy may be the closest thing in America to a "total institution."[5]

This chapter seeks to assess the role of such an institution in shaping the political views of those who enter it. By exploring the dynamics of opinion formation among the army's next generation of officers, we can see if institutional norms have developed that reinforce certain political views or affiliations with a specific political party, or if the attitudes of young officers are primarily a result of self-selection into military service.

Existing Research on Cadets and Socialization

An extensive body of research addresses the socialization of officers in precommissioning training. Unfortunately, no early studies of cadet attitudes address political party preference, although some address the idea of conservatism. Most focus broadly on the concept of militarism and cadet perceptions of the role of the military. And as might be expected, most of these studies were conducted in the 1960s and 1970s, which, with the Vietnam War and the end of the draft, was a fertile period for the study of civil-military relations. In summarizing the existing literature on the topic in 1976, Moskos concluded that "professional self-definitions are much more shaped by anticipatory and concurrent socialization than by social background variables."[6] The question here is the relative power of anticipatory socialization (a variant of self-selection) versus concurrent socialization. Specifically, does West Point shape the political and social attitudes of cadets, or do cadets arrive with preexisting attitudes that are not significantly altered by the West Point experience?

---

[5] Life at West Point seems to fit Erving Goffman's definition fairly well, although there is room for interpretation in both the definition and the implications of the concept of total institutions. Goffman outlined the four characteristics of a total institution as

First, all aspects of life are conducted in the same place and under the same single authority. Second, each phase of the member's daily activity is carried on in the immediate company of a large batch of others, all of whom are treated alike and required to do the same thing together. Third, all phases of the day's activities are tightly scheduled, with one activity leading at a prearranged time into the next, the whole sequence of activities being imposed from above by a system of explicit formal rulings and a body of officials. Finally, the various enforced activities are brought together into a single rational plan purportedly designed to fulfill the official aim of the institution. (Goffman, *Asylums*)

[6] Moskos, "The Military," 59.

TABLE 8.1

Current and Projected Political Preferences, Cadets and Civilians (1969)

	Current preference		Projected preference	
	USMA cadets	Civilian freshmen	USMA cadets	Civilian freshmen
Left/Liberal	21%	36%	19%	41%
Middle of the road	40	39	30	28
Moderately/Strongly conservative	39	25	51	31
	100	100	100	100

Source: 1969 American Council on Education Annual Survey (cited in Hecox's "Comparison of Cadets").

Self-Selection

An internal study from West Point's Office of Research, published in 1970, dramatically highlights the role of self-selection and anticipatory socialization in explaining the attitudes of future officers.[7] A survey of 1,257 incoming freshmen, or plebes, concluded that 21% placed themselves on the liberal side of the ideological spectrum and 39% placed themselves on the conservative side.[8] This was nearly a mirror image of the self-identification of civilian college students from the same era. Thirty-six percent of civilian freshmen at four-year colleges identified themselves as liberal, and 25% identified themselves as conservative. More interesting than this initial difference in attitudes were the *self-projected* future attitudes of the two populations. Both groups were asked to describe the political preferences that they expected to have in four years' time. Among cadets there was a slight decrease in the proportion who expected to identify themselves as liberal in four years and a significant increase in the proportion who expected to identify themselves as conservative. In sum, cadets entered West Point more conservative than their peers at regular universities and expected to become more conservative during their time at West Point. Conversely, civilian freshmen projected a more even split in their expected political preferences.

Several other studies from this period highlight how differences in attitudes were largely a function of career choice. One technique for assessing the effect of career choice was to examine attitudinal differences between West Point cadets, students enrolled in ROTC, and regular college stu-

[7] Hecox, "Comparison of New Cadets."

[8] A total of 1,429 cadets completed the original survey, but only 1,257 cadets without prior college experience were included in Hecox's analysis.

dents. In 1971 Peter Karsten found that between these three groups, the academy cadets were most militaristic, followed by ROTC cadets and then the non-ROTC undergraduates.[9] In another study published at the same time, William Lucas found that self-selection into military service explained the finding of increased militarism more than socialization within the ROTC program.[10] Using data collected from West Point cadets in 1988, John Hammill, David Segal, and Mady Wechsler Segal found that the values of new cadets as they related to conformity and self-direction appeared to be the result of cadets' "internal preparation for and attitudes toward the West Point environment."[11] In other words, self-selection appeared to be the most important element in explaining the values of new cadets.

The Limits of Socialization

These studies do not preclude a socialization effect and a change in attitudes during college. While Karsten found significant differences between ROTC cadets and regular college students at the time of entry into college, he also discovered that the militarism of ROTC cadets declined in college; this suggests that the environment of civilian educational institutions can lead to changes in outlook.[12]

But what about an immersive military environment such as West Point? In 1964 John Lovell found that the West Point experience did not have a comprehensive impact on the attitudes of future officers. In his words, "Socialization at West Point produces only slight impact upon professional orientations and strategic perspectives of the cadet."[13] Unfortunately, Lovell did not address the social and political attitudes of cadets broadly but focused his investigation on attitudes specifically related to the military profession.[14] One might assume—although one cannot be sure—that his findings also imply little, if any, change in attitudes not directly related to military service.

---

[9] Karsten, "Professional and Citizen Officers."

[10] Lucas, "Anticipatory Socialization."

[11] Hammill, Segal, and Segal, "Self-Selection."

[12] Hammill, Segal, and Segal also speculated that cadets would value conformity less as they matured at the academy and assumed leadership positions, although they could not address the question with their data.

[13] Lovell, "Professional Socialization," 145.

[14] An interesting note in Lovell's study is his explanation for not delving deeply into social and political attitudes. In his words, "The measures that were selected for inclusion . . . would be unlikely to offend the respondent's sense of propriety. (Therefore cadets were not asked their preference of political party, for example, a commitment they are not expected to voice.)" Lovell, "Professional Socialization," 121.

In one of the rare, published longitudinal studies of the attitudes of West Point cadets, Robert Priest, Terrence Fullerton, and Claude Bridges analyzed the attitudes of cadets across four years at West Point in the 1970s. One of their primary findings was that cadets grow in "pragmatic, situation-dependent judgment over the course of four years."[15] This appears to happen among students in nonmilitary institutions as well and therefore should not be considered specific to an education at a military academy. However, the authors also found that West Point cadets described themselves as more politically conservative than their peers upon entry into the academy and became more likely to identify themselves as politically conservative over the course of four years there.

This highlights a potential institutional effect, although the 1970 Office of Research study raises the question of how much this population was predisposed to becoming more conservative, independent of its experience at West Point. There are also a few other caveats to the finding. First, the proportion of cadets identifying themselves as politically liberal also increased during four years at West Point, although the increase was not as great.[16] Furthermore, the meaning of "conservatism" to cadets during this period is open to interpretation.

Research on civilian students during this era found that heavy involvement with athletics correlated with an increase in political conservatism.[17] Cadets enter West Point with more athletic experience than their peers and undergo four years of significant and mandatory involvement in organized sports. During the time of this study, 64% of incoming cadets rated themselves as above average in athletic ability compared with 49% of males at civilian colleges.[18] By the end of their four years at West Point, 81% of cadets rated themselves as above average in athletic ability, reflecting the heavy emphasis on organized athletics at the academy. While unexplored in the study by Priest et al., this correlation implies that some of the cadets' understanding of conservatism may relate to concepts such as teamwork and hierarchy, which are common elements in organized athletics.

On the other hand, the study did uncover an important social dynamic that cannot be overlooked: the role of officers who teach at West Point. The study found that "at entrance cadets who would persist at the Acad-

---

[15] Priest, Fullerton, and Bridges, "Personality and Value Changes."

[16] Those rating themselves as higher than average in political conservatism rose from 34% in 1971 to 47% in 1975. Over the same period, those rating themselves as higher than average in political liberalism rose from 15% to 20%. Ibid., 638.

[17] Astin, *Four Critical Years.*

[18] West Point was not integrated until 1976. The first class to graduate with women was the class of 1980.

emy had values much like officers assigned to West Point; in contrast, cadets who later attrited were more like men in general."[19] Given that a strong majority of officers in the 1970s identified themselves as conservative, and given the influential role that officers play at the academy, it stands to reason that cadets would leave West Point emulating the role models they interacted with on a daily basis, and that cadets who perceived the greatest difference between themselves and their role models would be the most likely to resign from West Point. (The influential role of officers at West Point, both in and out of the classroom, will be discussed in more detail later in this chapter.)

A more recent study that examined cadet socialization also found some evidence of attitude changes among cadets, but in very limited areas. In analyzing data drawn from a survey of cadet attitudes in 1995, Volker Franke found evidence that West Point does play a role in the socialization of cadets, at least in terms of value orientation and outlook toward various military missions. Franke found that more senior cadets tended to have more "warrioristic" attitudes than freshmen cadets; they also almost unanimously agreed that the military's primary focus was the conduct of combat operations.[20] Data from the same study, however, showed that cadets in all four classes were most likely to list family or religious or church groups as their most important reference group and that there was "no consistent change in cadets' reference group affiliations across classes."[21] These findings suggest that while West Point socialization affects attitudes directly related to military service, the academy experience may have little impact on more basic values and elements of cadet identity.[22]

Shaping Political Attitudes?

Unfortunately there are no studies that directly address the social and political attitudes of West Point cadets, so we are left to extrapolate how findings of attitude changes, or the lack of attitude changes, in other areas

[19] Priest, Fullerton, and Bridges, "Personality and Value Changes," 640.

[20] One limitation of the study's effort to assess change over time was its comparison of cadets across the four classes, as opposed to a longitudinal study of individual classes as they went through the West Point experience. This is, unfortunately, a problem inherent in almost all studies of the military's role in attitude formation (including this one). Franke, "Warriors for Peace."

[21] Franke, "Duty, Honor, Country."

[22] In a third look at the data, Franke compared cadet attitudes with a sample of civilian undergraduate students and found that self-selection appeared to explain much of the attitudinal differences between the two groups, with only the aforementioned "warrioristic" outlook increasing with time spent at West Point. Franke, "Generation X and the Military."

might inform our understanding of the formation of political attitudes among West Point cadets.

The question of party affiliation was at least addressed, tangentially, in two recent studies of cadet attitudes. As part of the TISS project, Don Snider, Robert Priest, and Felisa Lewis investigated cadet attitudes as they related to civil-military relations. They found that cadets differed from civilian students on attitudes toward the use of force and topics related to moral standards in society, but that these differences stemmed primarily from divergences between the two populations in gender, religiosity, and political identification.[23]

In a 2006 study, David Rohall, Morten Ender, and Michael Matthews analyzed differences in attitudes between regular college students, ROTC cadets, and cadets at West Point. They examined specifically 2003 survey data on attitudes toward the war in Afghanistan and the then-impending conflict in Iraq and found greater support for military intervention among cadets at West Point and those enrolled in ROTC.[24] This was not unexpected. However, they did not find evidence that the differences between regular college students and future officers were due primarily to their military training (most of the survey respondents were in their freshmen year). On the contrary, the differences in attitudes between the populations were explained largely by the higher proportion of men and Republican Party identifiers in the future officer population—a finding that points to self-selection as the primary determinant of these attitudes.

The exception to this finding was the fact that ROTC cadets were somewhat less favorable toward the war than West Point cadets. The authors suggest that this finding may be attributable to the exposure of ROTC cadets to civilian students, who do not necessarily share the attitudes of largely male and Republican populations. This indirectly raises the question of peer-group and informal officer/instructor influence on the attitudes of cadets at West Point.

On balance, all of these studies suggest that the West Point experience does have an effect on cadet attitudes, but in fairly limited ways. It is clear that the academy may shape a cadet's outlook on military missions and foster a "warrioristic" attitude. It is not clear how much the academy experience affects basic affiliations or shapes attitudes that are tangential to military service, such as ideology and political affiliation. The 1970 ORA study reveals how new cadets at West Point were more ideologically conservative than their civilian peers and had an *expectation* of greater conservative self-identification after their West Point experience. Further, the Ro-

---

[23] Snider, Priest, and Lewis, "Civilian-Military Gap."
[24] Rohall, Ender, and Matthews, "Effects of Military Affiliation."

hall, Ender, and Matthews study shows that a preponderance of cadets in 2003 brought Republican Party affiliation with them to the academy.

However, there is some evidence that West Point does indirectly influence political and ideological attitudes through exposure to other cadets and the informal influence of officers teaching at West Point. The Karsten and Rohall et al. studies hint at a "reinforcing," or affiliation, effect, whereby West Point cadets may be more uniform in their political views due to a lack of exposure to different viewpoints. When combined with the findings of Priest et al. that cadets with a worldview more similar to that of officers are more likely to graduate from West Point and become officers themselves, it becomes clear that more attention needs to be paid to how both peers and instructors may indirectly shape the political outlook of cadets.

In a review of studies highlighting perceptions of liberal bias among American academic institutions, Cathy Young highlighted how if a minority of students reported perceptions of intolerance among instructors for dissenting views, it could be indicative of a broader climate of hostility toward those not in line with campus orthodoxy.[25] A similar dynamic may be occurring at West Point, albeit in the opposite direction. Furthermore, the potential exists for instructors and professors at West Point to have a much greater impact on their students than do faculty at civilian institutions. At the conclusion of their analysis of officer education at the precommissioning level, Snider, Priest, and Lewis stated,

> Although not part of our quantitative analysis, there is a very large, informal influence by staff and faculty at the precommissioning military institutions on the attitudes and perceptions of military students, in some cases perhaps even more influential than the content of academic curricula or training programs.[26]

This echoes the thoughts of Moskos, who in 1983, when discussing political education in the military, wrote, "Education about political affairs seems to be more affected by the context of instruction—the conditions of learning surrounding teachers and students—than by the content of the instruction."[27] Given these observations, in the rest of this chapter I will focus explicitly on the nature of cadet political attitudes and affiliations and the influence that peers and instructors have on those attitudes.

[25] Young, "Impact of Academic Bias."
[26] Snider, Priest, and Lewis, "Civilian-Military Gap," 270.
[27] Moskos, "All-Volunteer Force," 318.

The 2004 Cadet Preelection Survey

The 2004 survey of cadets was originally designed to provide cadets the experience of a public opinion poll in the midst of an election season.[28] Using the C&S Survey as a guide, it covered (1) general attitudes about West Point and the army, including morale and career intentions; (2) cadets' reasons for seeking admission to West Point; (3) cadets' perceptions and experiences of discrimination and their opinions on gender, racial, and ethnic relations in the army and civilian society; and, for the purposes of the current study, (4) cadets' opinions of social and political issues, including foreign and defense policy and, especially, uses of the military in world affairs. Wherever useful and possible, the survey replicated questions in existing American national surveys to allow for comparisons with the civilian population.

In addition to gathering this baseline information on attitudes, the survey assembled extensive demographic information that the army has not normally collected. These included questions on language proficiency, the military service of family members, the political affiliations of family members, and the socioeconomic status of cadets' families. The survey also explored the extent to which cadets feel pressure to identify with one of the two major political parties.

All first-, second-, and third-year cadets enrolled in obligatory core economics and political science courses were eligible to complete the survey.[29] Due to the way these courses are scheduled, this meant that the entire sophomore class, half of the junior class, and a small number of freshmen were eligible to take the survey. We chose the timing of the survey to coincide with a period when politics and opinion polls would be most salient. The survey was administered at a secure Web site from Saturday, October 30, until 5 p.m. on Tuesday, November 2 (Election Day).[30]

---

[28] The survey was designed by Craig Cummings and me with the assistance of Robert Shapiro. It was supported by the Department of Social Sciences at USMA, which allowed for the inclusion of the entire sophomore class in the survey sample and an essentially random selection of half of the junior class.

[29] The survey did not specifically ask cadets what year they were attending at West Point. We did, however, know which core course respondents were taking when they responded to the survey through the use of access codes that were given out by instructors. From these, we estimated that 73% of respondents were sophomores and 27% were juniors. There is some room for error in these numbers, as a small number of cadets enter with advanced standing and do not have to take all the required courses. For this reason a very small percentage of the cadets categorized as sophomores are probably freshmen. Similarly, a small percentage of those cadets taking junior-level classes are probably sophomores.

[30] This probably increased cadet interest in the survey, and it should be noted that our data may reflect more pronounced feelings of partisanship than would usually be present in the cadet population.

TABLE 8.2
Composition of West Point Survey Respondents

| | West Point survey respondents | | | | | |
| | Men | | Women | | Total | |
	N	%	N	%	N	%
White	596	68.7	96	11.1	692	79.8
Hispanic	55	6.3	13	1.5	68	7.8
Black	13	1.5	5	0.6	18	2.1
Other/Unknown	74	8.5	15	1.7	89	10.3
Total	738	85.1	129	14.9	867	100

Source: 2004 Cadet Preelection Survey.

Responses to the survey yielded a final sample size for analysis of 885, including 738 men and 129 women.[31] The response rate of the survey was 54 percent; the composition of the final sample is shown in table 8.2, broken down by gender and race.[32] These subsample sizes closely approximate the demographics of the entire population of cadets at West Point, which will be discussed in more detail in the next section.[33]

The online survey was also followed up with an open-ended survey, administered to eighty-seven cadets, that focused more specifically on attitude change while at West Point. The questions in that follow-up survey covered cadet perceptions of the role that peers and instructors play in shaping political attitudes.[34] These were collected at the beginning of seven focus-group sessions that discussed cadet perceptions of attitude change while at West Point. Although the primary surveys and follow-up questionnaires provide only a snapshot of cadet attitudes in 2004, together they offer a unique and unprecedented perspective on the social and political attitudes of future officers.

Cadet Demographics

Table 8.3 shows the racial/ethnic and gender distribution of West Point in 2005 (as of March 2005, four months after the preelection survey). As

[31] Eighteen respondents chose not to respond to the question on gender.
[32] In all, an e-mail about the survey was sent to approximately 1,628 eligible cadets. An additional 18 foreign cadets received the survey, but these responses were excluded from the analysis. The response rate for American cadets was therefore 54.4%
[33] Results presented in the rest of the chapter reflect weighted values to account for discrepancies in response rates among racial and ethnic groups.
[34] The questions included in the follow-up survey are shown in appendix B.

TABLE 8.3
Race/Ethnicity and Gender of West Point Cadets, 2005

| | U.S. Corps of Cadets | | | | | |
| | Men | | Women | | Total corps | |
	N	%	N	%	N	%
African American	175	4.3	73	1.8	248	6.1
Caucasian	2,746	67.4	429	10.5	3,175	77.9
Hispanic	207	5.1	45	1.1	252	6.2
Unknown/Other	331	8.1	70	1.7	401	9.8
Total	3,459	84.9	617	15.1	4,076	100.0

Source: United States Military Academy, March 2005.

may be expected, the demographic composition of the Corps of Cadets closely resembles the composition of the active-duty officer corps. Because of the limited number of occupational specialties open to women in the army, West Point is constrained in the number of women it can accept each year. The number of women allowed to be cadets at West Point is linked to the number of women currently serving on active duty in the army.

Aside from this imbalance in gender and slightly fewer African Americans, the population of students at West Point is similar to the population of American college students (see table 8.4). Using the respondents to Harvard University's Institute of Politics (IOP) 2004 survey of college undergraduates across the United States as representative of the greater American undergraduate population, one can see that the racial and ethnic composition of the Corps of Cadets at West Point is fairly similar to the larger undergraduate population.[35]

Cadets are required to enter the academy prior to their twenty-third birthday, guaranteeing a relatively young cohort. The mean age of survey respondents was 19.8 years. Furthermore, each West Point class represents the United States in a very literal way, in that every person who enters is required to obtain a nomination from his or her congressional representative, his or her senator, or the president.[36] This ensures that every state is represented at the Military Academy. Reflective of this is the

[35] Because West Point is typically rated as one of the top ten most selective undergraduate institutions in the United States, a better comparison may be with colleges that are similarly ranked. Institute of Politics, "Coming of Age."

[36] There are a few other sources of obtaining a nomination, in addition to these primary sources. See www.usma.edu for a more detailed explanation of the nomination process.

TABLE 8.4
Race/Ethnicity and Gender of Institute of Politics Respondents, 2004

| | IOP 2004 survey respondents | | | | | |
| | Men | | Women | | Total | |
	N	%	N	%	N	%
African American	41	3.4	93	7.7	134	11.2
Caucasian	418	34.8	467	38.9	885	73.6
Hispanic	34	2.8	40	3.3	74	6.2
Other/Unknown	39	3.2	70	5.8	109	9.1
Total	532	44.3	670	55.7	1,202	100.0

Source: 2004 Harvard University Institute of Politics Survey of College Undergraduates across the United States.

fact that our survey included cadets from all fifty states in addition to Washington, D.C.

A large percentage of cadets have a tradition of military service in their families. In the survey, 41% of cadets had a mother or father who served in the military at some point. A full 15% of cadets had a father or mother who made a full career of military service, and about 10% of nominations for the Military Academy each year are reserved for the sons and daughters of veterans. About 7% of cadets report that one of their parents was a graduate of West Point, and 26% report having a brother or sister who has served, or is serving, in the military. As discussed briefly in chapter 4, having a tradition of military service in the family influences how soldiers and officers perceive military service. The same applies to cadets. Simply from the perspective of why cadets choose to come to the military academy, having parents who were officers or careerists correlates with a greater likelihood that cadets will list "Desire to serve my country" as their primary reason for coming to West Point.[37] How this also correlates with social and political attitudes will be discussed later in the chapter.

In terms of socioeconomic status, 71% of cadets describe their family as middle class. Another 19% describe their families as lower or working class, and the remaining 10% describe themselves as coming from an upper-class family. And while we do not have data on household income, we do know that 21% of USMA graduates in 2007 came from neighborhoods with a median income greater than $100,000. Over half, 55%,

---

[37] Forty-six percent of those cadets with parents who were either currently serving or who had made a career of the military reported this as their primary reason for coming to West Point, compared with 38% of those without career-military parents. A similar pattern emerges among those whose parent(s) served as an officer (47% and 37%, respectively).

come from neighborhoods that are in the top quintile of household incomes.[38] One in five cadets reports having attended a private high school. Seventy-eight percent of cadets report growing up in the suburbs or a small city, and only 8% report coming from a big city.

As for why they came to West Point, a plurality of cadets, 39%, said that a "desire to serve my country" was the most important reason. The second most common reason, chosen by 20% of respondents, was to receive a "top tier education."

The Composition and Role of West Point Instructors

In addition to describing the Corps of Cadets, it is important to characterize the composition of the staff and faculty at West Point and to note how critical the role of officers at West Point is to the professional development of cadets. Officers at West Point fall into two primary categories: instructors and tactical officers. Tactical officers are charged with supervising the military and leadership development of cadets. Historically, tactical officers were not afforded the opportunity to attend graduate school at a civilian university but instead attended a satellite civilian university program taught on the West Point campus, where they earned a master's degree in education (with a focus on counseling and leader development).[39] Upon the completion of this program, tactical officers are charged with supervising a company of cadets (typically about 120 students) and overseeing their daily lives, in addition to monitoring and facilitating their military training.

The other officers at West Point teach cadets academics (similarly to professors at civilian universities). Instructors typically attend a civilian graduate school for two years to earn a master's degree and then return to West Point to teach for three years. These officers make up 59% of the teaching faculty and are commonly referred to as the "rotating faculty." West Point also has a "permanent faculty," consisting of senior military officers who have typically earned doctoral degrees in their respective fields and are assigned to West Point until they retire from the military. These senior military officers make up about 19% of the faculty. In 2004 just under 20% of the faculty at West Point was made up of civilian pro-

---

[38] This is from analysis of the USMA graduating class of 2007 using census track data. Although not necessarily an accurate predictor of individual household wealth, at minimum it should serve as a proxy for the type of support networks and school systems that cadets grow up in. Watkins and Sherk, "Who Serves in the U.S. Military?"

[39] Currently, tactical officers receive their training and education from the Teachers College at Columbia University.

TABLE 8.5
Ideological Distribution of General Population, 18–24-Year-Olds, Cadets, and
Army Lieutenants

	Civilians	Civilians 18–24	Cadets	Army LTs
Liberal	24%	32%	20%	24%
Moderate	39	39	19	23
Conservative	37	29	61	53
Total	100	100	100	100
N =	51,933	3,793	871	82

Source: C&S Survey, 2004 Cadet Preelection Survey, and 2004 National Annenberg Election Survey.

Note: The difference in the self-identification of either army group (cadets or lieutenants) compared with either civilian group (civilians or civilians 18–24) is significant at the 0.001 level. The differences between cadets and lieutenants are not significant.

fessors. These instructors teach at West Point on a contractual basis, with the length of the contract generally determined by seniority.

Given that the daily lives of cadets are managed by active-duty army officers and that about 78% of the teaching faculty are also officers, it is important to note that officers at West Point serve first and foremost as role models for the cadets. The majority of the officers teaching and serving as tactical officers are captains and majors with about ten years of army experience, most of whom have recently commanded tactical army units. The cadets, upon graduation, start along the very same career path as these officers. As a result, the role of officers at West Point extends beyond the teaching of a subject to serving as a role model and mentor to cadets. And given the hierarchical nature of the military, cadets tend to follow the examples of the officers above them. In a sense, cadets are being shaped to emulate the officers who instruct them. Thus, we would expect the attitudes and beliefs of the officer corps as well as the army as an institution to influence the attitudes and beliefs of the cadets to a far greater extent than the effect professors have on students at civilian universities.

Ideology and Party Affiliation

On the eve of the 2004 election, cadets were much more likely than their civilian counterparts to describe themselves as conservative and to identify with the Republican Party. When asked to self-identify along the ideological spectrum, 61% of cadets identified themselves as conserva-

TABLE 8.6
Party Affiliation among IOP College Students, Cadets, and Army Lieutenants

	Civilian students	Cadets	Army LTs
Republican	30%	61%	44%
Independent/Other	34	27	36
Democrat	35	12	19
Total	100	100	99
N =	1,159	871	79

Source: C&S Survey, 2004 Cadet Preelection Survey, and 2004 Harvard University Institute of Politics Survey of College Undergraduates across the United States.

Note: The difference in Republican identification between civilian students and cadets is significant at the 0.001 level. The difference between civilian students and army lieutenants is significant at the 0.05 level. The difference between cadets and army lieutenants is significant at the 0.01 level. Totals do not sum to 100% due to rounding.

tive. Nearly 19% of the cadets identified themselves as liberal, and another 20% identified themselves as moderate. Cadets are more than twice as likely as youth in the general population to identify themselves as conservative.

Consistent with this finding, a strong majority of cadets, 61%, also identified themselves as Republican. Only 12% identified themselves as Democrat. The remaining 27% identified themselves as independent or "other," with—when asked further—14% saying that they leaned toward the Republican side and 10% toward the Democratic side. In comparison, 35% of the students surveyed in the Harvard Institute of Politics poll identified themselves as Democrat. Thirty percent identified themselves as Republican, and 34% chose to identify themselves as independent.[40] Maybe even more striking, given that it might be unexpected, is the difference between cadet attitudes and those of current army lieutenants. Cadets are both more conservative and more Republican than the population of current lieutenants.

Indoctrination or Self-Selection?

What is the cause of such divergent political views between West Point cadets and their college-age peers? Is West Point encouraging conservative and Republican self-identification in cadets, or do only those predisposed toward these views decide to attend the military academy? The remainder of this chapter will examine these questions from a number of angles.

[40] Numbers for the IOP survey reported here were calculated excluding nonresponses to make them comparable with the other data.

TABLE 8.7

Republican Party Identification by Race/Ethnicity and Gender

	Male	Female	White	Black	Hispanic
Cadets	64%	47%	66%	22%	45%
Civilians	35	25	35	2	28

Source: C&S Survey and 2004 Harvard University Institute of Politics Survey of College Undergraduates across the United States.

Note: Differences between cadet and civilian subgroups are significant at the 0.001 level, except for the differences between cadets and civilians who are either black or Hispanic. Differences between these groups are significant at the 0.05 level.

Demographics

Given the gender and racial/ethnic differences between West Point and university students as reported in the IOP study, party identification was compared within racial and gender groups to take into account these demographic differences. Whereas only 25% of women in the IOP study identified themselves as Republican, nearly half, 47% of women in the West Point survey did so. Similarly, cadets of all racial and ethnic groups were more likely to identify as Republican than their civilian counterparts. Sixty-six percent of white cadets identified themselves as Republican compared with 35% of white respondents to the IOP survey. Hispanic civilians reported identifying with the Republican Party at a rate of 28%, compared with 45% of Hispanic West Point cadets. A similar pattern appeared among African Americans, but the number of African Americans in each sample was too small to reach definitive conclusions.

These results hold in a multivariate regression using race/ethnicity and gender to predict party affiliation. While whites and males are more likely to identify as Republican in both the civilian and the cadet populations, being a cadet trumps these other demographic characteristics as a correlate of party identification.

Although not unexpected, this finding reinforces the fact that differences between cadet and civilian attitudes cannot be explained solely by differences in gender and race and ethnicity. Another demographic factor that may explain some of cadet attitudes is the party affiliation of their parents. Previously I have shown that career officers who began their military service in the late 1970s and early 1980s are overwhelmingly Republican in their self-identification. The children of these officers who have entered West Point are likely to echo the political beliefs of their parents. Given that 7% of cadets surveyed in 2004 had parents who attended West Point, and that a full 15% of respondents had parents who made a career of military service, this may explain some of the overwhelming preference that cadets have for the Republican Party. Indeed, in a multivariate analy-

TABLE 8.8
Parents' Party Affiliation

Republican	61%
Democrat	16
Independent	6
Split affiliation	12
Other	1
Not political/Don't know	4
Total	100

Source: 2004 Cadet Preelection Survey.

sis controlling for race/ethnicity and gender, having a father who served in the military as an officer was a significant predictor of both conservative self-identification and Republican Party affiliation.

Looking more broadly at parental attitudes independent of previous military service, we see that the majority of cadets, 61%, reported that their parents were affiliated with the Republican Party.[41] Only 16% of cadets reported that their parents were affiliated with the Democratic Party, 7% were independent or other, and the remaining 12% came from families with split party affiliations. These numbers point to a self-selection effect in that West Point appears to attract students from Republican families. We should expect young people to share many of the same political views as their parents.

However, there is possible evidence of institutional pressure. As shown in table 8.9, cadets with Democratic parents were far more likely to "defect" to the Republican Party than were cadets with Republican parents. Sixteen percent of cadets with Democratic parents identified themselves as Republican, whereas only 1% of cadets with Republican parents identified with the Democratic Party.

Eighty-three percent of cadets with Republican parents also identified as Republicans, and only 55% of cadets whose parents are Democrats

[41] There are well-known problems in the accuracy of these self-reports of parental partisanship. Individuals typically overreport that their parents share their partisan identification. This correlation has been found to be overestimated by about 0.10 (see footnote 10, page 40, of Jennings and Niemi's *Political Character*, based on Niemi's "Collecting Information," chapter 19). Even allowing for this systematic measurement error, I am confident in inferring that the cadets' parents are overwhelmingly Republican and that the findings reported in tables 8.8 and 8.9 are not very far off the mark. Any error would overestimate parental influence on a cadet's partisanship and underestimate the other influences considered below. Jennings and Niemi, *Political Character*. Niemi, "Collecting Information."

TABLE 8.9
Parent-Cadet Party Affiliation Match

Party affiliation of parents	Party affiliation of cadets				
	Republican	Democrat	Independent	Other	Total
Republican	83%	1%	12%	4%	100%
Democratic	16	55	24	5	100
Independent	10	6	80	4	100
Split	51	14	28	7	100
Not political	33	8	43	16	100

Source: 2004 Cadet Preelection Survey.

Note: Differences in cadets' self-identified party identification on the basis of reported affiliation of parents are significant at the 0.001 level.

also identified as Democrats. Therefore, cadet party affiliation appears to be largely driven by parental party affiliation. Yet the fact that cadets whose parents are Democrats were more likely to defect from their parents' party affiliation than cadets whose parents were Republicans indicates that other influences may be at work. Furthermore, cadets who ostensibly faced no pressure from their parents to affiliate with a certain party (those whose parents identified as independent, split, or apolitical) showed a tendency to identify with the Republican Party. However, it is possible that the shift in party affiliation away from parents may have occurred prior to the cadets' arrival at West Point, which, again, would point toward a selection bias. Indeed, some of the more interesting findings that emerged from our focus-group discussions were cadets' stories of becoming conservative and Republican in *rebellion* against their parents and capping off their quest for independence by going to the military academy. These cadets described West Point as a moderating experience.

Although not explored in the main survey, these anecdotes were supported by responses to the follow-up questionnaire. We asked respondents to describe their political orientation prior to coming to West Point. Of the 87 respondents, 35 described themselves as Republican. More interesting is that when asked to describe changes in their views since coming to the academy, 20 of those 35 related that they had become more moderate at West Point.

Institutional Pressure?

To examine the possibility that cadets may sense pressure to identify with a single political party, the survey asked cadets: "Do you believe there is pressure to identify with a particular party as a West Point cadet?" Over-

TABLE 8.10
Pressure to Identify with a Certain Political Party

	All cadets		Non-Repub.		Democratic		Republican	
	N	%	N	%	N	%	N	%
No pressure	449	51	107	34	16	19	342	62
Pressure to ID Republican	411	48	214	66	75	80	197	37
Pressure to ID Democrat	5	1	2	1	2	2	3	1
		100		101		101		100

Source: 2004 Cadet Preelection Survey.
Note: Differences in perceptions of pressure between cadets on the basis of self-identification are significant at the 0.001 level. Numbers do not sum to 100% due to rounding.

all, nearly half of the Corps of Cadets, 48%, thought there was pressure to identify as a Republican (see table 8.10). This number is especially telling in light of the fact that the majority of the corps already self-identifies as Republican. When controlling for cadet party affiliation, the results are even more dramatic. Among all cadets who did not identify with the Republican Party, two out of three, or 66%, believed there was pressure to identify themselves as Republican. Among those who identified themselves as Democrats, the proportion who felt pressure to identify as Republican was fully 80%. What is amazing about these responses is the complete lack of any reported counterpressure to identify with the Democratic Party, even among cadets who self-identify as Republican. This suggests not just an affinity for the Republican Party but an outright aversion to speaking out in favor of the Democratic Party at West Point. In the comments section of the survey, many cadets spoke of the pressure they felt to identify with a certain political ideology. A cadet who self-identified as a Republican even suggested, "Democrats are more likely to speak their mind on a survey because their opinion cannot be expressed well amongst a strongly Republican and intolerant Corps."

Comments such as these confirm the existence of pressure to identify with the Republican Party, yet imply that the source of these pressures is only indirectly institutional and may primarily be peers. To obtain a better picture of the source of this pressure, we looked at responses to the open-ended questionnaire. This questionnaire asked, "Do you feel free to openly discuss your political views among other cadets? In the classroom? (If not, please explain why)" and "Do officers openly discuss their political affiliation with you? Have any officers at West Point encouraged you to vote one way or another? How so?"

Of the 87 cadets who responded to these questions, 19, or about 22%, indicated that they felt pressure from their peers to identify as a conservative or Republican. Only 12 out of 87 respondents related instances of officers discussing their personal political preferences or encouraging cadets to vote a certain way. However, because the 87 cadets were essentially part of a convenience sample—drawn from cadets enrolled in political science courses—the responses can be used only to give context to the finding of perceived pressure at the military academy.

In these questionnaires and follow-up discussions with cadets, most of this pressure appeared to come from the dynamics of barracks life and from peers. West Point and the army emphasize cohesion and teamwork, and cadets may feel pressure to conform to the views of the majority of their peer group, especially given how frequently they interact with and work as members of a team. It is natural to expect 18- to 24-year-old students to be especially sensitive to group pressure. These pressures may be independent from those of the institution or the officers at West Point. That said, cadets did describe instances in which officers overtly expressed partisan preferences. Although limited in number, even a single instance of this is troublesome given the inherent authority that officers have over cadets, and even isolated instances, if uncorrected, can quickly reinforce the perception of a group norm.

While discussing the influence of officers on their political attitudes, many cadets commented:

> I have yet to hear an officer here endorse a political party. Some are obviously partial to the administration (gathered from comments on policy), but this has never turned into an overt endorsement. Most are very careful to hide their affiliations.

> The officers at West Point tend to be very guarded about their political affiliations.

> The officers here seem pretty good at staying neutral.

However, there were also several reported instances of officers openly endorsing the Republican Party; tellingly, there were no examples of officers endorsing Democrats. Among the examples of officer advocacy were statements such as

> . . . due to the fact that we are "supposed" to be conservatives in the military; not only do I fear repercussions from classmates, but instructors as well.

> I really don't get the impression most officers feel the need to stay neutral. The prevailing attitude among officers, in my judgment, is that only Republicans support the military, so we have no reservations about showing support for Republicans.

These comments highlight both the historical dynamic at work in military attitudes and the apparent failure of the army to emphasize appropriate norms of behavior for officers in general, and instructors at West Point in particular. The difficulty in teasing out sources of "pressure" from the experiences of cadets in 2004 is made more difficult by the fact that at the time the government was controlled by one party, with the commander in chief obviously identified with the Republican Party. As one cadet put it, "I feel that because I do not wholeheartedly support everything that the government and the army does that my views are discouraged." The power of this sentiment should not be taken lightly, particularly during wartime.

However, it is clear that by 2004 identification with the Republican Party was more than an objective phenomenon reflecting an appreciation for specific policies. Many officers and cadets had begun to conflate officership with Republican Party identification. And in a military that does not educate officers on the boundaries between professional duties and personal political preferences, to say nothing of maintaining an open, critical, and inquisitive classroom environment, there is the danger that the group's identity will be based at least partly on partisan political preferences.

In the comments section of the online survey, one cadet took the opportunity to articulate the competing demands on cadet loyalties and the difficulty of balancing duty to country with personal beliefs.

> I think that it is important for people in the military to be aware of their own political beliefs and not feel pressured into supporting the current administration. A distinction can be made between gladly serving the country, and disagreeing with whatever current administration is in power. It annoys me when people assume that i [sic] think a certain way just because i [sic] am a part of the army. I can serve my country while disagreeing with the president's policies.

Perceptions and Expectations

Although it appears that not all cadets experienced overt officer endorsement of the Republican Party—or, as in 2004, the Republican candidate for president—the fact that such endorsements are not uncommon has a profound effect on the social climate at the military academy. The fact that there is no counterpressure to identify as a Democrat, as seen in table 8.10, probably hinders open discourse and might give cadets a skewed perception of army attitudes. Most cadets view the army as slightly conservative or conservative (86% of cadets place "the Army as a whole" in one of these two categories on the seven-point extremely liberal to extremely conservative scale). Yet we know from the C&S Survey that a plurality of soldiers and officers, 41%, describe themselves as moderate. Likewise, 87% of cadets place "West Point cadets in general" on the conservative side of the spectrum. And although this is an accurate assessment, given that 61% of cadets do describe themselves as conservative, most cadets might be surprised to learn that one in five of their peers describes him or herself as liberal.

As one cadet perceptively put it in the open-ended questionnaire, "It is assumed that a vast majority of the officers and the corps is republican [*sic*] when this is not truly the case. Most are, but politics are not discussed openly and the Democrat minority is isolated and doesn't know how big it actually is." In essence, cadets may be experiencing a variant of "pluralistic ignorance," whereby people are collectively incorrect in their assessments of the views of others.[42] In this instance, although cadets may be correct in their assessment of the broad contours of the ideological identification of their fellow cadets, they probably either overestimate the degree to which other cadets share their views if they identify as a conservative or Republican or underestimate the degree to which their views are shared by others if they do not. Furthermore, the comments of cadets provide strong evidence of many cadets' unwillingness to speak up if they perceive that their views are out of line with the majority opinion.

This issue is clearly one that West Point and the army need to address, particularly for the cadre of officers at West Point, but it also reflects a dynamic that extends beyond the direct control of the military. The last question in the open-ended questionnaire was "What assumptions, if any, do people make about your political views?" In comparison with the 27 cadets who responded to previous questions with the statement that they felt pressure from peers or instructors to think a certain way, 58 of the 87 cadets who answered the questionnaire stated that people always assumed they were conservative and/or Republican.[43] The following is a sample of responses to that question.

I go to West Point, I am in the army, therefore, I must be a republican [*sic*] is what most people think about me.

People most likely assume that I am a conservative Republican because of several stereotypes. This could be because I am a Caucasian, Protestant, in the Army and a man. This is not cool.

---

[42] The term "pluralistic ignorance" was coined by Floyd Allport. I use the term in the context of Elisabeth Noelle-Neumann's work on how people adjust their behavior and reported attitudes based on the perceptions that they have of aggregate public opinion. Noelle-Neumann, *Spiral of Silence*.

[43] Seven cadets also indicated that others assumed they were liberal, or Democrats, although four of those cadets were clearly referring to the assumptions that other cadets made of them, and attributed their expectations to the fact that they were minorities or from the Northeast.

> That since I am in the military, people outside it assume I'm conservative. My cadet friends, who have a different perspective from those outside the military, assume I'm liberal because I don't openly say I'm conservative.

> I think they assume that, as a cadet, I am a Republican. . . . I think some people even see it as a military duty to be loyal to the Republican Party.

These responses point to an external influence and must be viewed both as a contributing factor in determining who self-selects into military service and as descriptive of how internal group norms can be imposed or reinforced by people outside the institution.

Conclusion

This chapter sought to assess the role of West Point in shaping the political views of future officers. In the popular culture there has always been a sense that military service is exceptionally transformative, but the scholarly literature suggests that institutions such as West Point are fairly limited in their ability to shape attitudes on issues tangential to military service. Previous research has suggested that cadet attitudes on various topics were largely the result of anticipatory socialization or self-selection and that the military has little influence on attitudes and affiliations. Unfortunately, few studies have addressed the ideological outlook of cadets, and fewer still have asked cadets about their preferences for political parties.

One of the more interesting findings from previous research was that cadets in 1970 expected to become more conservative during their time at West Point. This highlights the fact that future officers might anticipate becoming more like the officers in the institution they are entering. As the officer corps has historically been viewed as conservative, this was not an unexpected finding. As discussed previously, however, the concept of conservatism in 1970 was not yet strongly linked to Republican Party identification. In the intervening years, cadets at West Point have become even more likely to identify themselves as conservative, and most cadets now correlate conservative self-identification with Republican Party affiliation. By contrast, the ideological self-identification of civilian college students has not changed dramatically since the 1970s.

This shift in West Point cadets mirrors changes in the army's officer corps. But how, exactly, have these changes influenced the attitudes of cadets? The findings discussed in this chapter suggest four mechanisms by which future officers at the military academy emulate the social and political attitudes of senior officers.

The first is demographic but is tied to family more than to external characteristics such as race and gender. With the exception of a significant gender imbalance, the population of the Corps of Cadets generally matches the civilian undergraduate population in racial and ethnic composition. However, it is clear that even if the populations were evenly matched on these characteristics, West Point cadets would still be dramatically more likely to identify themselves as conservative and Republican than their civilian peers. Cadets also differ from their civilian peers in the proportion of students who come from military families. And because military officers have become more likely to identify themselves with the Republican Party over the last few decades, it stands to reason that having a father who is a military officer correlates strongly with Republican self-identification among cadets.

The second explanation is internal and reflects peer-group dynamics at West Point. Cadets sense pressure to identify with the Republican Party. Because the majority enter West Point as self-identified Republicans, many cadets apparently hesitate to challenge the group norm.

The third explanation relates directly to the actions of officers at West Point, enough of whom have become so comfortable with Republican Party identification that they have blurred the boundary between officership and political affiliation. Although this trend is not widespread, enough officers overtly endorse the Republican Party that many cadets apparently conflate an identification with the Republican Party with officership. As one cadet commented on the follow-up questionnaire, "I really don't get the impression most officers feel the need to stay neutral. The prevailing attitude among officers, in my judgment, is that only Republicans support the military, so we have no reservations about showing support for Republicans." These three explanations, however, are ultimately minor and merely reinforce the primary cause of overwhelming Republican Party affiliation among West Point cadets. Cadets enter West Point *expecting* to become part of an institution solidly identified with the Republican Party. An overwhelming majority of them sense that people expect them to be conservative and Republican because they are in the military. This is reflected in their responses to the follow-up questionnaire and is in keeping with public perceptions of the military. In 2006 we asked respondents to a national survey which party they felt had the support of most members of the military. A strong majority, 74%, replied that most members of the military supported the Republican Party.[44] This is important, independent of actual military affiliations, because it reflects how perceptions may play a role in shaping institutions like the army.

[44] Ansolabehere, Rivers, and Luks, "Cooperative Congressional Election Study."

Given this public perception of the military, it should come as no surprise that those predisposed toward Republican Party identification would be more likely to apply to West Point. We should also not be surprised by the extent to which cadets mimic the conservative and Republican self-identification suggested by public perceptions of the institution. Indeed, the act of committing to West Point suggests a degree of self-selection beyond that seen in other circumstances, which I describe as hyperselection. For a high school graduate to agree to spend the next nine years of his or her life in the army (four years at West Point and another five years on active duty) is indicative of a very significant commitment. One would expect those who agree to such an obligation to have favorable views of most aspects of the institution to include the perceived political and ideological preferences of those already serving.

In essence, then, the political attitudes of West Point cadets are the result of two feedback mechanisms, one of which is now out of the military academy's direct control. The direct mechanism, and the one easiest to influence, is the role of West Point instructors and the way that West Point instructs or fails to instruct cadets on the appropriate boundaries between personal political preferences and professional identification. Officers at West Point, particularly those who teach, must promote the free exchange of ideas and remain vigilant against any suggestion that an affiliation with a political party is part of an officer's professional identity.

A much larger, and primary, feedback mechanism also emanates from army officers but flows through public perceptions of the military. If the majority of Americans believe that most of the army supports the Republican Party, then it follows that party identification will play a role in recruitment. It also follows that it will play a pronounced role among those poised to make the greatest commitment of time and effort to the institution. In many ways this public perception is now beyond the direct control of the army but is nevertheless the result of the behavior of army officers. Army leaders should therefore expect the perception of the military as an institution dominated by Republicans to influence the pool of applicants to the military academy until the army regains control of its public image.

Army Attitudes in 2004 and Beyond

THE ARMED FORCES OF THE United States have played a central, if at times symbolic, role in the last five national elections. In 2000 some observers believed that the presidential election hinged on the status of ballots from overseas military personnel. In 2002 the nation was dealing with the aftermath of a major terrorist attack on U.S. soil, was engaged militarily in Afghanistan, and was considering military action against Iraq. The 2004 election coincided with the ongoing conflict in Iraq, and the election campaigns focused heavily on support from the military and the military service records of the two presidential candidates. In 2006 the election overlapped with a deteriorating situation in Iraq and the continuing conflict in Afghanistan, and in 2008 we witnessed a significant debate over our ultimate goals and strategy in the region. Throughout these campaigns, the conventional wisdom held that members of the military voted at high rates and overwhelmingly identified with the Republican Party, though there was no reliable evidence that this was the case.

This simplistic view of military attitudes is not due to a lack of scholarly studies detailing military demographics and the views of those who serve. A renaissance of interest in and studies of the American military has been ongoing since at least the early 1990s. The end of the Cold War and the election of the first president to have spent his formative years during the Vietnam War, as opposed to World War II, sparked several intense debates on civil-military relations. Many of the resulting studies, such as the project completed by the Center for Strategic and International Studies in 1995 and the Triangle Institute for Security Studies project in 2001, relate directly to the topic at hand. Indeed, much of what I have outlined in this book confirms previous scholarship. Unfortunately, there are no studies of military attitudes that take a comprehensive look across the ranks and focus extensively on the social and political attitudes of the active-duty force.

This project, therefore, serves as a deliberate effort to fill the gaps in our understanding by taking an in-depth look at one branch of military service—the U.S. Army—and examining the attitudes of military personnel as they relate to partisan politics. The results presented here have in many ways confirmed preexisting perceptions of senior military leaders, but in other, more important ways they either directly refute or add nuance to our understanding of the attitudes of military personnel.

Conventional Wisdom and the Reality of Army Attitudes

In 2004 the Military Times Company reported that 60% of the military identified with the Republican Party, and an additional 13% identified with the Democratic Party. Given the dearth of existing data on military attitudes, these figures were taken, without any detailed assessment, and often repeated as an accurate picture of the partisan attitudes of all military personnel.[1] The results presented by the surveys seemed to confirm existing data, notably from the TISS surveys, which probably contributed to their acceptance despite disclaimers from the Military Times Company that the survey results applied only to the population who subscribed to its chain of newspapers. This book makes clear that the results of these surveys need to be evaluated with caution.

Although very useful for gauging the opinions of senior military personnel, the samples of the Military Times surveys were not representative of service members of all ranks.[2] A look specifically at the subset of respondents who were active-duty members of the army shows that officers made up 42% of army respondents to the survey even though they comprise only 14% of the army population. Similarly, 23% of the army respondents to the survey were senior NCOs, who only make up about 10% of the army. The army's junior enlisted ranks are dramatically underrepresented. About 47% of the army serves in the ranks of E-1 through E-4. These ranks comprised only 7% of the active army population included in the 2004 Military Times survey. Racial and ethnic minorities and women were also underrepresented in the sample. This does not mean that the Military Times surveys are useless (far from it). Rather, it highlights that the Military Times survey results have often been inappropriately extrapolated to the entire military population.

The findings from the C&S Survey also indicate that previously reported rates of political participation by uniformed personnel are probably inaccurate. The conventional wisdom has generally been based on reported results from the Federal Voting Assistance Program (FVAP), the agency charged with facilitating voting by service members and Americans overseas. The FVAP has released reports of stunning participation rates in the last two presidential elections. These reports fit perceptions of a strongly partisan and politically active military and therefore were not seriously questioned. However, the methodology of the FVAP survey

---

[1] These perceptions persisted through 2007. As examples of the widespread use of the Military Times data, see Brooks, "Weaning the Military from the GOP," and The Economist's " Iraq War."

[2] See appendix C for a more detailed discussion of the Military Times surveys.

has since come under criticism by the Government Accountability Office, and the administrators of the FVAP survey have acknowledged that the survey samples are unrepresentative of the military population.[3] We should be exceptionally wary of claims that members of the military vote at rates approaching 80%. The idea that a population composed primarily of 18–24-year-old males would be more politically active than practically every other segment of the American public should have been questioned immediately upon the release of the FVAP report. That it was not is indicative of the distance and lack of understanding between the military and the public.

The C&S Survey reveals that rates of identification with the two major political parties and political participation are in fact lower in the army than in the civilian population. The C&S Survey data show that in 2004 only 43% of the army identified with the Republican or Democratic Party—much less than the 73% the Military Times reported and less than the 65% reported for the civilian population in the NAES surveys. Additionally, Republican Party affiliation across the army is probably about half of the rate reported in the Military Times and TISS surveys and is comparable to the percentage of Republican Party identifiers found in the civilian population. Last, the C&S Survey reveals that the army lags behind the civilian population in the proportion of soldiers who vote. This study shows that in contrast with the 80% of civilian respondents to the 2004 NAES survey who reported voting in the 2000 election, only 43% of the army reported voting in the same election.

A quick back-of-the-envelope calculation can help illustrate how common perceptions are skewed by the inappropriate use of preexisting data. If we take 60%, the reported rate of Republican Party identification in the 2004 Military Times surveys, and multiply that by FVAP's reported voting rate, we might be led to believe that almost half of the military is Republican *and* votes (41% if we use the 69% reported voting participation rate from 2000, or 47% if we use the 79% figure from 2004).

Data from the C&S Survey, however, paint a different picture. Starting from 29%, the rate of Republican Party identification within the army, means that the proportion of the army that is Republican *and* votes is significantly lower than these other surveys suggest. As discussed in chap-

[3] As discussed in chapter 7, in 2005 the Federal Voting Assistance Program (FVAP) reported exceptionally high rates of participation across the military services during the 2000 and 2004 elections (Brunelli, "Federal Voting Assistance Program"). A 2006 Government Accountability Office report suggested that the FVAP report was questionable due to low survey response rates and a lack of analysis of the survey sample and potential nonresponse bias (see the discussion on pages 7 and 8 of the GAO report). U.S. Government Accountability Office, "Elections." See also Langer, "Taking Aim."

ter 7, reported rates of voting differ by partisan affiliation, with Republicans in the army voting at a higher rate than other groups (60%). Combining this participation figure with the proportion of the army that self-identifies as Republican means that only about 17% of service members are both Republican and active voters. The inclusion of those army voters who align themselves ideologically with the Republican Party but do not feel they belong to either party, that is, "leaners," brings the total to 23%—still much less than contemporary commentary suggests.[4]

Why are perceptions of the political attitudes and activities of members of the army so dramatically distorted? The primary reason is the tendency of researchers to focus on senior military leaders, who do identify themselves as Republican and vote at rates greater than the rest of the army. This focus on senior leaders is an acceptable approach given limited access to military personnel and a desire to write about elite-level interactions. It has not provided us with a comprehensive view of attitudes across the army or insight into how soldiers and officers might develop their attitudes toward social and political issues. A secondary reason probably relates to perceptions of the "all-inclusive" nature of military life. Since the military exerts a high degree of control over the lives of its members, many believe that this control extends to opinions on social and political issues.[5] The assumption is that all members of the military mimic the views of those above them.

Writing in response to the "gap" literature spawned by the TISS project, Lance Betros implied in 2001 that it might be best if officers refrained from participating in surveys on officer voting patterns.[6] This study, however, shows that the interests of the army are best served by open and frank discussion about the political attitudes of members of the military and how those attitudes should best be reconciled with their professional obligations to the army and civilian leaders. Were it not for the C&S Survey and others like it, our perceptions of the military would be drawn largely from anecdotal evidence and limited interaction with military per-

---

[4] Comparable calculations suggest that only about 6% of soldiers and officers consider themselves members of the Democratic Party and vote. The inclusion of Democratic-leaning service members means that just over 10% of the force could be considered active voters for the Democratic Party. Together with Republicans and Republican "leaners," this means that only a third of the army, 33%, identifies with or leans toward one of the two major parties and votes.

[5] In 1983 Moskos lamented the overreach of observers who believe the influence of the military over its members extends to political and social attitudes. He observed that "we frequently find both supporters and opponents of the goals of the military organization giving great weight to the total or all-inclusive features of military life." His research revealed strong limitations to the ability of formal military socialization to shape attitudes. Moskos, "All-Volunteer Force," 310.

[6] Betros, "Political Partisanship," 515.

sonnel and the military lifestyle. This perception would be distorted in ways detrimental to any meaningful discussion of how best to maintain a military in a democracy.

Because the proportion of citizens with military service has declined, especially after the end of conscription in 1973, it is important for the military to be more proactive in increasing civilian understanding of military leaders and military life in general. The danger of not doing so can be seen in the comments of Thomas Ricks about the attitudes of enlisted personnel. Based on observations of one marine platoon at basic training, Ricks asserted it was likely that younger members of the military were more conservative than its more senior members.[7]

The C&S Survey reveals that junior officers in 2004 were much less likely to identify as conservatives than their more senior colleagues. The army appears to match the civilian population in the proportion who identify with the Republican Party, although there is a noticeable absence of Democratic Party identifiers in the service. The data also show that even when soldiers or officers identify themselves as conservative or identify themselves with the Republican Party, it is not always possible to predict their outlook on specific issues. Furthermore, this study shows that even in the absence of universal service and the draft, the army's enlisted ranks share many of the same attitudes on social and political issues as their civilian peers.[8]

Most important, the results of this study bring into question the extent to which the army engages in overt political socialization. Although anecdotes of active-duty officers disparaging the Democratic Party or openly professing affiliation with the Republican Party have been a staple of military service since at least the 1990s and often receive media attention, it appears that this was a byproduct of an especially pro-Republican cohort coming of age in the army. Although it is not possible to prove conclusively without panel data, the political attitudes and party affiliations of members of the military seem primarily to be a result of self-selection and shift with each generational cohort. Because the Republican Party was perceived as stronger on issues of national security and national defense in the years since the Vietnam War, it should come as no surprise that during this era decisions to join the military and to affiliate with the Republican Party often went hand in hand. The trends of increased identifi-

[7] Ricks, *Making the Corps,* and Holsti, "Of Chasms and Convergences," 3.

[8] As discussed in chapter 2, many scholars feared that with the end of the draft the links between the army and society would become much more tenuous. This study shows that at least in terms of their outlook on social and political issues, soldiers in the enlisted ranks are very much like their civilian peers. And although untested here, it is likely that the increase in the number of minorities and women in the army, which resulted from the advent of the all-volunteer force, helped mitigate the gravitation of the officer corps toward the Republican Party that began in the 1970s.

cation with the Republican Party in the army also corresponded with similar shifts among young American males more broadly, particularly those bound for college and therefore most likely to be officers.[9]

Despite the prevalence of Republican Party identifiers in the army's senior ranks in 2004, the C&S Survey data do not reveal an institution where officers who do not share the political views of their senior leaders are less motivated or have less faith in the ability of senior leaders to make good decisions on behalf of the army. One would expect to find decreased morale among ideological "outliers" or a lack of faith in army leaders among this group if the institution were engaged in deliberate political socialization.

However, this does not mean that overt and overwhelming support for the Republican Party among the army's senior ranks has not affected the institution in more subtle, yet ultimately more profound, ways. Within the high-pressure environment of West Point, Republican Party identification has become conflated with the professional identity of the officer corps. And while occasional lapses into partisan advocacy by the instructing officers are surely a contributing factor, much of the perceived pressure to identify as Republican at West Point comes from peers and a generalized expectation that identification with the Republican Party and conservatism are integral pieces of an officer's identity. That the academy and the army have not proactively addressed these perceptions and attempted to reestablish the army's erstwhile reputation for political neutrality means that a preference for a political party will probably influence the environment at West Point and the pool of potential applicants for some time to come.

While the more nuanced picture of military attitudes this book provides should remove some of the apprehension and distance that Americans may feel between themselves and their army, this study—and particularly the cadet data—should highlight to senior military leaders the danger of conflating either conservatism or affiliation with the Republican Party with military service. But beyond the military's reputation and the effect on officer recruiting, the political affiliations of senior army leaders have the potential to influence internal army policy and elite-level civil-military relations as well. Huntington himself warned against the danger of "substituting extraneous values for professional values" if the military became politicized, and there is clearly the potential for senior military officers to approach some questions related to the military from a partisan perspective.[10]

As discussed in chapter 6, among officers of different ideological stripes, there is little disagreement over how the military should be uti-

---

[9] Segal, Freedman-Doan, Bachman, and O'Malley, "Attitudes."
[10] Huntington, *Soldier and the State*, 71.

lized. This is indicative of a coherent professional viewpoint on this topic that trumps party affiliation or ideological self-identification. However, there is disagreement along party lines over issues related to gender and racial and ethnic minorities. These issues fall directly within the jurisdiction of military leaders as they formulate personnel policies and make recommendations to civilian leaders about the composition of the force. As officers either proactively or reactively engage in debates on any of these issues, they need to be aware that they may be defaulting to partisan or ideological cues instead of strictly professional concerns when they voice opinions or make recommendations to civilian leaders. Senior officers need to be especially attuned to how they approach these issues, as it may be difficult, given the political homogeneity of the current cohort of senior leaders, to distinguish between a professional and a political consensus on how the army should address these questions.

Officers also split along party lines on the issue of defense spending and the status of the national economy. This is probably good news for civil-military relations in that it is indicative of a military that does not train officers to make assessments and decisions related to national strategy—the purview of civilian leadership. Unfortunately, political elites often use the opinions of officers on these issues to justify policy proposals. The military must therefore be especially careful in how officers engage in such debates.

This concern ties into the question of how the military should educate officers on appropriate norms of behavior. The concern that Janowitz had about the deficiencies of the military's system of professional education sill holds true in that "military education has little interest in discussing the standards that should govern the behavior of officers vis-à-vis civilian appointees and Congress. There is little emphasis on the complex problems of maintaining administrative neutrality."[11] Indeed, officers must recognize that education about the political process and appropriate norms of behavior is essential to maintaining the professional reputation of the military. The army's education system generally fails to offer any instruction on these topics until officers are well into the latter stages of their careers, at which point they may be wedded to the "moralistic exhortations" and "ideal goals" that comprise the bulk of early education about the political process.[12] This failure to receive an appropriate education on

[11] Janowitz, *Professional Soldier,* 429.

[12] This assertion stems primarily from my own participation in the first four levels of the army's Professional Military Education program, involving precommissioning, basic officer training, the captain's career course, and attendance at the Command and General Staff College as well as in my previous role as an assistant professor at the United States Military Academy. It is also reinforced by observations gained while lecturing to senior officers in various forums. For a more comprehensive assessment of education on civil-military relations, see the following three papers presented at a panel entitled "Teaching Civil-Military Relations to the US Military: Balancing Scholarship, Policy, and Politics." Ulrich, "Civil-

the realities of practical politics opens the door for American officers to either inadvertently politicize the institution or fail to understand the dangers of overt party affiliation.

One of the more straightforward examples of this neglect to proactively address appropriate norms of behavior can be seen in the army's stance toward voting. It was the position of army icons Omar Bradley and George Marshall that officers should not vote in order for them to maintain their political neutrality. The theory behind this position was that having a stake in partisan politics would inappropriately influence the professionalism, or apolitical service, of the officer corps. Today the army routinely reminds and encourages soldiers to vote.[13] There are arguments to be made on each side, but the point here is that the army position appears to have shifted without any argument at all.[14] It is no longer uncommon to hear a general mention that soldiers and officers should vote. However, this message is rarely, if ever, accompanied by a discussion of how engagement with the political process must be carefully balanced with the need to maintain the apolitical reputation of the army. Evidence of this is revealed in the cadet survey. The message to get out and vote is clearly getting to the next generation of officers, as 94% of cadets think officers should vote while on active duty. However, the lack of a follow-on message is also apparent in that only 70% of cadets agree that members of the military should not publicly criticize a senior member of the civilian branch of the government.

A Generational Shift

Recently the Republican Party has begun to lose its edge over the Democratic Party on national security issues in the eyes of the public. For the first time in decades the public has rated the Democratic Party equal to or higher than the Republican Party on issues such as Iraq or on the handling of national defense in general.[15] It appears that this shift in primacy on national security issues correlates with a distancing from the Republi-

---

Military Relations Education." Mahoney-Norris, "Civil-Military Relations." Coletta, "Teaching Civil-Military Relations."

[13] An example of such a message sent over electronic mail can be found in appendix F.

[14] The counterargument to not voting is that the act of voting allows for the voice of soldiers and officers to be heard in a discreet manner. In this sense voting can act as a safety valve, preventing members of the military from engaging in other, more public, displays of partisan loyalty.

[15] Rasmussen, "On Iraq." The 2006 CCES data asked about confidence in handling national defense, to which respondents gave the Democratic Party a slight edge. Whereas 41% reported that they had hardly any confidence in the Democrats' handling of national defense, 44% felt the same way about the Republican Party.

can Party by a significant portion of the army. Even at the time of the 2004 election, the party preferences of veterans were closer than many people would suppose. Exit polls from that election show that veterans broke 57% to 41% for Bush—a wide margin by electoral standards but more balanced than many would guess.[16] Furthermore, Jeremy Teigen's in-depth analysis of the veteran vote in 2004 revealed that veterans were very similar to their nonveteran peers in party identification, but did appear to be significantly influenced by the "Swift Boat" ad campaign.[17] Additionally, recent surveys of military families have found that while they still tend to identify as Republican slightly more than their civilian counterparts, a plurality, 40%, consider themselves independent.[18]

The 2006 election was striking in that traditionally Republican districts with a high proportion of military voters, such as Kansas's Second Congressional District (which includes Fort Leavenworth), elected Democratic representatives. For political analysts like Amy Gershkoff this indicates that the military vote is "up for grabs" and should be treated as a swing vote in upcoming elections.[19]

While comprehensive data on the attitudes of active members of the military (and not just veterans or families) over the last few years do not exist, there are indicators that the shift among military families is echoed within the ranks. Indeed, it is here that the Military Times surveys can be useful in two ways. First, these surveys can gauge opinion trends. Although the results of these surveys may not present an accurate estimate of overall military attitudes in a given year, over time they reflect how the opinions of a portion of the military are shifting. By extension, we might assume that the rest of the military is shifting to a similar degree.[20] Second, if we limit our analysis of the survey data to senior officers, then the "subscriber bias" is likely to be minimal, in that the attitudes of senior officers in the Military Times subscriber database are likely to be similar to the attitudes of senior officers in general.[21]

If one agrees these surveys can be useful as a gauge of opinion *trends*, if not a comprehensive view of aggregate attitudes, then one can see that

---

[16] CNN, "America Votes 2004."

[17] Teigen, "Veteran's Party Identification."

[18] Among military families in 2006 (those with at least one person currently serving in Iraq or Afghanistan), 30% reported a Republican identification and 22% considered themselves Democrats. Among nonmilitary families, 25% and 28% considered themselves Republican and Democratic, respectively. These are the results of a survey conducted by the Pew Research Center for the People and the Press as cited in Gershkoff's "Up for Grabs."

[19] Ibid.

[20] Page and Shapiro, *Rational Public*. For a discussion of "parallel publics," see chapter 7 of *Rational Public*.

[21] Whereas a junior soldier or officer who subscribes to the *Army Times* is likely to have a more careerist outlook than his or her peers, the difference between subscribers and nonsubscribers is likely to be more muted in the senior officer ranks.

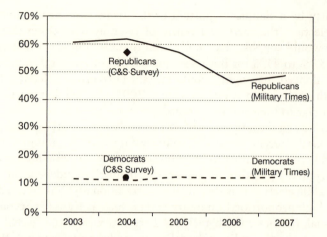

Figure 9.1 Party Identification among Senior Officers in the Military Times Surveys, 2003–2007 (Army Respondents above the Rank of Captain)
Source: C&S Survey and Military Times Polls
Note: Differences between years statistically significant at the .001 level. This chart reflects the affiliations of only the subset of army personnel above the rank of Captain (O–3) included in the Military Times surveys. The C&S data presented also excludes anyone under the rank of Major. There are 249 respondents above the rank of Captain in the C&S Survey. The subsample sizes for the Military Times surveys are; 2003=168, 2004=198, 2005=182, 2006=154, 2007=198.

the military is experiencing a shift comparable to what occurred between 1976 and 1980. During that period military leaders shifted decidedly toward the Republican Party. By the end of Carter's presidency, the proportion of senior military leaders who identified with the Republican Party had increased by 13%.[22] George W. Bush is this era's Jimmy Carter, in that the military appears to be undergoing an equally dramatic shift—only this time away from the Republican Party. Over the last three years the Military Times surveys have shown a decline in Republican Party identification of 14% among active-duty army respondents and an overall decline of 13% among senior army officers (see figure 9.1).

These survey results show that support for the Republican Party among senior members of the army, the group most likely to identify as Republican, declined significantly between 2004 and 2006 before leveling off at about 49% in 2007. Also interesting is that the data show no corresponding change in support for the Democratic Party. In other words, a number of army officers are leaving the Republican Party, but it is unclear where they are going.

[22] Holsti, "A Widening Gap."

The Way Forward

The Future of American Civil-Military Relations

Members of the army are increasingly considered "up for grabs" in terms of their political affiliations. This presents a unique opportunity, and challenge, for the military. For the first time in a generation, the institution's leaders have a chance to shape how members of the military approach politics and, by extension, the public's perception of the "politics" of the army. Military leaders should embrace examinations of the military's diversity, reinforcing the ideal that the army is a servant of the country and beholden to neither political party. Army leadership must also recognize that they need to be proactive in reestablishing the institution's reputation for partisan neutrality. In doing so, the recent shift away from Republican Party affiliation could translate into a restoration of the military's apolitical reputation. The other, less desirable option would be either a shift to an "antipolitical" military or a period of partisan infighting that would politicize the active force.

The shift to an apolitical military would correspond with an understanding that it is not in the military's interest to be overly affiliated with one particular party, while still maintaining a healthy respect for the political process. The shift to an antipolitical military would correspond with a disenchantment with and disdain for the political system. Unfortunately, it is possible the military will at least flirt with this second option. Not only has the recent conflict led many to question the value of democratic processes and institutions, particularly the media, but the ongoing partisan divide and lack of clear resolution to current conflicts may lead members of the military to recoil in disgust from all things political. Such a reaction is not uncommon, and officers have often been predisposed to this outlook throughout American history.[1]

The risk of a period of partisan infighting is a distinct possibility for a couple of reasons. First, recent research on how Americans think about foreign policy suggests that the link between partisan politics and national

---

[1] Beginning with the institution's formative years prior to the Civil War, officers have often viewed politicians as "shifty, divisive, self-serving, and too willing to compromise principles." Skelton, "Officers and Politicians," 29.

security issues has recently grown stronger and may persist beyond the war in Iraq.[2] When debates over foreign policy harden along strictly partisan lines, it becomes increasingly difficult for people who are directly invested in a military conflict to maintain a position of neutrality, but this dynamic also makes it much more important to the military's long-term reputation that they do so.[3] It is therefore crucial for the military to educate its members on appropriate norms of behavior at a time when military leaders must carefully navigate a contentious domestic political environment that is sharply divided on issues of national security.

The second dynamic that may promote partisan infighting in the military relates to the political attitudes of veterans and active-duty soldiers. There are indications that the army's newest cohort may be more politically active and more ideologically balanced than older cohorts. This development presents two challenges for senior army leaders. First, they must be proactive in delineating the boundary between professional judgment and political advocacy. The army should neither lose young soldiers and officers because of differences in political opinions between generations nor allow partisan differences to interfere with professional obligations. A good starting point for this endeavor, pointed out by Ulrich in 2002, would be to follow the guidance outlined in West Point's strategic vision, which states:

> Officers strictly obey the principle that the military is subject to civilian authority and do not involve themselves or their subordinates in domestic politics or policy beyond the exercise of the basic rights of citizenship. Military officers render candid and forthright professional judgments and advice and eschew the public advocate's role.[4]

The challenge in doing so is easier said than done, as many officers have grown up in an army that has come to view overt displays of partisan affiliation as an acceptable norm. Likewise, the perception of the military as an institution dominated by the Republican Party is so ingrained in the minds of scholars and the public that counteracting it will require more effort than the army's typically passive approach to these issues. However, increasing support for the Democratic Party among former members of the military means that competition for military voters between the two parties has taken on an increasingly high profile, and the military may be forced to address the issue to prevent conflict within the ranks.

---

[2] Shapiro and Bloch-Elkin, "Political Polarization."

[3] As of March 19, 2008, just over two-thirds of Republicans felt the war in Iraq was worth fighting compared with only one-third of independents and one in eight Democrats. Agiesta, "Iraq."

[4] Office of Policy Planning and Analysis, "United States Military Academy."

It is now more common for retired generals to speak out in support of Democratic candidates, and numerous veterans have thrown their hat in the electoral ring as Democrats themselves. Adding to this dynamic are acts like the high-profile defection from the Republican Party by James Webb, an iconic military figure from the Vietnam era, who made a point of highlighting instances where he felt that Republicans had denigrated the service of veterans for political aim.[5] In sum, supporters of the Democratic Party in the military community can no longer be dismissed as outliers, which is likely to reduce the aversion to overt Democratic Party affiliation among members of the active force.

In light of this increased risk of partisan infighting, taking a more aggressive approach and being ruthless about the importance of partisan neutrality is imperative for the military's continued success. Admiral Michael Mullen, chairman of the Joint Chiefs of Staff, made a tentative step in the right direction in 2008 with a letter to military officers admonishing them to maintain their political neutrality and to keep partisan leanings private, but more discussion is needed.[6] The army is entering a new era when respect and understanding of the political system will become even more important to the ability of officers to fulfill their duties in addition to shaping the future relationship between the army and political elites. Not only are military officers increasingly assuming missions and responsibilities that explicitly require a greater understanding of the interplay between politics and military force, but they are doing so in an environment where debates over national security are sharply divided along party lines.

The blurring of the divide between politics and military force is certainly not a new development in American history, but it represents a distinct departure from the self-conception that most officers have had about their professional role over the last few decades. Similarly, we must remember that today's senior officers grew up in an era dominated by the Cold War. Given the comparably minor national defense and foreign policy differences between the two parties at the time (the "Cold War consensus"), it comes as no surprise that military leaders are not attuned to navigating more contentious debates over the use and role of military force. Officers must be able to navigate this terrain without compromising their professional ethic or the reputation of the military.

Senior officers must therefore openly embrace these challenges and aggressively educate members of the military on appropriate methods for engaging in the political process. Army officers can no longer be comfortable in believing that their political views do not influence public

---

[5] Webb, "Purple Heartbreakers."
[6] Mullen, "From the Chairman."

perceptions of, or elite-level interactions with, the institution, particularly when those views become fodder for competition between political parties. Unlike the 1950s, when it appeared that officers held an ideology separate and distinct from common political discourse and were therefore insulated from partisan debates, this research shows that today's officers are clearly capable of aligning themselves with a mainstream political party. Discussions of civil-military relations must therefore start with an acknowledgment that members of the military are not naturally separate and distinct from the civilian population. This should alleviate any concerns of "distance" between the military and the society it serves, but it also requires a reassessment of how the army maintains its professional ethic.

For many years a number of political scientists and sociologists have addressed the question of civil-military relations with a focus on the overlap between the military and society, as opposed to starting from an assumption of a fundamental separation. One such scholar, John Lovell, wrote in 1964: "Professional socialization is no longer consecration to beliefs and values that distinguish the professional group from other groups, but rather a process of adapting the values and beliefs held rather widely in the society to the specialized roles associated with a skilled profession."[7] Such an approach to professionalism represents a distinct break from Huntington's conception, but it is more helpful in focusing military officers on the requirement for proactively managing the military's relationship with society and, subsequently, its reputation for apolitical service. Officers must recognize this and guide the profession with an awareness that a reputation for political neutrality best serves the army and ultimately the nation's interest.[8]

Unfortunately, there is no shortage of examples of how the army is ill served by its continuing neglect of its reputation for partisan neutrality. Several events that have caught the public's attention in recent years serve as case studies of clumsy advocacy and a failure to understand the roles and responsibilities of military leaders in a democracy. In the examples of the endorsements of candidates by recently retired generals at the 2004 political conventions, the "revolt of the generals" in 2006, and current efforts by active and former soldiers to influence the political process, there is ample evidence of an institution that has not devoted sufficient time or effort to understanding the interplay between the army, partisan politics, and the army's relationship with the nation it serves.

---

[7] Lovell, "Professional Socialization."

[8] For a much more detailed discussion of the concept of the army as a profession, readers are encouraged to examine the two editions of *The Future of the Army Profession,* the first edited by Snider, Watkins, and Matthews, and the second by Snider and Matthews.

Leveraging the Institution for Political Gain

When Tommy Franks stepped onto the stage of the Republican National Convention in 2004, he was there not because of his speaking abilities or to offer a unique and personal worldview but because he was the face of the army. Only recently out of uniform, Franks had no identity other than that of a soldier, and in agreeing to endorse the Republican candidate for president he implicitly traded on a commodity that he should have realized was not his to trade. And in his comments, he explicitly drew upon the reputation of the army to enhance the prospects of his personal choice for president of the United States. Unfortunately, Franks was not the only retired general speaking at a political convention in 2004. Former chairman of the Joint Chiefs of Staff John Shalikashvili stood at the opening of the Democratic convention and declared, "I do not stand here as a political figure. Rather, I stand here as an old soldier," before moving on to an endorsement of the Democratic candidate.

There is room for retired officers in politics, but when they enter the political arena as soldiers first and citizens second, they do a disservice to those still in uniform. The army, and those in the general officer ranks particularly, must come to terms with how retired members of the military can enter the political arena without implicitly trading on the reputation of the active force.

Since it is clear that there are no internal norms for regulating such speech among military retirees, the army should consider imposing a symbolic penalty on generals who step directly out of uniform and use the military's prestige to endorse partisan political candidates or parties. Although retired officers share all the rights of their fellow citizens, they should be reminded that recently retired officers, and particularly generals, are perceived first and foremost as spokespersons for the institution. The simple act of removing the title of general from official military correspondence to any general who chooses to publicly endorse a party or political candidate within five years of leaving active service would suffice to remind the public that these officers no longer speak for the military. Another option is to exclude these generals from the many mentorship roles that retired general officers are often asked to perform. At the very least, more professional opprobrium should be meted out to those who step in front of national political conventions and have the temerity to claim to be "simple soldiers."

Fulfilling Professional Obligations

Such a moratorium on partisan political activity in the period immediately after retirement may have helped guide the men involved in 2006's so-called revolt of the generals. When several generals abruptly left the army and began speaking out against the secretary of defense, subsequently calling for a Democratic takeover of Congress in the 2006 election, they once again exposed the army's lack of clear norms for providing professional judgments to civilian leadership. That John Batiste and Paul Eaton felt military advice on Iraq had been ignored could reasonably lead one to wonder if the remaining generals on active duty were competently engaging civilian leadership. It also injected the views of senior military leaders into a political arena over which officers have little control. As officers are confronted with a line between politics and military strategy that is increasingly porous, they must familiarize themselves with ways to engage the various seats of political power. It seems that many current leaders are so afraid of politics they cannot find a way to respectfully air their judgments to civilian policy makers while on active duty. In 2007 retired Lieutenant General Ricardo Sanchez added himself to the list of retired officers speaking out against the handling of the war in Iraq, which led Senator John McCain pointedly to ask why he had not aired his views while still on active duty.[9]

This failure to engage the political process responsibly while in uniform will ultimately result in the loss of professional autonomy and, paradoxically, the increased politicization of the active force. If retired generals continue to leave the force and enter the partisan political fray as a means to settle unresolved grievances, they are likely to inspire elected leaders to further vet the political affiliations of those officers considered for promotion. Furthermore, when officers endorse parties or candidates as a means of resolving conflicts with their former bosses, they may lead other elected officials to question the motivation of military advice in other contexts.

In sum, we are witnessing the result of a generation of officers who have not considered the intricacies of civil-military relations beyond an abbreviated and bastardized version of Huntington's dictum to keep the military and politics separate. Having taken Huntington out of context, many in the army shun all things political to the point where they cannot competently operate in the often nonhierarchical and fluid environment of contemporary Washington. The result is that the army must now act to shore up the confidence of both elected political leaders and those junior officers who are left wondering about the direction in which their senior leaders are taking the institution.

Translating Service into Privilege

Unfortunately, generals are not the only service members who have entered the political arena. In fact, it seems the actions of prominent gener-

---

[9] Memmott and Lawrence, "McCain."

als, paired with institutional silence on the issue, have established a new norm whereby service members of all ranks feel freer to add their voices to the partisan fray. Beginning in 2007, active members of the military began publicly to appeal to Congress for the withdrawal of forces from Iraq. Although it is not uncommon for individual members of the military to contact their senators or representatives with problems, it is unique for active members of the military to organize and lobby Congress as a group. The danger of such a development lies in its very appeal to those service members seeking a voice in Congress. In embracing the "Appeal for Redress," Representative Dennis Kucinich has said, "*No one speaks with more moral authority* or understanding of the complexity of Iraq than the brave men and women who serve in our armed forces" (emphasis mine).[10]

In a twist, members of the military have translated service to the state into a privileged voice within the state, at least in the view of a few members of Congress. In essence, they are no longer defending the democratic process but using military service as a means to gain an advantage over others with competing views. Such activity not only threatens the army's internal cohesion but denigrates the apolitical and professional nature of military service.

The 2008 presidential election also saw a series of ads put out by a conservative advocacy group using combat veterans to voice support for the continuation of the war in Iraq.[11] Ironically, the implications of using military service in this manner can also be seen in an opposing ad put out by a liberal advocacy group. There are no veterans in the ad, simply a mother who declares that her son will not be available for military service.[12] The implication of the ad is that military service is an endorsement of a specific foreign-policy view, and that there is little value in a military that stands ready to follow the directives of the people's democratically elected representatives, regardless of the party in power.

This is a dangerous development for both internal army relations and the military's reputation for being apolitical. If the direction of national strategy comes to be determined by members of the military, or rather those members of the military with the best access to civilian policy makers, the armed forces risk being torn apart by internal political conflicts in addition to squandering the military's reputation for unwavering subservience to the democratic process.[13] And when 1% of the popula-

---

[10] Bacevich, "Warrior Politics."

[11] Tapper and Miller, "Selling the War."

[12] Kuhnhenn, "AFSCME."

[13] By 2007 there had been significant growth in the number of both pro- and antiwar veterans' groups who habitually lobbied politicians on Iraq war policy. The danger is that this activity will spill into the active-duty force. See Fairbanks, "Friendly Fire."

tion seeks to dictate national security strategy to elected officials, can the military still be said to honor the ideals of sacrifice and service to the nation?

Lessons from the Army's Birthday

In conclusion, it is worth looking back at the experiences of George Washington to inform our understanding of these current challenges to civil-military relations. But first it is necessary to pinpoint the birth of the American army. Officially, the U.S. Army considers June 14, 1775, as its date of birth. On that day the Continental Congress authorized the formation of ten companies of riflemen to serve the colonies. This is an important day in our history, but it is not unique to the American experience. Throughout history, groups have formed militaries to protect collective interests and assert their independence. As far as militaries go, nothing especially unique was created on that day in 1775. It was after the Revolution, on March 15, 1783, that the American army truly came into being.

On that day Washington brought to a halt a burgeoning conspiracy among veterans of the Revolutionary War assembled in Newburgh. The veterans had reason to be aggrieved, as it was becoming clear that the Continental Congress would not provide them the pay they had been promised for their service during the war. Many felt that they needed to take matters into their own hands and demand payment, presumably through the threat of force. Upon hearing of a planned gathering to discuss their grievances, Washington canceled the meeting and called for another on the fifteenth, to which he unexpectedly arrived.[14] It was there in the "Temple" at the New Windsor encampment that Washington quashed an incipient movement to organize the military against the elected leaders of the new republic.

In this, Washington set several important precedents for the American army and its future relationships with elected officials and the government it serves. Most immediately, he established that a soldier's sacrifice to the nation is first and foremost just that, a sacrifice. The service of the officers of the Revolutionary Army had been to the ideal of a new and independent democratic republic. The fact that the new government could not repay them adequately for their service did not give them the right to

[14] Unexpectedly for the officers present, but clearly a calculated move on Washington's part to put the conspirators off balance. Ellis describes the advance placement of supporters in the crowd to clap appropriately at key lines in Washington's planned speech. Ellis, *His Excellency*, 146.

usurp the people's duly appointed representatives. To do so would "lessen the dignity, and sully the glory" that they had achieved from the nobility of their service. Furthermore, Washington understood that the military should not act as an interest group independent of civilian authorities because such action would "sow the seeds of discord and separation between the Civil and Military powers of the Continent."[15]

Washington's ability to quell the conspiracy was also due, in large part, to his knowledge of the political process and the faith that his subordinates placed in his ability to work with the Continental Congress to achieve a just resolution to their grievances. In this, Washington did not shy away from direct contact and frank exchanges with political leaders. He stayed in close contact with a variety of politicians and did not hesitate to make his views known to those he felt needed to hear them. For Washington, faithful service to the political system and intimate knowledge of that system were not mutually exclusive concepts. And in keeping with the first precedent, Washington made it clear that even if his appeals failed, this would not constitute a justification for the military to work against the government.

The last and most important precedent that Washington set was his willingness to forgo the direct translation of military prestige into political power. His dramatic exit from army life and his post–Revolutionary War years in Mount Vernon allowed for a distance to grow between Washington the military commander and Washington the private citizen. This ensured that when he later joined the political struggle over the new Constitution, he did not do so on his authority as a military leader. He did it as a citizen who had also been a soldier.

---

[15] George Washington, "Speech to Officers at Newburgh," http://www.pbs.org/george-washington/milestones/newburgh_read.html (accessed March 23, 2009).

Update: The 2008 Election _____

WHEN ANALYZING DATA THROUGH 2007, the compelling question was where the military was going if it was shifting away from the Republican Party. The results of the 2008 election suggest that the army is moving toward a more balanced distribution of Republican and Democratic identifiers. Representative poll data for the military in 2008 are unavailable, but the Military Times surveys are again useful for assessing trends within the military population. In September 2008 the Military Times sent e-mails to about 69,000 subscribers and collected responses from 2,982 active-duty members of the military, 1,543 of whom were in the army.[1] As with previous Military Times surveys, the 2008 respondents were not representative of the active-duty military population but were disproportionately white, male, and of the officer ranks.[2] So shifts in opinion among these subscribers are probably indicative of shifts in the larger officer population. They may also indicate trends in the broader army population, even if they cannot be used as a measure of aggregate military opinion.

The primary headline to come out of the Military Times surveys was that 68% of respondents backed the Republican presidential candidate, John McCain.[3] However, lost in the analysis was a significant shift in support for the Democratic nominee. Respondents to the survey were asked both whom they supported in the last election and whom they planned to vote for in 2008. These two questions therefore provide a unique opportunity to assess shifts in opinion, and possibly party affiliation, between the two elections (unfortunately, the survey did not ask for respondents' party affiliations). A look at just the subset of active-duty

---

[1] The Military Times sent original messages to about eighty thousand, but many came back as undeliverable. Some of this should be expected, and appropriately discounted, given the high mobility of the active-duty military community, but it is not clear how many potential respondents with invalid addresses were active as opposed to being retirees or in the guard or reserve. These numbers also include 316 respondents who were left out of the analysis put out by the Military Times due to the fact that they were not likely voters. Data reported here include these respondents.

[2] As discussed in chapter 3, the actual army population is about 85% male; 14% are regular commissioned officers (not including warrant officers), and 60% are white. The active-duty members of the army who responded to the Military Times poll were 90% male; 45% of them were regular commissioned officers, and 71% white. Furthermore, the army's junior enlisted ranks are dramatically underrepresented in the Military Times surveys. About 47% of the army serves in the ranks of E-1 through E-4 (see table 3.1). These ranks comprise only 6% of the active army population included in the 2008 Military Times survey.

[3] McGarry, "Military Times Poll."

members of the army in the 2008 Military Times preelection poll shows that 64% of these respondents reported voting for George Bush in 2004 and 15% reported voting for John Kerry. As for the 2008 election, 66% planned to vote for McCain and 25% reported planning to vote for Barack Obama. Although these percentages do not indicate a reversal of military preferences among officers, the increase in support for the Democratic candidate signals a significant shift in military opinion and demonstrates that military aversion to the Democratic Party may be on the wane. About 40% of this increase in support for Obama over Kerry came from respondents who reported voting for Bush in 2004. The other 60% reported either not voting at all or voting for someone other than Bush or Kerry in the 2004 election. Of those who shifted their allegiance from Bush to Obama, 95% were male and 55% were white. Among those who voted for neither the Republican nor the Democratic candidate in 2004 but planned to vote for Obama in 2008, 77% were male and 39% were white. This indicates that the increased support for the Democratic presidential candidate is due to a shift of a portion of the army's traditional voting bloc away from the Republican Party as well as an infusion of new, predominantly minority voters into the Democratic column. An extrapolation from these trends to the broader army population, which is much younger and is composed of a higher proportion of minorities than respondents to the Military Times surveys, suggests that the increase in Democratic Party voters in the military was probably larger than the 10% we can glean from this survey.

The second significant conclusion to draw from the results of this preelection survey is that McCain was able to hold on to a significant portion of the votes of senior military officers at a time when the Republican Party was hurting nationally. At the time of the survey, McCain was holding a slightly higher portion of the senior officer vote than Bush did in 2004. This was probably not indicative of a shift back to the 60% of senior officers who identified with the Republican Party during that election but was due more to McCain's veteran status. Among active-duty army respondents, 73% felt that the veteran status of the candidates was important in their voting decision. (Thirty-two percent said it was very important. Another 41% felt it was somewhat important.) Thus the veteran status of the candidates correlated highly with voting patterns. Furthermore, in a multi-variate regression controlling for gender, race, rank, and education level, the importance of the service records of the two candidates to military voters was statistically significant and the most powerful predictor of vote choice among these factors. This finding is not surprising, but it does suggest that the military's support for McCain in 2008 may not indicate a return to the Republican camp after trending away during the second Bush administration. It is likely that postelection assessments of the party identification of senior officers will be closer to the figures reported in the 2007 Military Times survey.

Further evidence that military voters are moving toward parity can be seen in tallies of the veteran vote in exit polls. Whereas in 2004 veterans preferred Bush to Kerry by a sixteen-point margin (57% to 41%), that gap decreased to nine points in 2008. Exit polls reflect that 54% of veterans voted for McCain, compared with the 44% who voted for Obama. This may also indicate stronger trends toward voting for the Democrats within the active-duty ranks, given that veterans are much older, more likely to be white, and more likely to be male than either the general population or the population of those actively serving.[4]

With the ascent of a Democrat to the position of commander in chief, we should expect this trend not only to continue but to accelerate. Much of the military's disillusionment with the Republican Party can be attributed to the war in Iraq.[5] It is therefore likely that the current focus on the Iraq endgame, paired with renewed attention to the conflict in Afghanistan, will bring more members of the army into the Democratic column. The new president has also clearly sought to build a bridge to the military, most notably with the appointments of a former chief of staff of the army to head the Department of Veterans Affairs and a previous commandant of the Marine Corps as national security advisor (Generals [Ret.] Eric Shinseki and Jim Jones, respectively).

Many service members are also likely to experience newfound respect for, or at least tolerance of, the Democratic Party as a byproduct of the centrality of the commander-in-chief position to military identity. Much as General George Patton felt compelled to vote for his commander in chief, regardless of party affiliation, President Obama is poised to collect the political loyalties of many service members as a byproduct of the mili-

---

[4] There were 524 veterans in the 2008 exit poll. In this poll the population of veterans is about 76% white and 89% are men. Thirty-five percent of veterans are over sixty-five, triple the share among nonveterans and obviously well above the fraction of a percentage of active-duty service members who are in their sixties. At the other end of the age spectrum, only 5% of vets are under the age of thirty. Langer, "The Veteran Vote."

[5] Approval for Bush's handling of the war in Iraq among respondents to the Military Times surveys broadly tracks trends in Republican Party identification. In 2003, the first year of the surveys, 52% of respondents approved of the president's handling of the conflict and 25% expressed disapproval. Approval ratings rose considerably in 2004, to a 63% approval and 20% disapproval, before dropping in 2005 to a 54% approval and 25% disapproval. Approval ratings plummeted in 2006 to 35%, and the disapproval rate was 42%. In 2007, the last year for which data are available on this question, 40% of respondents to the Military Times surveys approved of Bush's handling of the war in Iraq and 38% registered disapproval.

tary's inherent respect for the chain of command.[6] And although current conditions might resemble those during the disastrous relationship between President Carter and the military in the late 1970s, such as a constrained military budget and an opposition poised to promote the narrative of a Democratic unwillingness to "finish the fight," this development is not a foregone conclusion. With an agreement between Iraqi leaders and the Bush administration setting a timetable for the withdrawal of U.S. forces and a strong consensus about renewing our efforts in Afghanistan, the incoming new president has a unique opportunity to restore balance to the affiliations of members of the military.

What is clear from all of this is that the military vote is now in play more than it has been since before the Carter administration. It is certain that military voters will continue to be heavily courted by the political parties. Although this newfound balance may deter both parties from trying to claim the "prestige" of the military vote, the military should not rely on the restraint of outside actors to protect its professional reputation. Without positive action from military leaders, partisan fights over the military vote may spill over into the active force.

The way the military responds to this period of increased balance and contestation will set the tone for civil-military relations for years to come. Admiral Michael Mullen and General David Petraeus, the two highest-profile officers in the military, in an effort to demonstrate their neutrality, made a point of declaring that they would not vote in 2008.[7] This is a good first step that should spark further discussion among military professionals about their personal rights and professional obligations as they relate to the political process.

---

[6] See the discussion in chapter 2. Galloway and Johnson, *West Point,* 237.

[7] Glanton, "Campaigns Wage War."

Afterword

Thoughts on Sparta . . .

The tone of discussion about American civil-military relations has changed considerably since this project began. At the time, the central concern of scholars and observers of military affairs was how to check a military that seemed to be challenging civilian control. The pendulum has swung. Scholars are now writing about the dangers of neglecting military advice and the limits within which members of the military may challenge commands from civilian authorities. This shift in scholarly discourse is reflective of a period of instability in American civil-military relations.

Over the last eight years, we have witnessed a period in which the secretary of defense largely directed the means by which the military would execute its mission, followed by a backlash from many of the officers involved in that decision-making process or in the execution of the resulting plans. We then entered a period when a single military officer, General Petraeus, represented the face of American strategy in the Middle East. Each of these developments is troubling in its own right. They become more troubling when combined with both the passions of partisan politics and the substantial distance between the American population and its army.

Blunting the use of the military as a weapon in partisan politics is therefore an essential first step to improving American civil-military relations. Part of this can be accomplished through education and greater interaction between the American people and their military. Members of the military should encourage and embrace studies of the institution and its relationships with American society. If nothing else, such studies serve to inoculate against stereotypes that capture the popular imagination. Military personnel should not be viewed as champions of any specific faction, nor derided as bullies or patronized as victims. Service members come from, and are shaped by, American society. As such, they should be understood as Americans who serve their country under arms, and not as a distant or alien population.

This increased understanding can come only from a more diverse engagement with the military. Since fewer Americans have experience with military service, we must be more proactive in keeping the dialogue open. Relying on the small number of existing narratives of military life can leave observers with an incomplete or a misleading impression. Even well-intentioned portrayals often miss the larger picture or use snapshots of military life to advance a tangential agenda. Such was the case with Samuel Huntington's closing comments in *The Soldier and the State*. Describing the architecture of West Point, and by extension its ethos, as culminating in the gothic chapel on the hill above the parade grounds, Huntington conjured a monastic image of military life sharply delineated from the discord of civil society and suggested that American society would be better off emulating military standards. But is the military that different from society? At least a few officers keep Huntington's portrayal of the academy on their walls as a source of pride, but does this mean that life at West Point flows to the chapel, or that members of the military share the hierarchy of values Huntington extrapolated from the layout of buildings around the parade field?

It is true that on any given weekend a visitor is likely to find thousands of cadets flowing up from the barracks and toward the chapel, but they are more likely to walk past the chapel toward the cathedral of college football than they are to stop for prayer. In this and myriad other dimensions of life, they are just like the rest of America.[1] After witnessing the ordered serenity of morning formations or parade practice, visitors would do well to witness the exodus of cadets on evening or weekend pass. There they can observe firsthand the great dash for the gates and the palpable desire of cadets to maintain their sense of connection with the world they have temporarily left behind. For cadets, military life does not supplant the American experience but augments who they are. The military ethos does not reshape their fundamental views but offers an avenue for them to serve the broader ideals of America.

It is only at first glance that civilians and the military appear to be sharply divided. Officers and officers in training do not abandon their core American identities but learn to fuse who they are with the obligation to serve their country. Similarly, the academy itself cannot be understood as an obelisk that magically appeared on the Hudson (as with the black stone in Stanley Kubrick's *2001: A Space Odyssey*, sent in more gothic form by a divine hand to enlighten the primitives). Instead, we must acknowledge that each stone at West Point has been shaped and placed by American hands seeking to build an enduring institution whose purpose is to protect the people and lands from which our military leaders are drawn.

---

[1] Readers wishing to understand more about life at West Point are highly encouraged to read the recent works of Elizabeth Samet and David Lipsky. See Samet, *Soldier's Heart,* and Lipsky, *Absolutely American.*

. . . and Babylon

Having experienced firsthand the disconnect between life in the army and portrayals of that life in popular culture, I thought I was prepared for more of the same while attending graduate school at the institution that surely occupies the opposite pole in the imagination of a red and blue America: Columbia University in the City of New York.[2] Columbia's history of protest politics, dating primarily from 1968, along with its continued opposition to the Reserve Officers' Training Corps, may suggest to some that the visions of West Point and Columbia are diametrically opposed. Indeed, several minor tempests on campus in the aftermath of September 2001 seemed to reinforce the image of Columbia as dutifully reprising its role from the culture wars of the 1960s. However, a closer look reveals a more nuanced environment and a few developments that suggest we may finally be moving beyond the divides of the Vietnam War.

As New York City regained its composure in the fall of 2001, so students at Columbia began to express their opinions of the war in Afghanistan. For a few months, the dominant theme was sobriety, but as the shock of September 11 slowly faded, campus activists began to find their voice. At times one might have been excused for thinking that the United States was still at war in Vietnam as both the slogans and images of that conflict found their way to rallies and onto posters adorning the campus. This recycled rhetoric was indicative of the time and distance that have grown between the American military and academia. With the end of the draft and the closure of ROTC programs at many elite universities in the aftermath of Vietnam, the gap between the nation's armed forces and academia left many on campus with no point of reference for the military beyond the tired stereotypes.

As the war went on, it appeared that the Solomon Amendment, a law mandating that institutions receiving federal funds could not bar military recruiting, would force a greater accommodation of the military on campus. But it was not the Solomon Amendment that ultimately brought a discussion of military service to the academic community, and for this we should be grateful. By all appearances the Solomon Amendment was written as a punitive measure by a conservative congressman seeking to strong-arm universities into supporting the military. Yet the idea of leveraging the power of the federal government to police academic life seems

---

[2] Credit for using Sparta and Babylon as foils for a discussion of the differences between civilians and members of the military must ultimately go to Huntington, but readers are also encouraged to explore the deeper exploration presented by Driver in *Sparta in Babylon*.

diametrically opposed to traditionally American ideals as well as to efforts at fostering mutual understanding.

Conversely, academic disengagement from questions of national defense has done little to change military personnel policies and in fact has widened the gulf between today's academic and military elites. Although there are valid criticisms of the policy known as "Don't ask, don't tell," overt opposition to the law prohibiting the service of open homosexuals in the military seems to appear only when it is needed as an excuse to keep ROTC off campus.

It is therefore a relief that the move to return ROTC to Columbia has been driven by students proactively seeking to reengage with issues of military service and representation on their own.[3] Their discussions about the presence of ROTC at Columbia have moved beyond the rhetoric of the Vietnam generation. Therefore they reflect a welcome change from the false choice presented by those who equate a lack of support for the military with treason and those who feel that any engagement with the military is automatically an endorsement of militarism and discrimination. By all indications, today's students are ready to engage in these questions from a position that recognizes these either-or options as impediments to constructive dialogue.[4] These students were given a tremendous boost when President Obama attended a campaign event at Columbia, his only campaign appearance at his alma mater, along with Senator John McCain. As part of the ServiceNation Presidential Forum, both candidates expressed their support for the return of ROTC to Columbia. This endorsement, combined with ongoing student engagement on the issue, led to a student referendum that revealed a close split on the issue of ROTC's return.[5]

Although a renewed engagement between the military and academia will not directly lead to the resolution of debates over military manpower policies, to say nothing of the external security challenges we face, the immediate benefit of such discussions is the dissolution of the stereotypes that suggest an unbridgeable gap between the Left and the Right in America. Indeed, the appropriate starting point is to realize that there is no Left or Right, or red or blue, America. Only on the most superficial level can one suggest that Columbia and West Point are not

[3] It is significant that the push for ROTC at Columbia has been picked up by a large number of students with no previous military experience and no family connections with the military, in addition to being supported by students who have served in uniform. There is also significant support from members of the faculty. See Silver, "Why ROTC Should Return to Columbia."

[4] For an especially compelling argument, see Foote, "A Bias-Free Campus?"

[5] Schneider, "Students Roughly Split."

complementary and connected parts of the fabric of American life. Moving beyond debates over symbolic differences and engaging from a position of mutual interest are therefore essential first steps in ensuring that we each fulfill our role in providing for the security and sustained health of our democracy.

Appendix A

Citizenship and Service: 2004 Survey of Army Personnel

Survey Method

As discussed in chapter 1, the Citizenship and Service: 2004 Survey of Army Personnel (C&S Survey) was conducted primarily via mail questionnaires between April 3 and July 24, 2004. The survey sample was drawn from an army database. The database contained extensive demographic information, which allowed for a random selection of the sample and for an oversampling of key demographics. Every soldier and officer on active duty whose name was in the army personnel database as of February 2004 was eligible for the survey with the exception of personnel who were deployed in combat zones; those serving in units deploying to and from Iraq and Afghanistan during April and May 2004; and soldiers and officers in a few selected ranks.[1]

Due to the high turnover and sustained deployment of forces into Iraq and Afghanistan, the exclusion of soldiers in a combat zone did not prevent me from surveying combat veterans. Fully 376 of the respondents, or 32% of the sample, were veterans of either Operation Iraqi Freedom (2003–2004) or Operation Enduring Freedom in Afghanistan (2001–2004), and 143 indicated that they had been involved in direct ground combat in the previous two years.

I excluded sergeants major and generals due to the small population size of these ranks and the high visibility of generals.[2] I also excluded the

[1] After drawing the names of soldiers from the February 2004 database, we obtained mailing addresses for those soldiers from a separate December 2003 database, the pay database, which reportedly contained more accurate contact information. The tradeoff was that we added another four months between the database entry and the time the survey was mailed to the soldier. This was not an insignificant tradeoff, given that up to a third of the army changes duty stations every year. After drawing the mailing addresses from the pay database, I went through and identified all incomplete or suspect addresses and then looked for more accurate addresses in both the personnel database and the army white pages (an online directory).

[2] In analyses that might report on survey respondents from small populations, it may be difficult to protect fully the anonymity of such respondents as required by rules regarding the use of human subjects, to which this study conforms. There were only 312 generals and 3,333 sergeants major in the army at the time of the survey.

lowest two enlisted ranks, private E1 (PV1) and private E2 (PV2), because of the very high mobility of these soldiers. Specifically, soldiers generally serve in these ranks for less than a year upon entering the army, spending the majority of their time in basic and advanced individual training before arriving at their first regular unit.[3] The soldiers and officers in the four ranks just cited make up only approximately 10% of the army on active duty, which left 90% of the army population, by rank, eligible to be included in the survey.[4]

Because of the inherent mobility of army personnel and the fact that I drew mailing addresses from a three-month old database, I built into the sample size a substantial buffer to allow for cases lost due to undeliverable mail. Twenty-four percent of the surveys that were sent (856 cases) came back as undeliverable. This number was well within the range of what I expected, given that individual soldiers move every two to three years and that during a given period a sizable portion of the army is in training, is deployed, or is in transit. As mentioned above, the two lowest ranks in the army, PV1 and PV2, are typically very mobile and the hardest to reach by postal mail as they go through initial training, which is why I excluded them from the sample.[5] After arriving at their first unit, however, soldiers are subject to a fairly uniform rotation schedule. There is a tendency for soldiers to keep their mailing addresses in personnel records more accurate and up to date as they move up the ranks, but every soldier has an almost equal chance of being in transit between units at any given time. Soldiers across the army are generally equally likely to receive moving orders from the army, effectively making it a random occurrence. Therefore it is reasonable to exclude soldiers with invalid mailing addresses in evaluating the survey's response rate and the quality of the sample. I calculated the final response rate to be 45% among those soldiers and officers whose mail was not returned as undeliverable.[6] (A discussion and analysis of which subgroups were more likely to have invalid addresses in the army database is in the next section.)

---

[3] The exclusion of privates from the sample will particularly affect the reasons soldiers report for joining the army, as a soldier's thoughts about why he or she joined will evolve over time.

[4] The total population of the army as of February 2004 was 486,811. Excluding PV1s, PV2s, CSMs, and generals from the sample left 435,851 in the ranks included in the survey.

[5] Representatives from the Army Research Institute, the army's clearinghouse for internal polling, indicated that they normally do not even try to reach anyone below the rank of corporal through regular mail. I decided to include privates first class anyway. They ended up having the lowest proportion of valid addresses and the lowest response rate of any rank included in the survey, but the resulting database does include responses from fifty soldiers in that rank.

[6] If we include undeliverable addresses in the calculation, the response rate is 34%.

TABLE A.1
Sample Breakdown by Race/Ethnicity and Gender

Race	Rank			
	Enlisted	Warrant	Officer	Total
White	197	14	209	420
Hispanic	192	32	173	397
Black	130	37	126	293
Other	44	7	27	78
Total	563	90	535	1,188
Male	*432*	*81*	*407*	*920*
Female	*131*	*9*	*128*	*268*

Source: C&S Survey.

I designed the survey sample to emphasize and focus on the dimensions of race and rank.[7] I first drew a random sample and then oversamples of certain groups based on projected return rates. Specifically, I drew additional white, black, and Hispanic officers as well as additional black and Hispanic enlisted soldiers in an attempt to get close to 200 respondents in each category.[8] In the end, responses from the basic sample plus the oversample, taken together, yielded a final sample size for analysis of 1,188. The composition of the final sample, including the oversamples, broken down by rank, gender, and race and ethnicity, is shown in table A.1.

The survey was conducted primarily via questionnaires delivered in the mail. Computer use is not consistent across the army; nor do all soldiers have access to computers and e-mail.[9] Similarly, the army does not keep track of personal phone numbers, making targeted surveying over the phone impossible (not the mention the expense and difficulty of reaching soldiers stationed overseas).[10]

[7] In retrospect, it was a mistake not to oversample women soldiers as well. Although women had a greater likelihood of having a valid address in the army database and were also more likely to respond to the survey, the low numbers of women in certain rank and racial categories made weighting on the dimensions of race, rank, and gender difficult.

[8] The six primary groups I wanted to compare were white officers, white enlisted soldiers, black officers, black enlisted soldiers, Hispanic officers, and Hispanic enlisted soldiers.

[9] The army gives all soldiers a Web-based e-mail account, but not all soldiers own personal computers or have regular access to computers at work.

[10] Sending a mail survey to a soldier stationed overseas costs the same as sending a mail survey to a soldier stationed in the continental United States. This is due to the Army Postal Service, which receives overseas-bound mail at army post offices located in the United States and then delivers the mail to soldiers overseas—all for the price of domestic delivery.

Each respondent received an introductory letter that was followed, in sequence, by the primary survey mailing, a reminder postcard, and then a second survey mailing. The last contact was a fifth letter offering respondents the option of completing the survey online.[11] Each of these mailings was done using the principles outlined by Don Dillman in *Mail and Internet Surveys: The Tailored Design Method*. The introductory letter, the letters accompanying the two survey mailings, and the letter in the final follow-up mailing were hand signed in an effort to personalize the mailing. I also affixed a first-class postage stamp to every return envelope in an effort to promote a higher response rate.[12] In all, the survey consisted of 15,748 separate mailings.[13]

The survey mailings went out from April 3 through July 24, 2004. Although ideally I would have liked to make all of the mail contacts within a shorter period, I had the challenge of sending mail to soldiers stationed overseas. Twenty-six percent of the survey mailings went to overseas personnel. Although domestic mailings are delivered normally, mail to overseas personnel goes through an army post office (APO) located in the continental United States. From there, the Military Postal Service takes control of the mail and delivers it overseas. While this reduces the costs of mailing letters outside the continental United States, it does add to the delivery time. There was therefore a significant time lag between the first three mailings and the two follow-ups as returned surveys and undeliverable mail trickled in through the month of May. During this time the names of soldiers who returned the survey and those with nondeliverable addresses were struck from the list of those who would receive the fourth and fifth mailings.

Survey Response

A multivariate regression shows that being male decreased the odds that a potential respondent would return the completed survey, and being older increased the odds of a response. Officers were more likely than soldiers

---

[11] Every soldier in the army has an e-mail account, although the use of that account is not required. The internal organizations that regularly poll army personnel still use mail as a primary means of contact, although offering potential respondents the opportunity to complete the poll online is becoming much more common.

[12] These are the most commonly accepted techniques for reducing nonresponse. See Dillman, *Mail and Internet Surveys,* and Moore and Turnai, "Evaluating Nonresponse Error."

[13] Primary thanks go to my wife, Laura, and a small crew of overworked and under-paid students for helping to make this happen on an initial budget of about $14,000.

TABLE A.2
Timing of Response Solicitations

Mailing	Date sent
Introductory letter	3 April
1st survey mailing	8 April
Reminder postcard	12 April
2nd survey mailing	12 June
Letter w/ Web response option	24 July

to return the survey.[14] Blacks were less likely to respond than soldiers and officers of other races or ethnicities.[15] Recent deployment to a combat zone did not influence response rates directly, although soldiers in this category were slightly less likely to have a valid address in the army's database. Response rates by demographics are shown in table A.3. The table shows response rates calculated both as a percentage of those with valid addresses in the database and as a percentage of all soldiers of that demographic in the original sample.

I ran several models to assess how survey nonresponse may have influenced the reported results of the survey, including weighting for nonresponse and including survey wave indicators in regression models.[16] None of these models suggested any significant attitudinal differences between early and late responders to the survey.[17] This may imply, by extension, that differences between those who responded and those who did not are minimal.[18] And, by having extensive demographic information on the

[14] The higher proclivity of officers to respond makes sense for two reasons. First, officers have a higher educational level, as all officers are required to have at least a bachelor's degree. We know that lower educational levels are correlated with a response of "no opinion," and we can assume that a similar dynamic may occur in the response-nonresponse decision in that those with better cognitive skills may be both more interested in the survey and more able to navigate through it quickly and easily. The second reason is that officers are more likely to feel closely identified with the army institution, and are therefore more trusting and compliant in fulfilling requests for information. Assuming that potential respondents viewed the survey as official, we should expect that in a collectivist culture such as the army the response rates would increase. See Leeuw and Heer, "Trends in Household Survey Nonresponse." See also Krosnick, "Causes of No-Opinion Responses."

[15] This is in keeping with the response rate of blacks in the civilian population. See Johnson, O'Rourke, Burris, and Owens, "Culture and Survey Nonresponse."

[16] For more details, see Dempsey, "Effects and Mitigation."

[17] Another mitigating factor may have been offering respondents a chance to fill out the survey online in the fifth survey mailing. This alternative mode may have enticed those who were interested but felt too busy to fill out a paper copy and return it in the mail.

[18] This technique is obviously somewhat problematic and assumes that one can extrapolate from the differences in views between early and late responders to the views of nonrespondents. See Filion, "Estimating Bias."

TABLE A.3
Response Rates by Key Demographic

Demographic	With valid addresses %	Overall %
Male	43.6	32.5
Female	47.9	38.5
Enlisted total	**35.4**	**25.4**
Jr. enlisted	30.3	20.2
NCO	35.6	25.7
Sr. NCO	46.5	39.2
Officer total[a]	**58.0**	**47.9**
Warrant	54.0	44.6
Lieutenant	50.3	34.8
Captain	58.0	47.8
Major	60.6	52.2
Lt. colonel	65.2	61.5
Colonel	59.3	58.2
White	46.5	35.6
Hispanic	45.2	33.7
Black	41.3	31.7
Other	45.8	32.0
Under 25	30.3	18.8
25 to 29	36.6	26.0
30 to 34	48.2	36.8
35 to 39	45.9	38.3
40 to 44	55.9	47.8
Over 45	63.6	59.8
Overall	**44.6**	**33.7**

Source: C&S Survey.
[a] Includes warrant officers.

population being studied, I have been able to adjust, through weighting, for indicators that often play a factor in survey nonresponse (such as gender, age, and race).

As for item nonresponses, 76 respondents out of 1,188 left one of the five political scaling questions blank.[19] As three of these scaling questions

[19] In a bivariate analysis it appeared that increased education levels, increased age, being male, being white, and being an officer corresponded with a reduced chance of leaving these questions blank. However, in a multivariate analysis, all of these indicators were statistically insignificant, and the only statistically significant factor in predicting nonresponses to these questions was whether a respondent returned the second survey mailing, as opposed to responding to the first mailing or over the Internet. This leads me to believe that the reason for a higher rate of item nonresponse to these questions was primarily survey fatigue and question complexity; this group required several contacts to complete the survey and was probably less motivated to respond than those who responded after the first contact.

TABLE A.4
Case-Wise Deletion and Multiple-Imputation Comparison

| | Predictions of Republican Party identification | |
	Regular	Imputed
Average person	28%	27%
Significant SES variables		
Black, nonreligious, working class, high school	4	4
White, religious, upper class, some college	72	68
Significant army variables		
Combat support, junior enlisted	12	13
Combat arms, lieutenant colonel	58	55
SES and army factors combined		
Extreme low	1	2
Extreme high	90	87

Source: C&S Survey.

were essential to predicting party identification, I wanted to see if item nonresponses, particularly to these questions, biased the reported results. To assess the potential impact of item nonreponses, I compared the results of regression models using case-wise deletion and multiple imputation.[20] Predictions of Republican Party identification using the two methods are shown in table A.4.

The results are nearly similar, reflecting the changes that come from a relatively small increase in the number of respondents in the data set with the use of multiple imputation (a 14% increase from 1,045). What differences there are, however, move in the direction one would expect in that there is a lower tendency to identify with the Republican Party after imputing the attitudes of those who would normally have been dropped from the equation.

Although it would have been preferable to achieve a 100% response rate and have every respondent answer every question, my analysis of survey and item nonresponses leads me to believe that the reported attitudes of the respondents in the C&S Survey sample fairly accurately reflect the attitudes of the army population. The most important factor in the quality of the C&S Survey results is unquestionably the fact that potential respondents were drawn randomly from a comprehensive list of everyone in the army. The next most important tool I had was extensive demographic information about the army, which allowed me to weight the sample to reflect the army population.

[20] Hill, "Missing Data."

Survey Weighting

All regression models in this study control for key demographic factors, making weighting unnecessary. However, aggregate army attitudes reported here reflect weighted data. For this, I constructed a proportional weighting scheme on the dimensions of race/ethnicity, rank, and gender. Using the army database, I was able to construct proportional weights so that the C&S Survey sample exactly reflected the army population (minus the ranks of PV1, PV2, sergeant major, and general) on these three dimensions. The minimum cell population used in the weighting scheme was six respondents. In the case of minorities who did not fit one of the three oversampled groups (white, black, or Hispanic), as well as women and Hispanics in the senior officer ranks, cells were combined to meet the minimum cell-size requirement.[21]

One disadvantage of this weighting scheme is that the variance of weights is large. This will cause standard errors to be larger than those shown in unweighted estimates.[22] However, it is accepted that this loss of precision is outweighed by the reduction in bias that weighting achieves. This is particularly true given that in this instance we know the true population values of the army on the dimensions used to construct this weighting scheme.[23]

[21] In all, fifty-three permutations of race/ethnicity, rank, and gender were used to create the weighting scheme. Additional weighting schemes tested with as few as sixteen separate cells showed no significant differences in reported marginals.

[22] Sturgis, "Analysing Complex Survey Data."

[23] Ibid. Also thanks to Karol Krotki for his insights offered during his short course on survey weighting offered at the 2006 annual conference of the American Association of Public Opinion Researchers.

SURVEY APPROVAL AUTHORITY: U.S. ARMY RESEARCH INSTITUTE
FOR THE BEHAVIORAL AND SOCIAL SCIENCES
SURVEY CONTROL NUMBER: DAPE-ARI-AO-04-11
RCS: MILPC-3

INSTRUCTIONS:

1. READ CAREFULLY EACH QUESTION AND ALL THE POSSIBLE RESPONSES before selecting your response.

2. YOU MAY USE A PEN OR PENCIL TO ANSWER. Please mark your choice clearly by filling in the appropriate bubble. When it says "MARK ALL THAT APPLY" you may mark more than one answer.

3. PROVIDE YOUR BACKGROUND INFORMATION. The information asked in the section "Your Background" on the last two pages is essential for analyzing the data. Please answer these questions.

4. YOUR PARTICIPATION IS NEEDED. We need everyone to answer this survey so that the data will be complete and representative of all soldiers.

5. USE THE RETURN ENVELOPE. After you have completed the survey, please place the questionnaire in the pre-paid envelope provided and return it.

THIS SURVEY SHOULD TAKE APPROXIMATELY 15 MINUTES
↓ BEGIN SURVEY HERE ↓

CAREER MATTERS

1. **Do you agree or disagree with the following?**
   MARK A RESPONSE FOR EACH.

   Column headers (right to left): Strongly agree / Agree / Neither agree nor disagree / Disagree / Strongly disagree

   a. I believe that the Army leadership will make the best decisions to maintain a quality Army
   b. The Army will protect my benefits and retirement
   c. I am confident I will be promoted as high as my ability and interest warrant if I stay in the Army
   d. I am very likely to get assignments that match my skills and interests if I stay in the Army

2. **At your current rank, how fair are the selections for...**
   MARK A RESPONSE FOR EACH

   Column headers (right to left): Very unfair / Unfair / Neither fair nor unfair / Fair / Very fair / Not applicable at my rank

   a. training/developmental courses?
   b. developmental assignments?
   c. promotion?

3. **Which ONE of the following describes your current active duty Army career intentions? MARK ONE.**
   O DEFINITELY stay in until retirement
   O PROBABLY stay in until retirement
   O DEFINITELY stay in beyond my present obligation, but not necessarily to retirement
   O PROBABLY stay in beyond my present obligation, but not necessarily to retirement
   O PROBABLY leave upon completion of my present obligation
   O DEFINITELY leave upon completion of my present obligation

Please continue on next page ➡

YOU AND YOUR UNIT

4. How would you rate <u>your</u> current level of morale?
- O Very high
- O High
- O Moderate
- O Low
- O Very low

5. How would you rate your current level of morale compared to your morale one year ago?
- O Much higher
- O Higher
- O About the same
- O Lower
- O Much lower

6. How would you rate the climate in your unit regarding... MARK A RESPONSE FOR EACH.

Very poor
Poor
Neither good nor poor
Good
Very good

- a. unit cohesion? ____ O O O O O
- b. respect <u>from</u> the chain of command? ____ O O O O O
- c. respect <u>for</u> the chain of command? ____ O O O O O
- d. the overall EO environment? ____ O O O O O
- e. concern for soldiers' families? ____ O O O O O

DEPLOYMENTS

7. Have you been deployed as part of Operation Enduring Freedom or Operation Iraqi Freedom?
- O Yes
- O No
- O Don't know

The Army defines **direct ground combat** as engaging an enemy on the ground with individual or crew served weapons, while being exposed to hostile fire and to a high probability of direct physical contact with the hostile force's personnel.

8. Have you been involved in direct ground combat in the last 2 years?
- O Yes
- O No
- O Don't know

REASONS FOR JOINING

Listed below are some reasons why persons join the Army. For Questions 9, 10 and 11 below, please select the three reasons which <u>most</u> influenced you to join the Army.

1. Travel
2. Army advertising
3. Army recruiter
4. Desire to serve my country
5. Develop self-discipline
6. Earn more money than previous job(s)
7. Educational benefits
8. Family support services
9. Get away from a personal problem
10. Influence of family
11. Influence of friends
12. Lack of civilian employment opportunities
13. Medical care benefits
14. Military tradition in family
15. Need to be on my own
16. Retirement pay and benefits
17. Security and stability of a job
18. Training in job skills
19. To become a U.S. citizen
20. Other (write in below)

9. Fill in the item number of the FIRST most important reason for joining

____ (if you picked #20, please describe below)

10. Fill in the item number of the SECOND most important reason for joining

____ (if you picked #20, please describe below)

11. Fill in the item number of the THIRD most important reason for joining

____ (if you picked #20, please describe below)

Description of #20, 'Other', *if used*:

_____
_____
_____
_____
_____

PERSONAL BELIEFS

12. The following are some possible uses of the military. Please indicate how important you consider each potential role of the military.

Don't know
Not at all important
Somewhat unimportant
Somewhat important
Very important

a. To fight and win our country's wars ⬤ ⬤ ⬤ ⬤ ⬤

b. As an instrument of foreign policy, even if that means engaging in operations other than war (such as nation-building or peacekeeping) ⬤ ⬤ ⬤ ⬤ ⬤

c. To provide disaster relief within the U.S. ⬤ ⬤ ⬤ ⬤ ⬤

d. To address humanitarian needs abroad ⬤ ⬤ ⬤ ⬤ ⬤

e. To intervene in civil wars abroad ⬤ ⬤ ⬤ ⬤ ⬤

f. To combat drug trafficking ⬤ ⬤ ⬤ ⬤ ⬤

g. To deal with domestic disorder in the U.S. (if it arises) ⬤ ⬤ ⬤ ⬤ ⬤

h. Enforcing immigration laws along the nation's borders ⬤ ⬤ ⬤ ⬤ ⬤

i. To fight terrorism ⬤ ⬤ ⬤ ⬤ ⬤

13. Please indicate whether you agree or disagree with the following statements:

Disagree
Agree

a. Sometimes politics and government seem so complicated that a person like me can't really understand what's going on ⬤ ⬤

b. People like me don't have any say about what the government does ⬤ ⬤

c. Public officials don't care much what people like me think ⬤ ⬤

14. Some people feel that the government in Washington should see to it that every person has a job and a good standard of living...Others think the government should just let each person get ahead on his/her own. Where would you place yourself on this scale?

Govt. Guarantee Job & Standard of Living → | Everyone on Their Own ↓

1 2 3 4 5 6 7
⬤ ⬤ ⬤ ⬤ ⬤ ⬤ ⬤

15. For each of the following government programs, indicate whether you feel it should be expanded, kept about the same, or cut back.

Don't know
Cut back
Kept about the same
Expanded

a. Education ⬤ ⬤ ⬤ ⬤

b. Defense spending ⬤ ⬤ ⬤ ⬤

c. Social Security ⬤ ⬤ ⬤ ⬤

d. Military aid to other nations ⬤ ⬤ ⬤ ⬤

e. Economic aid to other nations ⬤ ⬤ ⬤ ⬤

f. Health care ⬤ ⬤ ⬤ ⬤

g. Programs to combat violence and crime ⬤ ⬤ ⬤ ⬤

h. Homeland security ⬤ ⬤ ⬤ ⬤

16. How would you rate the condition of the national economy these days?
- ⬤ Very good
- ⬤ Fairly good
- ⬤ Fairly bad
- ⬤ Very bad
- ⬤ Don't know / no opinion

17. Do you think the economy is getting better or worse?
- ⬤ Getting better
- ⬤ Getting worse
- ⬤ Staying about the same
- ⬤ Don't know / no opinion

18. How would you compare your personal financial situation today with your financial situation one year ago?
- ⬤ Better
- ⬤ Worse
- ⬤ About the same
- ⬤ Don't know / no opinion

19. Looking ahead, how do you think your personal financial situation will be one year from now?
- ⬤ Better
- ⬤ Worse
- ⬤ About the same
- ⬤ Don't know / no opinion

Please continue on next page ➡

20. Please indicate your position on the following domestic issues

Don't know/ No opinion
Strongly Oppose
Oppose
Favor
Strongly Favor

a. Banning the death penalty_____ O O O O O

b. Relaxing environmental regulations
   to stimulate economic growth _____ O O O O O

c. Allowing prayer in public schools _____ O O O O O

d. Placing more restrictions on gun
   ownership_____ O O O O O

e. Outlawing abortion entirely_____ O O O O O

21. How much guidance does your religion provide in your day-to-day living?
- O I am not religious
- O No guidance
- O Some guidance
- O Quite a bit of guidance
- O A great deal of guidance

GENDER RELATIONS

22. Generally, do you think there is more or less sexual discrimination in the military as in civilian society at large?
- O More sexual discrimination in the military
- O About the same
- O Less sexual discrimination in the military
- O Don't know / no opinion

23. Some people feel that women should have an equal role with men in running business, industry and government. Others feel that women's place is in the home. Where would you place yourself on this scale?

Equal Role for   Woman's Place is
Women   in the Home
   ↓   ↓
   1   2   3   4   5   6   7
   O   O   O   O   O   O   O

RACIAL / ETHNIC RELATIONS

24. Generally, do you think there is more or less racial and ethnic discrimination in the military as in civilian society at large?
- O More racial and ethnic discrimination in the military
- O About the same
- O Less racial and ethnic discrimination in the military
- O Don't know / no opinion

25. Consider the people you come in contact with in the social or community groups to which you belong. What percentage of the people you spend your free time with are of the same racial or ethnic group as you?

0% 10   20   30   40   50   60   70   80   90   100%
O   O   O   O   O   O   O   O   O   O   O

26. What percentage of the people you spend your free time with are in the military?

0% 10   20   30   40   50   60   70   80   90   100%
O   O   O   O   O   O   O   O   O   O   O

27. Thinking about the people you work with on a day-to-day basis, what percentage of the people you work with are of the same racial or ethnic group as you?

0% 10   20   30   40   50   60   70   80   90   100%
O   O   O   O   O   O   O   O   O   O   O

28. During your Army service, have you had anyone you would describe as a mentor (that is, a senior ranking person who regularly assisted you and gave you advice on your career)?
- O Yes
- O No
- O Don't know

29. If you had a mentor, was he or she of the same racial or ethnic group as you?
- O Yes
- O No
- O Don't know

30. Thinking about the last time you were considered for promotion, do you think your race or ethnicity helped or hurt you in the selection process?
- O My race or ethnicity helped
- O No effect
- O My race or ethnicity hurt
- O Don't know / No opinion

RACIAL / ETHNIC RELATIONS
IN SOCIETY & THE ARMY

The next set of questions asks about racial and ethnic relations in society and the Army. For the first question in each pair, think about society in general—not including the Army. The second question in each pair asks specifically about that aspect of racial and ethnic relations in the Army.

Society

31. How frequently or infrequently do you feel that you are subject to racial or ethnic discrimination by people *outside of the Army*?
- O Not frequently at all
- O Somewhat infrequently
- O Somewhat frequently
- O Very frequently

33. Thinking about society in general: In order to make up for past discrimination, do you favor or oppose programs which make special efforts to help minorities get ahead?
- O Favor
- O Neither favor or oppose
- O Oppose
- O Don't know / no opinion

35. Thinking about society in general: How would you describe relations between whites and Hispanics?
- O Generally good
- O Neither good nor bad
- O Generally bad
- O Don't know / no opinion

37. Thinking about society in general: How would you describe relations between blacks and Hispanics?
- O Generally good
- O Neither good nor bad
- O Generally bad
- O Don't know / no opinion

39. Thinking about society in general: On the whole, do you think affirmative action programs help or hurt Hispanics?
- O Help Hispanics
- O Don't affect Hispanics
- O Hurt Hispanics
- O Don't know / no opinion

41. Have you personally experienced discrimination in the civilian world because of your race or ethnicity?
- O Yes
- O No
- O Don't know

The Army

32. How frequently or infrequently do you feel that you are subject to racial or ethnic discrimination by people *in the Army*?
- O Not frequently at all
- O Somewhat infrequently
- O Somewhat frequently
- O Very frequently

34. Thinking about the Army: In order to make up for past discrimination, do you favor or oppose programs which make special efforts to help minorities get ahead?
- O Favor
- O Neither favor or oppose
- O Oppose
- O Don't know / no opinion

36. Thinking about the Army: How would you describe relations between whites and Hispanics?
- O Generally good
- O Neither good nor bad
- O Generally bad
- O Don't know / no opinion

38. Thinking about the Army: How would you describe relations between blacks and Hispanics?
- O Generally good
- O Neither good nor bad
- O Generally bad
- O Don't know / no opinion

40. Thinking about the Army: On the whole, do you think affirmative action programs help or hurt Hispanics?
- O Help Hispanics
- O Don't affect Hispanics
- O Hurt Hispanics
- O Don't know / no opinion

42. Have you personally experienced discrimination in your *current unit* because of your race or ethnicity?
- O Yes
- O No
- O Don't know

Please continue on next page ➡

CIVIC PARTICIPATION

43. Are you currently registered to vote?
- O Yes (if Yes, go to question 44)
- O No (if No, skip to question 45)

44. If you are registered to vote, where are you registered?
- O Registered where I currently live
- O Registered at home-of-record
- O Don't know

45. In 2000, Al Gore ran for President on the Democratic ticket against George W. Bush for the Republicans and Ralph Nader for the Green Party. Did you vote in that election?

O Yes, I voted in 2000   O Don't remember   O No, I did not vote (if no, skip to question 47)

46. If you voted in the 2000 Presidential Election: How did you vote?

O In person   O By absentee ballot   O Don't remember

47. Thinking back to that election, did your unit voting officer brief you on procedures for registering to vote?
- O Yes
- O No
- O Don't remember
- O I was not in the Army at the time

48. As a private individual (not representing the Army or otherwise not in your official capacity), have you ever done any of the following during an election or campaign?

	YES	NO	Don't Know
a. Given money to a political organization party, or committee favoring a particular candidate or slate of candidates?	O	O	O
b. Worn a campaign button, put a campaign sticker on your car, or placed a sign in your window?	O	O	O

49. In terms of politics and political beliefs, we hear a lot of talk these days about liberals and conservatives. Where would you place the Republican Party on the following scale?

Extremely Liberal — Liberal — Slightly Liberal — Moderate — Slightly Conservative — Conservative — Extremely Conservative
O   O   O   O   O   O   O

50. In terms of politics and political beliefs, where would you place the Democratic Party?

Extremely Liberal — Liberal — Slightly Liberal — Moderate — Slightly Conservative — Conservative — Extremely Conservative
O   O   O   O   O   O   O

51. In terms of politics and political beliefs, where would you place enlisted soldiers in general?

Extremely Liberal — Liberal — Slightly Liberal — Moderate — Slightly Conservative — Conservative — Extremely Conservative
O   O   O   O   O   O   O

52. In terms of politics and political beliefs, where would you place officers in general?

Extremely Liberal — Liberal — Slightly Liberal — Moderate — Slightly Conservative — Conservative — Extremely Conservative
O   O   O   O   O   O   O

53. In terms of politics and political beliefs, where would you place yourself?

Extremely Liberal — Liberal — Slightly Liberal — Moderate — Slightly Conservative — Conservative — Extremely Conservative
O   O   O   O   O   O   O

54. Do you think of yourself as someone who identifies with one of the major political parties (i.e. Republican or Democratic Party)?

O Yes   O No   O Don't Know

    (if No, or Don't Know, skip question #55 and go to question #56 on next page)

55. If yes, how strong would you describe your attachment to this party?

O Strong   O Weak   O Don't Know

YOUR BACKGROUND

The information requested in this section is essential for analyzing the data. All of your responses will remain confidential.

56. Are you male or female?
- O Male   O Female

57. Are you of Hispanic, Latino, or Spanish origin or ancestry (of any race)? MARK ALL THAT APPLY.
- O No, not of Hispanic, Latino, or Spanish ancestry
- O Yes, Mexican, Mexican American, Chicano
- O Yes, Puerto Rican
- O Yes, Cuban
- O Yes, other Hispanic / Spanish / Latino

58. If you are married, is your spouse of Hispanic, Latino, or Spanish origin or ancestry (of any race)? MARK ALL THAT APPLY
- O I am not married
- O No, not of Hispanic, Latino, or Spanish ancestry
- O Yes, Mexican, Mexican American, Chicano
- O Yes, Puerto Rican
- O Yes, Cuban
- O Yes, other Hispanic / Spanish / Latino

59. What is your race? MARK ALL THAT APPLY.
- O American Indian or Alaska Native (e.g., Eskimo, Aleut)
- O Asian (e.g., Asian Indian, Chinese, Filipino, Japanese, Korea, Vietnamese)
- O Black or African American
- O Native Hawaiian or other Pacific Islander (e.g., Samoan, Guamanian, Chamorro)
- O White
- O Hispanic / Spanish / Latino
- O Other (Write here:_____)

60. If you are married, what is the race of your spouse? MARK ALL THAT APPLY.
- O I am not married
- O American Indian or Alaska Native (e.g., Eskimo, Aleut)
- O Asian (e.g., Asian Indian, Chinese, Filipino, Japanese, Korea, Vietnamese)
- O Black or African American
- O Native Hawaiian or other Pacific Islander (e.g., Samoan, Guamanian, Chamorro)
- O White
- O Hispanic / Spanish / Latino
- O Other (Write here:_____)

61. Do most of your immediate family members live in the United States or in another country?
- O Most live in another country
- O Most live in the United States
- O Equally divided between U.S. and another country

62. What is your current U.S. citizenship status?
- O I am a U.S. citizen
- O I am not a U.S. citizen
- O Don't know

63. Where were you born?
- O United States
- O Another Country (Write here:_____)

64. If you were *not born in the U.S.*, were you born abroad of U.S. parents?
- O Yes
- O No
- O One parent was a U.S. citizen, the other was not
- O I was born in the U.S.

65. Please indicate where the following people were born:

	In the United States	Somewhere other than the U.S.	Don't Know
a. Your mother	O	O	O
b. Your father	O	O	O
c. Your mother's mother	O	O	O
d. Your mother's father	O	O	O
e. Your father's mother	O	O	O
f. Your father's father	O	O	O

66. What was the first language you learned while you were growing up?
- O English
- O Spanish
- O Both English and Spanish
- O Other- If other, what was the first language you learned? _____

67. How would you describe how well you speak the following languages?

	I cannot speak the language at all	I can only speak in simple phrases	I can only handle basic conversations	I can generally handle complex conversations	I am completely fluent
a. English	O	O	O	O	O
b. Spanish	O	O	O	O	O
c. Other Language (Write here:_____) (If none, leave blank)	O	O	O	O	O
d. Other Language (Write here:_____) (If none, leave blank)	O	O	O	O	O

68. Do you have any siblings (brothers or sisters) that have served or are serving in the military?
- O Yes
- O No

69. If you are married, has your spouse ever served in the military?
- O Yes
- O No
- O I am not married

Please continue to last page ➡

70. What was your father (or stepfather's) military service status?
- O No military service or Don't Know
- O Served less than 20 years; no longer in active service
- O Now on active duty
- O Served 20 years or more; retired from active service
- O Now on Reserve / National Guard status

71. What was your mother (or stepmother's) military service status?
- O No military service or Don't Know
- O Served less than 20 years; no longer in active service
- O Now on active duty
- O Served 20 years or more; retired from active service
- O Now on Reserve\National Guard status

72. If you were asked to use one of three names for your family's social-economic class, which would you say best describes your family?
- O Working class
- O Middle class
- O Upper class

73. Which of the following best describes the place where you grew up?
- O A big city
- O The suburbs or outskirts of a big city
- O A small city or town
- O A country village
- O A farm or home in the country

74. What is your rank?

Officers	Warrant Officers	Enlisted	
O 2LT	O WO1	O PV1	O SFC
O 1LT	O CW2	O PV2	O MSG/1SG
O CPT	O CW3	O PFC	O SGM/CSM
O MAJ	O CW4	O CPL/SPC	
O LTC	O CW5	O SGT	
O COL+		O SSG	

75. What is your source of commission?
- O Does not apply; I am not a commissioned officer
- O OCS
- O ROTC
- O USMA
- O Direct Appointment
- O Appointed (Warrant Officer only)
- O Other

76. What was your age on your last birthday?
- O Under 20
- O 20-24 years old
- O 25-29 years old
- O 30-34 years old
- O 35-39 years old
- O 40-44 years old
- O 45-49 years old
- O 50 or over

77. What is the highest level of education you have completed? MARK ONE.
- O Some high school or less, but no diploma, certificate, or GED
- O High school diploma or GED
- O From 1 to 2 years of college, but no degree
- O Associate degree
- O From 3 to 4 years of college, but no degree
- O Bachelor's degree
- O A year or more of graduate credit, but no graduate degree
- O Master's degree
- O Doctorate degree
- O Professional degree, such as MD, DDS, or JD

78. To what kind of unit are you currently assigned?
- O Combat Arms (CA) (TOE units only)
- O Combat Support (CS) (TOE units only)
- O Combat Service Support (CSS) (TOE units only)
- O Joint Command
- O Allied Command
- O Other Command (TDA units)
- O Do not know

79. What is your current unit leadership position?
- O Does not apply; I am not in a leadership position.
- O Brigade Commander
- O Battalion Commander
- O Company/Battery Commander
- O Detachment Commander
- O Platoon Leader
- O Command Sergeant Major
- O First Sergeant
- O Platoon Sergeant
- O Squad Leader
- O Team Leader
- O Other leadership position
  (Please write here_____)

80. How many total years of active military service have you completed? MARK ONE

O 1 or less	O 8	O 15	O 22
O 2	O 9	O 16	O 23
O 3	O 10	O 17	O 24
O 4	O 11	O 18	O 25
O 5	O 12	O 19	O 26
O 6	O 13	O 20	O 27
O 7	O 14	O 21	O 28 or more

81. What is your Military Occupational Specialty (MOS), Branch, or your primary Area of Concentration (AOC)?

_____

(11B for Infantry, for example. If you do not know the letter code for your MOS, just describe it.)

THANK YOU FOR TAKING THE TIME TO COMPLETE THIS SURVEY. PLEASE RETURN THIS SURVEY IN THE INCLUDED PRE-PAID RETURN ENVELOPE.

If you would like to make any comments on the topics of this survey please write them on the included comment sheet and return it with the survey.

The 2004 Cadet Preelection Survey

As discussed in chapter 8, the 2004 Cadet Preelection Survey was administered through a secure Web site from Saturday, October 30, until 5 p.m. on Tuesday, November 2 (Election Day). A total of 1,628 cadets, including the entire sophomore class, half of the junior class, and a small number of freshmen were eligible to take the survey. Responses to the survey yielded a final sample size for analysis of 885, including responses from 738 men and 129 women (18 respondents did not indicate their gender on the survey). The survey response rate was therefore 54.4%. Broken down by gender and race, the composition of the final sample is shown in table B.1. These subsample sizes roughly approximate the demographics of the entire population of cadets at West Point. Results presented in this book reflect weighted values to account for discrepancies in response rates among racial and ethnic groups.

The online survey was also followed up with 87 open-ended surveys that focused more specifically on attitude changes while at West Point. The questions in that follow-up survey covered cadet perceptions of the role that peers and instructors play in shaping political attitudes. These follow-up surveys were collected at the beginning of seven separate focus-group sessions that were spent discussing cadet perceptions of attitude changes while at West Point.

TABLE B.1
Gender and Race/Ethnicity of Cadet Survey Respondents

	Men		Women		Total	
	N	%	N	%	N	%
White	596	68.7	96	11.1	692	79.8
Hispanic	55	6.3	13	1.5	68	7.8
Black	13	1.5	5	0.6	18	2.1
Other/Unknown	74	8.5	15	1.7	89	10.3
Total	738	85.1	129	14.9	867	100

Source: 2004 Cadet Preelection Survey.

Pre-Election Survey

INSTRUCTIONS:

- READ CAREFULLY EACH QUESTION AND ALL THE POSSIBLE RESPONSES before selecting your response.

- Please mark your response by clicking on the appropriate button or checkbox(s). Provide written comments by clicking on the text box provided and typing your comments.

- PROVIDE YOUR BACKGROUND INFORMATION. The information asked in the section "Your Background" in the last section of the survey form is essential for analyzing the data. Please answer these questions.

- YOUR PARTICIPATION IS NEEDED. We need everyone to answer this survey so that the data will be complete and representative of all cadets.

- Answers are not recorded until you reach the end of the form and press the Submit button.

THIS SURVEY SHOULD TAKE APPROXIMATELY 15 MINUTES
↓ BEGIN SURVEY HERE ↓

CAREER MATTERS

1. Do you agree or disagree with the following?

MARK A RESPONSE FOR EACH	Strongly agree	Agree	Neither agree nor disagree	Disagree	Strongly disagree
a. I believe that the Army leadership will make the best decisions to maintain a quality Army	○	○	○	○	○
b. The Army will protect my benefits and retirement	○	○	○	○	○
c. I am confident I will be promoted as high as my ability and interest warrant if I stay in the Army	○	○	○	○	○
d. I am very likely to get assignments that match my skills and interests if I stay in the Army	○	○	○	○	○

2. Which ONE of the following describes your current active duty Army career intentions? MARK ONE.

○ DEFINITELY stay in until retirement

○ PROBABLY stay in until retirement

○ DEFINITELY stay in beyond my present obligation, but not necessarily until retirement

○ PROBABLY stay in beyond my present obligation, but not necessarily until retirement

○ PROBABLY leave upon completion of my present obligation

○ DEFINITELY leave upon completion of my present obligation

3. When you graduate from the Military Academy, you will enter one of the branches of the Army. Based on what you know now, which one of the following is most appealing to you? MARK ONE.

○ Combat Arms (Air Defense Artillery, Armor, Aviation, Engineers, Field Artillery, Infantry)

○ Combat Support (Chemical, Military Intelligence, Military Police, Signal)

○ Combat Service Support (Adjutant General, Finance, Medical Service, Ordnance, Quartermaster, Transportation)

○ Special (Judge Advocate General, Medical/Veterinary/Dental, Nurse)

○ Inter-service commission (e.g., USN, USAF, USMC)

YOU AND YOUR COMPANY

---

4. How would you rate your current level of morale?

○ Very high

○ High

○ Moderate

○ Low

○ Very low

5. How would you rate the current level of morale in your company?

○ Very high

○ High

○ Moderate

○ Low

○ Very low

6. How would you rate the current level of morale in the Corps of Cadets?

○ Very high

○ High

○ Moderate

○ Low

○ Very low

7. Did you serve in the Armed Forces prior to coming to West Point?

O No

O Yes

8. If you served in the Armed Forces prior to coming to West Point, how would you describe that service?

O I did not serve prior to West Point

O I served active-duty enlisted in the Army

O I served in the National Guard

O I served in a different branch (Navy, AF etc.)

O Other. Describe

[_____ ⬍]

REASONS FOR JOINING

Listed below are some reasons why persons come to West Point. For Questions 9, 10, and 11 below, please select the three reasons which most influenced you to attend West Point.

1. Top tier education
2. Desire to serve my country
3. Travel
4. No tuition
5. Future opportunities as a West Point Graduate
6. Get away from a personal problem
7. Influence of family
8. Influence of friends
9. Lack of civilian employment opportunities
10. Medical care
11. Military tradition in family
12. Pay and allowances
13. Prestige of West Point
14. Retirement pay and benefits
15. Security and stability of a job
16. Adventure
17. Challenge
18. Chance to play collegiate-level athletics
19. The events of September 11, 2001
20. Want to go to combat
21. Develop self-discipline
22. Other (write in below)

9. Fill in (select from the drop down box below) the item number of the FIRST most important reason for joining

[_____ ▼] **(if you picked #22, please describe below)**

10. Fill in (select from the drop down box below) the item number of the SECOND most important reason for joining

[▼] **(if you picked #22, please describe below)**

11. Fill in (select from the drop down box below) the item number of the THIRD most important reason for joining

[▼] **(if you picked #22, please describe below)**

Description of #22, "Other," if used:

[▲]
[▼]

PERSONAL BELIEFS

12. How much of the time do you think you can trust the government in Washington to do what is right—just about always, most of the time, or only some of the time?

O Just about always
O Most of the time
O Only some of the time
O Don't know/No opinion

13. Would you say the government is pretty much run by a few big interests looking out for themselves or that it is run for the benefit of all the people?

O A few big interests looking out for themselves
O Run for the benefit of all the people
O Don't know/No opinion

14. Do you think that people in the government waste a lot of the money we pay in taxes, waste some of it, or don't waste very much of it?

O Waste a lot of money
O Waste some of it
O Don't waste very much
O Don't know/No opinion

15. Do you think that quite a few of the people running the government are crooked, not very many are, or do you think hardly any of them are crooked?

O Quite a few
O Not very many
O Hardly any of them
O Don't know/No opinion

16. Please indicate whether you agree or disagree with the following statements:

	Agree	Disagree	Neither
a. Sometimes politics and government seem so complicated that a person like me can't really understand what's going on	O	O	O
b. People like me don't have any say about what the government does	O	O	O
c. Public officials don't care much what people like me think	O	O	O

17. Generally, do you think there is more, less, or about the same amount of racial discrimination in the military as in civilian society at large?
O More racial discrimination in the military
O About the same
O Less racial discrimination in the military
O Don't know/No opinion

18. Generally, do you think there is more, less, or about the same amount of sexual discrimination in the military as in civilian society at large?
O More sexual discrimination in the military
O About the same
O Less sexual discrimination in the military
O Don't know/No opinion

19. In order to make up for past discrimination, do you favor or oppose programs which make special efforts to help minorities?
O Favor
O Oppose
O Don't know/No opinion

20. Some people believe that we should spend much less money for defense. Others feel that defense spending should be greatly increased. Where would you place yourself on this scale?

Spend Much Less						Greatly Increase Spending
↓						↓
1	2	3	4	5	6	7
O	O	O	O	O	O	O

21. Do you think we should return to a military draft, or should we continue to rely on volunteers?
O Return to a military draft
O Continue to rely on volunteers
O Don't know/No opinion

22. Would you favor or oppose a law that would allow homosexuals to serve openly in the military?
O Strongly favor
O Somewhat favor
O Somewhat oppose
O Strongly oppose
O Don't know/No opinion

23. Would you favor or oppose a change in Army policy that would allow women to serve in the Infantry or Armor branches?
O Strongly favor
O Somewhat favor
O Somewhat oppose
O Strongly oppose
O Don't know/No opinion

24. The following are some possible uses of the military. Please indicate how important you consider each potential role of the military.

	Very important	Somewhat important	Somewhat unimportant	Not at all important	Don't know
a. To fight and win our country's wars	O	O	O	O	O
b. As an instrument of foreign policy, even if that means engaging in operations other than war (such as nation-building or peacekeeping)	O	O	O	O	O
c. To provide disaster relief within the U.S.	O	O	O	O	O
d. To address humanitarian needs abroad	O	O	O	O	O
e. To intervene in civil wars abroad	O	O	O	O	O
f. To combat drug trafficking	O	O	O	O	O
g. To deal with domestic disorder in the U.S. (if it arises)	O	O	O	O	O
h. Enforcing immigration laws along the nation's borders	O	O	O	O	O
i. To fight terrorism	O	O	O	O	O

25. Please indicate whether you agree or disagree with the following statements:

	Agree	Disagree	Don't know/ No opinion
a. Members of the military should not publicly criticize a senior member of the civilian branch of the government.	O	O	O
b. Members of the military should be allowed to publicly express their political views just like any other citizen.	O	O	O
c. Members of the military should vote while serving on active duty.	O	O	O

26. Should the United States try to change a dictatorship to a democracy where it can, OR should the United States stay out of other countries' affairs?

O Change to Democracy when it can

O Stay out of other countries' affairs

O Don't know/No opinion

27. How would you rate the condition of the national economy these days? Is it very good, fairly good, fairly bad, or very bad?

O Very good

O Fairly good

O Fairly bad

O Very bad

O Don't know/No opinion

28. Do you think the economy is getting better, getting worse, or staying about the same?

O Getting better

O Getting worse

O Staying about the same

O Don't know/No opinion

29. If you had to choose, would you rather have a smaller government providing fewer services, or a bigger government providing more services?

O Smaller government with fewer services

O Bigger government with more services

O Don't know/No opinion

30. If you had to choose, would you prefer reducing the federal budget deficit or cutting taxes?

O Reduce the federal budget deficit

O Cut taxes

O Don't know/No opinion

31. Some people feel that the government in Washington should see to it that every person has a job and a good standard of living... Others think the government should just let each person get ahead on his/her own. Where would you place yourself on this scale?

Govt. Guarantee Job & Standard of Living						Everyone on Their Own
↓						↓
1	2	3	4	5	6	7
O	O	O	O	O	O	O

32. Some people feel that women should have an equal role with men in running business, industry, and government. Others feel that women's place is in the home. Where would you place yourself on this scale?

Equal Role for Women   Woman's Place Is in the Home

1	2	3	4	5	6	7
O	O	O	O	O	O	O

33a. Which of the following opinions best agrees with your view?

O By law, abortion should never be permitted.

O The law should permit abortion only in case of rape, incest, or when the woman's life is in danger.

O The law should permit abortion for reasons other than rape, incest, or danger to the woman's life, but only after the need for the abortion has been clearly established.

O By law, a woman should always be able to obtain an abortion as a matter of personal choice.

33b. Which of the following views comes closest to your opinion on the issue of school prayer?

O By law, prayer should not be allowed in public schools.

O The law should allow public schools to schedule time when children can pray silently if they want to.

O The law should allow public schools to schedule a time when children as a group can say a general prayer not tied to a particular religious faith.

O By law, public schools should schedule a time when all children would say a chosen Christian prayer.

33c. Would you favor or oppose a law which would require a person to obtain a police permit before he or she could buy a gun?

O Favor

O Oppose

O Don't know/No opinion

33d. Do you agree or disagree that homosexual couples should have the right to marry one another?

O Favor

O Oppose

O Don't know/No opinion

33e. Do you favor or oppose the death penalty for persons convicted of murder?

O Favor

O Oppose

O Don't know/No opinion

34. Would you say your religion provides no guidance in your day-to-day living, some guidance, quite a bit of guidance, or a great deal of guidance in your day-to-day life?
O I am not religious
O No guidance
O Some guidance
O Quite a bit of guidance
O A great deal of guidance

35. Apart from occasional weddings, baptisms, or funerals, how often do you attend Church or religious services? Is it once a week or more, almost every week, once or twice a month, a few times a year, once a year or less, or never?
O Every week
O Almost every week
O Once or twice a month
O A few times a year
O Never
O I am not religious

36. Are you registered to vote?
O Yes
O No

37. Are you registered to vote in the state of New York or are you registered to vote in your home-of-record?
O Registered in New York
O Registered at home-of-record
O Not registered
O Don't know

38. What are your thoughts regarding the current size of the Active Duty Army?
O It should be increased
O It should be decreased
O It should stay the same
O Don't know/no opinion

39. How concerned are you about the following aspects of Army life?

	Very concerned	Somewhat concerned	Not at all concerned	Don't know/ No opinion
a. Service in a combat zone	O	O	O	O
b. Frequency of deployments	O	O	O	O
c. Adequate pay	O	O	O	O
d. Impact of Army on family life	O	O	O	O
e. Other (please describe below)	O	O	O	O

40. In terms of politics and political beliefs, we hear a lot of talk these days about liberals and conservatives. Where would you place the Democratic Party?

Extremely Liberal	Liberal	Slightly Liberal	Moderate	Slightly Conservative	Conservative	Extremely Conservative
O	O	O	O	O	O	O

41. Where would you place the Republican Party?

Extremely Liberal	Liberal	Slightly Liberal	Moderate	Slightly Conservative	Conservative	Extremely Conservative
O	O	O	O	O	O	O

42. Where would you place the Army as a whole?

Extremely Liberal	Liberal	Slightly Liberal	Moderate	Slightly Conservative	Conservative	Extremely Conservative
O	O	O	O	O	O	O

43. Where would you place West Point cadets in general?

Extremely Liberal	Liberal	Slightly Liberal	Moderate	Slightly Conservative	Conservative	Extremely Conservative
O	O	O	O	O	O	O

44. Where would you place officers that serve as instructors at West Point in general?

Extremely Liberal	Liberal	Slightly Liberal	Moderate	Slightly Conservative	Conservative	Extremely Conservative
O	O	O	O	O	O	O

45. Where would you place officers that serve as tactical officers at West Point in general?

Extremely Liberal	Liberal	Slightly Liberal	Moderate	Slightly Conservative	Conservative	Extremely Conservative
O	O	O	O	O	O	O

46. In terms of politics and political beliefs, where would you place yourself?

Extremely Liberal	Liberal	Slightly Liberal	Moderate	Slightly Conservative	Conservative	Extremely Conservative
O	O	O	O	O	O	O

47. Where would you place your parent(s) or guardian(s) on the following scale?

Extremely Liberal	Liberal	Slightly Liberal	Moderate	Slightly Conservative	Conservative	Extremely Conservative
O	O	O	O	O	O	O

48. Generally speaking, do you usually think of yourself as a Republican, a Democrat, an Independent, or what?

○ Republican

○ Democrat

○ Independent

○ Other. (Describe

[▲▼])

49. IF YOU IDENTIFY AS A REPUBLICAN OR DEMOCRAT— Would you say your attachment to the party is strong or not very strong?

○ Strong

○ Weak

50. IF YOU IDENTIFY AS INDEPENDENT OR OTHER— Do you think of yourself as closer to the Republican or Democratic party?

○ Closer to Republican Party

○ Closer to Democratic Party

51. Generally speaking, do you usually think of your parent(s) or guardian(s) as Republican, Democrat, Independent, or what?

○ Republican

○ Democrat

○ Independent

○ Split Affiliations (One parent is Republican, One is Democrat, etc.)

○ Other. (Describe

[▲▼])

○ Not political/Don't know

52. IF YOUR PARENT(S) OR GUARDIAN(S) IDENTIFY AS A REPUBLICAN OR DEMOCRAT— Would you say their attachment to the party is strong or not very strong?

○ Strong attachment

○ Weak attachment

53. IF YOUR PARENT(S) OR GUARDIAN(S) IDENTIFY AS INDEPENDENT OR OTHER— Do you think of them as closer to the Republican or Democratic party?

○ Closer to Republican Party

○ Closer to Democratic Party

54. Do you believe that there is pressure to identify with a particular party as a West Point cadet?

○ No

○ Yes, there is pressure to identify as a Republican

○ Yes, there is pressure to identify as a Democrat

YOUR BACKGROUND

The information requested in this section is essential for analyzing the data. All of your responses will remain confidential.

55. Are you male or female?

O Male   O Female

56. What is your race? MARK ALL THAT APPLY.

☐ American Indian or Alaska Native (e.g., Eskimo, Aleut)

☐ Asian (e.g., Asian Indian, Chinese, Filipino, Japanese, Korea, Vietnamese)

☐ Black or African American

☐ Native Hawaiian or other Pacific Islander (e.g., Samoan, Guamanian, Chamorro)

☐ White

☐ Hispanic (Latino or Spanish ancestry)

☐ Other (Write here: [＿＿＿＿＿＿＿＿＿＿＿ ▲▼])

57. What state do you call home?

[Select One ▼]

58. What was your family's reaction to your decision to attend West Point?

O Supportive

O Indifferent

O Opposed

59. Was either of your parents a graduate of USMA?

O No, neither parent was a USMA graduate

O Yes, my <u>father</u> was a USMA graduate

O Yes, my <u>mother</u> was a USMA graduate

O Yes, <u>both of my parents</u> are USMA graduates

60. What was your father's (or stepfather's) military service status?

O No military service or Don't Know

O Served less than 20 years; no longer in active service

O Now on active duty

O Served 20 years or more; retired from active service

O Now on Reserve/National Guard status

61. What was your father's (or stepfather's) military rank?

O Not applicable, father was never in the military

O Officer

O Non-Commissioned Officer (NCO)

O Enlisted

O Don't know

62. What was your mother's (or stepmother's) military service status?
O No military service or Don't Know
O Served less than 20 years; no longer in active service
O Now on active duty
O Served 20 years or more; retired from active service
O Now on Reserve/National Guard status

63. What was your mother's (or stepmother's) military rank?
O Not applicable, mother was never in the military
O Officer
O Non-Commissioned Officer (NCO)
O Enlisted
O Don't know

64. Do you have any siblings (brothers or sisters) that have served or are serving in the military?
O Yes
O No

65. How old are you today?
O 17
O 18
O 19
O 20
O 21
O 22
O 23+

66. What was the first language you learned while you were growing up?
O English
O Spanish
O Both English and Spanish
O Other—If other, what was the first language
you learned? [   ]

67. How would you describe how well you speak the following languages?

	I cannot speak the language at all	I can only speak in simple phrases	I can only handle basic conversations	I can generally handle complex conversations	I am completely fluent
a. English	O	O	O	O	O
b. Spanish	O	O	O	O	O
c. Other Language (Write here: [ ]) O (If none, leave blank)		O	O	O	O
d. Other Language (Write here: [ ]) O (If none, leave blank)		O	O	O	O

68. Are you a foreign cadet?
O No
O Yes

69. If you were asked to use one of four names for your family's social class, which would you say best describes it: the lower class, the working class, the middle class, or the upper class?
O Lower class
O Working class
O Middle class
O Upper class

70. Which of the following best describes the place where you grew up?
O A big city
O The suburbs or outskirts of a big city
O A small city or town
O A country village
O A farm or home in the country

71. What is your current GPA (Academic Only)?
O 1.99 or less
O 2.0 – 2.49
O 2.5 – 2.99
O 3.0 – 3.49
O 3.50+

72. What is your major and with which department are you majoring?

MAJOR:

Select one:	▼

DEPARTMENT:
O 1. D/Behavioral Sciences & Leadership
O 2. D/Chemistry & Life Science
O 3. D/Civil & Mechanical Engineering
O 4. D/Electrical Eng. & Computer Science
O 5. D/English
O 6. D/Foreign Languages
O 7. D/Geography & Environmental Eng.
O 8. D/History
O 9. D/Law

O 10. D/Mathematics
O 11. D/Physics
O 12. D/Social Sciences
O 13. D/Systems Engineering

73. Did you graduate from a public or private high school?
○ Public
○ Private
○ Other (home school)

If you would like to make any comments on the topics of this survey please write them in the block below. Especially annotate any questions that you did not understand or felt were confusing. If applicable, please indicate the question number to which your comment is related.

THANK YOU FOR TAKING THE TIME TO COMPLETE THIS SURVEY.

Click here to review your answers

Please complete your survey form by clicking on the button below.

Click Here to Submit Your Survey Form

Follow-on Questionnaire:

Type your answer below each question.

1. Have your political views changed significantly since you came to West Point? If so, how?

2. Did you affiliate with, or feel attached to, a political party before you came to West Point? Has that affiliation changed since you have been here? Why?

3. Do you feel free to openly discuss your political views among other cadets? in the classroom? (If not, please explain why.)

4. Do officers openly discuss their personal political affiliations with you? Have any officers at West Point encouraged you to vote one way or another? How so?

5. What assumptions, if any, do people make about your political views?

Any additional comments you would like to make:

Comparison Surveys

THE 2004 NATIONAL ANNENBERG ELECTION SURVEY

Whenever possible the 2004 National Annenberg Election Survey (NAES) was the primary survey used for comparison with the C&S Survey data due to the large size of the NAES sample. Because of the size and time span of the NAES (late 2003 through 2004), I deleted all surveys conducted prior to April 1, 2004, from the data set. This ensured that respondents to the NAES and C&S Survey were answering their respective surveys during approximately the same time period. I also excluded active members of the military from the NAES sample. The NAES does not provide weights with its data set, so I used the age and sex demographic information provided in the NAES codebook to allow for proportional weighting of the NAES subsample selected for comparison with the C&S Survey.

TRIANGLE INSTITUTE FOR SECURITY STUDIES, 1998–1999

When citing data on civilian attitudes or from the entire military sample from the Triangle Institute for Security Studies (TISS) survey, I reported marginals directly from the published works of those involved in the survey project. In an effort to compare army officers directly with army officers, I used the data and codebook to pull out only active-duty army officers. These data were not weighted.

MILITARY TIMES SURVEYS, 2003–2007

The Military Times Company has conducted surveys of its subscribers annually since 2003. As noted briefly in chapter 9, these surveys overrepresent officers, whites, and males. As an example, 42% of the sample in 2004 consisted of officers while officers made up only 14% of the army population in 2004. Similarly, the sample population was 77% white and 12% female while the army in 2004 was 60% white and 15% female. There is also the issue of the sample population consisting of the type of person who chooses to subscribe to a professional trade newspaper. In an effort to mitigate the biases inherent in the sample population, I limited comparisons between the Military Times and C&S survey data sets to the populations of majors and above. Within this population, the subscriber bias should be minimal in that most officers above the rank of major are likely to be fully committed to the army as a career and to be the type of people who subscribe to a publication dedicated to news about their profession. The 2008 data are from the Military Times Election Survey, which is conducted separately from the annual surveys and fields a more narrow range of questions focused specifically on the election.

GENERAL SOCIAL SURVEY, 2004, AND
NATIONAL ELECTION STUDY, 2004

The General Social Survey (GSS), 2004, and the National Election Study (NES), 2004, were used "as is," with the weights included in each data set (wt2004nr for the GSS data set and V040101 for the NES data set).

CHICAGO COUNCIL ON GLOBAL AFFAIRS
(PUBLIC AND ELITE DATA SETS), 2004

The Chicago Council on Global Affairs (CCGA) surveys were used similarly to the NES and GSS surveys. No recoding or weighting was done on these data. Weights used for analysis were those provided by the CCGA with the data sets ("weight" for the public sample and "wt" for the elite sample). Data from the elite sample should be used with caution, as the definition of "foreign-policy elites" is clearly subject to debate. The composition of the CCGA elite sample, as described by CCGA, was:

> 450 leaders with foreign policy power, specialization, and expertise. These included 100 Congressional members or their senior staff, 31 from the Senate and 69 from the House; 75 university administrators and academics who teach in the area of international relations, 59 journalists and editorial staff who handle international news, 41 administration officials such assistant secretaries and other senior staff in various agencies and offices dealing with foreign policy, 50 religious leaders, 38 senior business executives from Fortune 1,000 corporations, 32 labor presidents of the largest labor unions, 29 presidents of major private foreign policy organizations, and 25 presidents of major special interest groups relevant to foreign policy. For purposes of analysis, data for each of the individual groups were also reviewed separately for comparisons among them and with the leader sample as a whole as well as with the public.

COOPERATIVE CONGRESSIONAL ELECTION STUDY, 2006

The Massachusetts Institute of Technology ran the Cooperative Congressional Election Study, or CCES, in 2006. The CCES consisted of a thirty-thousand-person national stratified sample survey. The survey consisted of two waves. The preelection phase was administered in late September to late October and rolled out in three distinct time periods: the end of September, the middle of October, and the end of October. Survey data referenced in this study utilized a small set of questions drawn up by Craig Cummings, Robert Shapiro, and I to address civilian attitudes toward the military. The sample sizes for these questions ranged from 787 to 996 respondents.

SURVEY OF COLLEGE UNDERGRADUATES
ACROSS THE UNITED STATES, 2004

Harvard University's Institute of Politics surveyed 1,202 college under-graduates via telephone between October 7 and October 13, 2004. Students were randomly selected from a database of 5.1 million college students nationwide. Data used from this survey are as reported by the institute in 2004.

FOREIGN POLICY LEADERSHIP PROJECT SURVEYS, 1976–1996

When citing data on civilian attitudes or from the entire military sample from the Foreign Policy Leadership Project (FPLP) surveys, I reported marginals directly from previously published works. For analyses specific to this book, I used the raw FPLP data to extract only active-duty military respondents and, where possible, active-duty army respondents (the FPLP surveys did not ask specifically about branch of service in all years). Here is the description of the FPLP surveys from Holsti's *Public Opinion and American Foreign Policy*:

> The FPLP has conducted surveys by means of a mailed questionnaire in March of every fourth year between 1976 and 1996. The sample for each survey, repre-senting leaders in a wide range of occupations—including politics, business, the military, the media, the State Department and Foreign Service, labor unions, churches, academia, law and health care—was drawn in part from such stan-dard sources as *Who's Who in America, Who's Who of American Women, Who's Who in American Politics*, and the *State Department Directory*. Others were included by virtue of their positions in specific institutions—for example, membership in the current class at the National War College, chief editorial writers of newspapers with circulations of one hundred thousand or more, and labor union officers. . . . Each of the six surveys brought forth completed ques-tionnaires from more than twenty-one hundred opinion leaders.

A NOTE ON SIGNIFICANCE TESTS

Marginals reported in tables reflect weighted data unless otherwise speci-fied. Significance tests between internal army populations were conducted with weighted data. Significance tests between the C&S Survey and other surveys were conducted using unweighted data. The default test statistic used is Pearson's chi-squared.

Appendix D _____

The Virtual Army and Virtual Officer Corps

THE PRIMARY DATA SET USED for the Virtual Army analysis was the NAES one. When necessary for comparing questions from the C&S Survey that were not included in the NAES, I used the NES and CCGA data sets, although this was not preferred due to the relative small size of these two data sets in comparison with that of the NAES. The size of the NAES data set allowed for selection and weighting along key demographics without resulting in a sample that was too small to be reliable. Due to the demographic specifications of the officer ranks, it was not possible to create a Virtual Officer Corps with either the NES or CCGA data set.

THE VIRTUAL ARMY (NAES)

To create the Virtual Army from the NAES data set, I first took the NAES data set, as used for comparison in the rest of this study, and dropped all respondents whose incomes did not fall within the range of incomes found within the army population.[1] I also excluded anyone with an eighth-grade or lower education (a small percentage of the army does not have a high school diploma or the equivalent—typically around 1%), as well as anyone over the age of sixty-five.

I then tabulated the remaining respondents on the dimensions of race/ethnicity (four categories: white, black, Hispanic, and other), gender, and income (five categories between $25,000 and $150,000). Using a similar tabulation of the C&S Survey data, I was thereby able to construct a proportional weighting scheme so that the NAES respondents looked like the army on these three dimensions.

THE VIRTUAL ARMY (NES AND GSS)

The same general procedure was used for the NES and CCGA data sets, although not with the same fidelity due to the small sample size in these surveys. After dropping respondents whose incomes did not fall within the range of those found in the army, I also dropped all respondents over the age of sixty-five. I did not drop any respondents from these data sets

[1] This comparison data set consisted only of those respondents who were not serving actively in the military and answered the NAES survey after April 1, 2004.

based on education, as the education categories in the NES and CCGA data sets went down to only "non-HS graduates" and did not specify lower levels of education.

The procedure for creating the proportional weights was also the same as with the NAES data set, although due to the small sample sizes of the NES and CCGA, I was able to break race/ethnicity into only two categories (white and nonwhite).

THE VIRTUAL OFFICER CORPS (NAES)

The Virtual Officer Corps was created in the same manner as the Virtual Army, with more restrictive criteria for those included in the sample. In addition to excluding more respondents from the sample on the basis of income, I also excluded noncitizens, respondents younger than twenty-one, and respondents without a bachelor's degree to reflect the fact that officers must be citizens and must have gone through a precommissioning training program, which typically requires a college degree.

Rules Governing Political Participation of Members of the Army

FROM DOD DIRECTIVE 1344.10, "Political Activities by Members of the Armed Forces on Active Duty," enclosure 3:

Active duty members of the armed services *may*: 1) Register, vote, express a personal opinion on political candidates and issues, but not as a representative of the Armed Forces. 2) Promote and encourage other military members to exercise their voting franchise, if such promotion does not constitute an attempt to influence or interfere with the outcome of an election. 3) Join a political club and attend its meetings when not in uniform. 4) Serve as an election official, if such service is not as a representative of a partisan political party, does not interfere with military duties, is performed when not in uniform, and has the prior approval of the Secretary concerned or the Secretary's designee. 5) Sign a petition for specific legislative action or a petition to place a candidate's name on an official election ballet, if the signing does not obligate the member to engage in partisan political activity and is done as a private citizen and not as a representative of the Armed Forces. 6) Write a letter to the editor of a newspaper expressing the member's personal views on public issues or political candidates, if such action is not part of an organized letterwriting campaign or a solicitation of votes for or against a political party or partisan cause or candidate. 7) Make monetary contributions to a political organization, party, or committee favoring a particular candidate or slate of candidates. 8) Display a political sticker on the member's private vehicle. 9) Attend partisan and nonpartisan political meetings or rallies as a spectator when not in uniform.

Active duty members of the armed services *may not*: 1) Use official authority or influence to: interfere with an election, affect the course or outcome of an election, solicit votes for a particular candidate or issue, or require or solicit political contributions from others. 2) Be a candidate for civil office in Federal, State, or local government, (with some exceptions see regulations for them), or engage in public or organized soliciting of others to become partisan candidates for nomination or election to civil office. 3) Participate in partisan political management, campaigns, or conventions (except as a spectator when not in uniform) or make public speeches in the course thereof. 4) Make a contribution to another member of the Armed Forces or a civilian officer or employee of the US for the purpose of promoting a political objective or cause, including a political campaign. 5) Solicit or receive a contribution from another member of the Armed Forces or a civilian officer or employee of the US for the purpose of promoting a political objective or cause, including a political campaign. 6) Allow or cause to be published partisan political articles signed or written by the member that solicits votes for or against a partisan political party, candidate, or cause. 7) Serve in any official capacity or be listed as a sponsor of a partisan political club. 8) Speak before a partisan political gathering, including any gathering that promotes a partisan political party, candidate or cause. 9) Participate in any radio, television, or other program or group discussion as an advocate for or against a partisan political party, candidate, or cause. 10) Conduct a political opinion survey under the auspices of a partisan political group or distribute partisan political literature. 11) Use contemptuous words against the officeholders described in 10 USC. 12) Perform clerical or other duties for a partisan political committee during a campaign or on an election day. 13) Solicit or otherwise engage in fundraising activities in Federal offices or facilities, including military reservations, for a partisan political cause or candidate. 14) March or ride in a partisan political parade. 15) Display a large political sign, banner, or poster (as distinguished from a bumper sticker) on the top or side of a private vehicle. 16) Participate in any organized effort to provide voters with transportation to the polls if the effort is organized by, or associated with, a partisan political party or candidate. 17) Sell tickets for, or otherwise actively promote, political dinners and similar fundraising events. 18) Attend partisan political events as an official representative of the Armed Forces.[1]

[1] U.S. Department of Defense, "Political Activities."

Appendix F

Adjutant General's Absentee Voting Message

From: *voting.army@us.army.mil*
[mailto:*voting.army@us.army.mil*]
Sent: Friday, June 06, 2008 11:36 AM
Subject: Adjutant General's Absentee Voting Message

As the Army's Senior Service Voting Representative, I strongly encourage you to participate and cast your vote in the 2008 General Election. Voting is the essence of our democracy and one of our most fundamental Constitutional rights. Our elected officials have very important jobs; the good news is, you have a voice in who is elected to do them . . . if you vote. You can exercise your right to vote by completing the Federal Post Card Application (FPCA Standard Form 76) or complying with the ballot request procedures enacted by the state in which you vote. The FPCA Standard Form 76, or other request, should be mailed or sent electronically as soon as possible. You should then receive your absentee ballot as requested. The Federal Voting Assistance Program has been working with the states to allow ballots to be submitted and received electronically. Check with your Unit Voting Assistance Officer (UVAO) for your state requirements.

Mailing guidelines differ from state to state; therefore, we recommend you check your state's guidelines by contacting your UVAO, or by visiting the Army Voting Assistance Program website at *www.vote.army.mil*. It is imperative that you complete and send in your ballot immediately to ensure it is received by your hometown local election officials no later than your state's deadline. If you are an overseas voter and have not received your regular absentee ballot 30–45 days prior to your state's deadline, you should complete a Federal Write-in Absentee Ballot (FWAB) and send it to your local election official. If you later receive your absentee ballot, you should also complete and send it in for processing.

The 2008 General Election is quickly approaching, so please don't wait until the very last minute to register and or send in your absentee ballot.

BE SMART. DO YOUR PART. VOTE!

REUBEN D. JONES
Brigadier General, USA
The Adjutant General

DO NOT CALL THE AKO HELP DESK FOR VOTING ASSISTANCE INFORMATION. CONTACT YOUR UNIT VOTING ASSISTANCE OFFICER!

Bibliography

"The 2004 National Election Study [data set]." The National Election Studies, University of Michigan, Center for Political Studies. Ann Arbor, MI, 2004.

Abramowitz, Alan I., and Kyle L. Saunders. "Ideological Realignment in the U.S. Electorate." *Journal of Politics* 60 (August 1998): 634–52.

Abramson, Paul, Barbara Anderson, and Brian Silver. "Who Overreports Voting?" *American Political Science Review* 80 (1986): 12.

Agiesta, Jennifer. "Iraq: Public Opinion Five Years In." In *Behind the Numbers*. http://blog.washingtonpost.com/behind-the-numbers/2008/03/iraq_public_opinion_five_years_1.html (accessed March 23, 3009).

Almond, Gabriel, and Sidney Verba. *The Civic Culture: Political Attitudes and Democracy in Five Nations*. Princeton: Princeton University Press, 1963.

Anderson, Bruce. "An Admiral at the Court of St. James's." *Stanford Magazine*, September/October 1997.

Ansolabehere, Stephen, Doug Rivers, and Sam Luks. Cooperative Congressional Election Study. Massachusets Institute of Technology, Cambridge, MA, 2006.

Astin, Alexander W. *Four Critical Years: Effects of College on Beliefs, Attitudes, and Knowledge*. San Francisco: Jossey-Bass, 1977.

Bacevich, Andrew J. *The New American Militarism: How Americans Are Seduced by War*. New York: Oxford University Press, 2005.

———. "Warrior Politics." *Atlantic Monthly*, May 2007.

Bacevich, Andrew J., and Lawrence F. Kaplan. *Generals versus the President: Eisenhower and the Army, 1953–1955*. Syracuse: Syracuse University and Johns Hopkins University, 1997. http://exed.maxwell.syr.edu/exed/sites/nss/node/12 (accessed on March 23, 2009).

Bachman, Jerald G., John D. Blair, and David R. Segal. *The All-Volunteer Force: A Study of Ideology in the Military*. Ann Arbor: University of Michigan Press, 1977.

Betros, Lance. "Political Partisanship and the Military Ethic in America." *Armed Forces & Society* 27, no. 4 (2001): 501–23.

Betts, Richard K. "Are Civil-Military Relations Still a Problem?" Paper presented at the conference on American Civil-Military Relations: Fifty Years After "The Soldier and the State." West Point, New York, June 2007.

Bretschneider, John. "A Look at Today's Army." *Army Times*, October 15, 2007.

Brooks, Rosa. "Weaning the Military from the GOP." *Los Angeles Times*, January 5, 2007.

Brown, Richard. *Social Attitudes of American Generals, 1898–1940*. New York: Arno, 1979.

Brunelli, Polli. "The Federal Voting Assistance Program: Seventeenth Report." Vol. 4. Washington, DC: Department of Defense, 2005.

Burnham, David. "Pentagon Is Faulted for Action in 1984 Campaign." *New York Times*, March 23, 1986.

Campbell, Angus, Philip E. Converse, Warren E. Miller, and Donald E. Stokes. *The American Voter.* New York: John Wiley & Sons, 1960.

Campbell, Angus, Gerald Gurin, and Warren Miller. *The Voter Decides.* Evanston, IL: Row, Peterson, 1954.

CNN. "America Votes 2004: Election Results." *CNN.com.* http://www.cnn.com/ELECTION/2004/pages/results/states/US/P/00/epolls.0.html (accessed March 23, 2009).

Coffman, Edward. "The Course of Military History in the United States since World War II." *The Journal of Military History* 61 (1997): 16.

———. *The Old Army: A Portrait of the American Army in Peacetime, 1784–1889.* New York: Oxford University Press, 1986.

———. *The Regulars: The American Army, 1898–1941.* Cambridge, MA: Belknap Press of Harvard University Press, 2004.

Cohen, Eliot. *Supreme Command: Soldiers, Statesmen and Leadership in Wartime.* Paperback ed. New York: Random House, 2003.

Coletta, Damon. "Teaching Civil-Military Relations to Military Undergraduates: The Case of the United States Air Force Academy." Paper presented at the annual meeting of the International Studies Association 48th Annual Convention. Chicago, March 2007.

Collins, Joseph J., and Ole R. Holsti. "Civil-Military Relations: How Wide Is the Gap?" *International Security* 24, no. 2 (1999): 199–207.

Commager, Henry Steele. *The Blue and the Gray.* 2 vols. New York: Mentor, 1973.

Connelly, Donald B. *John M. Schofield and the Politics of Generalship.* Civil War America, edited by Gary W. Gallagher. Chapel Hill: University of North Carolina Press, 2006.

Converse, Philip. "Information Flow and the Stability of Partisan Attitudes." *The Public Opinion Quarterly* 26, no. 4 (1962): 578–99.

Crowe, William J., Jr., and David Chanoff. *The Line of Fire from Washington to the Gulf: The Politics and Battles of the New Military.* New York: Simon & Schuster, 1993.

Cummings, Craig, and Robert Shapiro. "Studying the Effect of Elite Leadership on the Public's Policy Preferences and Confidence in Elites with a Split-Ballot Design." Paper presented at the Annual Meeting of the American Political Science Association. Chicago, 2004.

Cushman, John H. "Top Military Officers Object to Lifting Homosexual Ban." *New York Times,* November 14, 1992.

Dempsey, Jason. "The Effects and Mitigation of Non-Response in a Mail Survey of Army Personnel." Unpublished paper, Columbia University, 2006.

———. "Public Evaluation of Presidential Performance during Foreign Policy Crises." *The Forum* 4, no. 1 (2006).

Dempsey, Jason, and Robert Y. Shapiro. "The Army's Hispanic Future." *Armed Forces & Society* 35, no. 3 (2009): 526–61.

Desch, Michael. "Explaining the Gap: Vietnam, the Republicanization of the South, and the End of the Mass Army." In *Soldiers and Civilians,* edited by Peter Feaver and Richard Kohn. Cambridge, MA: MIT Press, 2001.

———. "United States Civil-Military Relations in a Changing International Order." In *United States Civil-Military Relations: In Crises or Transition?* edited by Don Snider and Miranda Carlton-Carew. Washington, DC: Center for International and Strategic Studies, 1995.

Dillman, Don. *Mail and Internet Surveys: The Tailored Design Method.* New York: John Wiley & Sons, 2000.

Douglas, Clint. "Elect More Jim Webbs." *Washington Monthly,* June 2007.

Driver, Darrell. "Sparta in Babylon: Case Studies in the Public Philosophy of Soldiers and Civilians." PhD diss., Graduate School of Syracuse University, 2006.

Eisenhower, Dwight David. "Farewell Radio and Television Address to the American People." In *Public Papers of the President: Dwight D. Eisenhower, 1960–1961,* 1025–39. Washington, DC: Government Printing Office, 1961.

Ellis, Joseph J. *His Excellency: George Washington.* New York: Alfred A. Knopf, 2004.

Erikson, Robert, and Kent Tedin. *American Public Opinion.* Vol. 6. Boston: Allyn and Bacon, 2001.

Fairbanks, Eve. "Friendly Fire." *The New Republic,* October 12, 2007.

Faris, John. "The All-Volunteer Force: Recruitment from Military Families." *Armed Forces & Society* 7, no. 4 (1981): 14.

Feaver, Peter. *Armed Servants: Agency, Oversight, and Civil-Military Relations.* Cambridge, MA: Harvard University Press, 2005.

———. "Civil Military Conflict and the Use of Force." In *U.S. Civil-Military Relations: In Crises or Transition,* edited by Don Snider and Miranda Carlton-Carew, 113–44. Washington, DC: Center for Strategic and International Studies, 1995.

Feaver, Peter D., and Christopher Gelpi. *Choosing Your Battles: American Civil-Military Relations and the Use of Force.* Princeton: Princeton University Press, 2004.

Feaver, Peter, and Richard Kohn. *Soldiers and Civilians: The Civil-Military Gap and American National Security.* Cambridge, MA: MIT Press, 2001.

Filion, F. L. "Estimating Bias Due to Nonresponse in Mail Surveys." *Public Opinion Quarterly* 39, no. 4 (1976).

Foote, Learned. "A Bias-Free Campus?" *Columbia Spectator,* October 19, 2008.

Franke, Volker C. "Duty, Honor, Country: The Social Identity of West Point Cadets." *Armed Forces & Society* 26, no. 2 (2000): 28.

———. "Generation X and the Military: A Comparison of Attitudes and Values between West Point Cadets and College Students." *Journal of Political and Military Sociology* 29 (2001): 28.

———. "Warriors for Peace: The Next Generation of U.S. Military Leaders." *Armed Forces & Society* 24, no. 1 (1997): 24.

Franks, Tommy. "Text of Gen. Tommy Franks." September 2, 2004. http://www.latimes.com/nyc-franksspeech,0,6626805.story?page+1 (accessed May 23, 2009).

Frantzich, Stephen E. "Citizens in Uniform: Political Participation among Military and Civilian Samples." *Journal of Political and Military Sociology* 10, no.14 (Spring 1982).

Frum, David. Speech to cadets at West Point. September 21, 2005.

Galloway, Bruce K., and Robert B. Johnson. *West Point: America's Power Fraternity.* New York: Simon and Schuster, 1973.

Gellman, Barton. "Pentagon Intensifies Effort to Muster Military Voters." *Washington Post*, September 17, 1992.

"General Social Survey [database]." Chicago: National Opinion Research Center, 2004.

Gershkoff, Amy. "Up for Grabs: Changing Politics among Military Families." *Public Opinion Pros* (2007).

Glanton, Dahleen. "Campaigns Wage War to Win Military Families." *Chicago Tribune*, October 26, 2008.

"Global Views 2004 [U.S. public and elite data sets]." Chicago Council on Global Affairs, 2004.

"Global Views 2004: U.S. Leaders Topline Report." Chicago Council on Global Affairs, 2004.

Goffman, Erving. *Asylums: Essays on the Social Situation of Mental Patients and Other Inmates.* New York: Doubleday Anchor, 1961.

Goldstein, Kenneth, and Travis Ridout. "The Politics of Participation: Mobilization and Turnout over Time." *Political Behavior* 24, no. 1 (2002).

Hammill, John, David Segal, and Mady Wechsler Segal. "Self-Selection and Parental Socioeconomic Status as Determinants of the Values of West Point Cadets." *Armed Forces & Society* 22, no. 1 (1995): 13.

Hartz, Louis. *The Liberal Tradition in America.* New York: Harcourt Brace Jovanovich College Publishers, 1955.

Hecox, Walter E. "A Comparison of New Cadets at USMA with Entering Freshmen at Other Colleges: Class of 1973." Edited by Office of Research. West Point, NY: United States Military Academy, 1970.

Heinl, Robert Debs. *Victory at High Tide: The Inchon-Seoul Campaign.* 3rd ed. Baltimore: Nautical & Aviation Publishing Corporation of America, 1979.

Herspring, Dale R. *The Pentagon and the Presidency: Civil-Military Relations from FDR to George W. Bush.* Lawrence: University Press of Kansas, 2005.

Hill, Jennifer. "Missing Data: Now That You Know So Much About Missing Data . . . If You're Not Part of the Solution, You're Really a Part of the Problem." Presentation as part of the Robert Wood Johnson Health and Society Scholars Program, Columbia University, New York, February 17, 2005.

Hodierne, Robert. "Military Times Poll." Military Times Media Group, 2006.

Holsti, Ole R. "Of Chasms and Convergences: Attitudes and Beliefs of Civilians and Military Elites at the Start of a New Millennium." In *Soldiers and Civilians*, edited by Peter Feaver and Richard Kohn. Cambridge: Cambridge University Press, 2001.

———. *Public Opinion and American Foreign Policy.* Rev. ed. Ann Arbor: University of Michigan Press, 2004.

———. "A Widening Gap between the US Military and Civilian Society? Some Evidence, 1976–1996." *International Security* 23 (1998): 5–42.

Hunt, Albert R. "Letter from Washington: As U.S. Rich-Poor Gap Grows, So Does Public Outcry." *International Herald Tribune*, February 18, 2007.

Huntington, Samuel. *The Soldier and the State*. Cambridge, MA: Belknap Press, 1957.

———. *The Common Defense: Strategic Programs in National Politics*. New York: Columbia University Press, 1961.

Institute of Politics. "Coming of Age: The Political Awakening of a Generation." Harvard University, Cambridge, MA, 2004.

"The Iraq War: Collateral Damage." *The Economist*, March 22, 2007.

Jamieson, Amie, Hyon B. Shin, and Jennifer Day. "Voting and Registration in the Election of November 2000." Washington, DC: U.S. Department of Commerce, Economics and Statistics Administration, U.S. Census Bureau, 2002.

Janowitz, Morris. "The All-Volunteer Military as a 'Sociopolitical' Problem." *Social Problems* 22, no. 3 (1975): 432–39.

———. *The Professional Soldier: A Social and Political Portrait*. New York: Free Press, 1971.

Janowitz, Morris, and Charles Moskos. "Five Years of the All-Volunteer Force: 1973–1978." *Armed Forces & Society* 5, no. 2 (1979): 47.

Janowitz, Morris, and Stephen Wesbrook, eds. *The Political Education of Soldiers*. Beverly Hills, CA: Sage Publications, 1983.

Jennings, M. Kent, and Gregory Markus. "The Effect of Military Service on Political Attitudes: A Panel Study." *American Political Science Review* 71, no. 1 (1977): 136.

Jennings, M. Kent, and Richard G. Niemi. *The Political Character of Adolescence*. Princeton: Princeton University Press, 1974.

Jentleson, Bruce W., and Rebecca L. Britton. "Still Pretty Prudent: Post–Cold War American Public Opinion on the Use of Military Force." *Journal of Conflict Resolution* 42, no. 4 (1998).

Johnson, Timothy, Diane O'Rourke, Jane Burris, and Linda Owens. "Culture and Survey Nonresponse." In *Survey Nonresponse*, edited by Robert Groves, Don Dillman, John Eltinge, and Roderick Little. New York: John Wiley & Sons, 2002.

Kane, Tim. "Who Are the Recruits? The Demographic Characteristics of U.S. Military Enlistment, 2003–2005." Washington, DC: Heritage Foundation, 2006.

Kaplan, Lawrence F. "Generals Used to Be Neutral." *The New Republic*, September 13, 2004.

Karsten, Peter. "Professional and Citizen Officers." In *Public Opinion and the Military Establishment*, edited by Charles Moskos, 37–62. Beverly Hills: Sage Publications, 1971.

Katznelson, Ira. "Extremes Clash, Ambiguity Rules: Ballots for Soldiers." In *Fear Itself*. Forthcoming.

King, David C., and Zachary Karabell. *The Generation of Trust: How the U.S. Military Has Regained the Public's Confidence since Vietnam*. Washington, DC: American Enterprise Institute Press, 2002.

Kittfield, James. *Prodigal Soldiers: How the Generation of Officers Born of Vietnam Revolutionized the American Style of War*. New York: Simon & Schuster, 1995.

Kohn, Richard. "Out of Control: The Crises in Civil-Military Relations." *National Interest* 35 (1994): 3–17.

Krosnick, Jon. "The Causes of No-Opinion Responses to Attitude Measures in Surveys: They Are Rarely What They Appear to Be." In *Survey Nonresponse*, edited by Robert Groves, Don Dillman, John Eltinge, and Roderick Little. New York: John Wiley & Sons, 2002.

Krotki, Karol. "Short Course on Survey Weighting." Presentation at the Annual Conference of the American Association of Public Opinion Researchers, Montreal, Canada, 2006.

Kuhnhenn, Jim. "AFSCME, MoveOn Ad Targets McCain on Iraq War." Associated Press, June 17, 2008.

Langer, Gary. "Taking Aim at the Military Vote." *ABCNews.com*, July 22, 2008. http://blogs.abcnews.com/thenumbers/2008/07/taking-aim-at-t.html (accessed March 23, 2009).

———. "The Veteran Vote—an Update." *ABCNews.com*, December 24, 2008. http://blogs.abcnews.com/thenumbers/2008/12/the-veteran-vot.html (accessed March 23, 2009).

Laufer, Robert S. "The Aftermath of War: Adult Socialization and Political Development." In *Political Learning in Adulthood*, edited by Roberta S. Sigel. Chicago: University of Chicago Press, 1989.

Leal, David. "It's Not Just a Job: Military Service and Latino Political Participation." *Political Behavior* 21, no. 2 (1999): 153–74.

Leeuw, Edith de, and Wim de Heer. "Trends in Household Survey Nonresponse: A Longitudinal and International Comparison." In *Survey Nonresponse*, edited by Robert Groves, Don Dillman, John Eltinge, and Roderick Little. New York: John Wiley & Sons, 2002.

Leip, David. "Atlas of U.S. Presidential Elections." http://uselectionatlas.org/ (accessed March 23, 2009).

Lipset, Seymour, and William Schneider. "The Decline of Confidence in American Institutions." *Political Science Quarterly* 98, no. 3 (1983): 379–402.

Lipsky, David. *Absolutely American: Four Years at West Point*. Boston: Houghton Mifflin, 2003.

Locher, James R. *Victory on the Potomac: The Goldwater-Nichols Act Unifies the Pentagon*. College Station: A&M University Press, 2002.

Lovell, John P. "The Professional Socialization of the West Point Cadet." In *The New Military: Changing Patterns of Organization*, edited by Morris Janowitz, 119–57. New York: Russell Sage Foundation, 1964.

Lovell, John P., and Judith Hicks Stiehm. "Military Service and Political Socialization." In *Political Learning in Adulthood*, edited by Roberta S. Sigel. Chicago: University of Chicago Press, 1989.

Lucas, William. "Anticipatory Socialization and the ROTC." In *Public Opinion and the Military Establishment*, edited by Charles Moskos, 99–134. Beverly Hills: Sage Publications, 1971.

MacArthur, Douglas. "Address by General of the Army Douglas MacArthur to the Corps of Cadets Accepting the Thayer Award." General Douglas MacArthur Foundation, West Point, NY, 1962.

Mahoney-Norris, Kathleen. "Civil-Military Relations: Educating US Air Force Officers at the Graduate Level." Paper presented at Annual Meeting of the International Studies Association 48th Annual Convention. Chicago, March 2007.

Manchester, William. *American Caesar: Douglas MacArthur, 1880–1964*. New York: Random House, 1978.

Maxfield, Betty D. "Army Profile, FY04." Edited by Department of the Army Headquarters, Deputy Chief of Staff, Army G-1. Washington, DC: Office of Army Demographics, 2005.

Mazur, Diane. "The Bullying of America: A Cautionary Tale about Military Voting and Civil-Military Relations." *Election Law Journal* 4 (2005): 105.

McGarry, Brendan. "Military Times Poll: Troops Backing McCain." *Army Times*, October 8, 2008.

Memmott, Mark, and Jill Lawrence. "McCain: Gen. Sanchez Should Have Told Congress if He Thought Things Were Wrong in Iraq." *USA Today on Politics*, 2007. http://blogs.usatoday.com/onpolitics/ (accessed March 5, 2009).

Mills, C. Wright. *The Power Elite*. New York: Oxford University Press, 1956.

Mondak, Jeffrey, and Shannon Ishiyama Smithey. "The Dynamics of Public Support for the Supreme Court." *Journal of Politics* 59, no. 4 (1997): 1114–42.

Moore, Danna, and John Turnai. "Evaluating Nonresponse Error in Mail Surveys." In *Survey Nonresponse*, edited by Robert Groves, Don Dillman, John Eltinge, and Roderick Little. New York: John Wiley & Sons, 2002.

Moskos, Charles C. "The All-Volunteer Force." In *The Political Education of Soldiers*, edited by Morris Janowitz and Stephen Wesbrook. Beverly Hills: Sage Publications, 1983.

———. "The Military." *Annual Review of Sociology* 1976, no. 2 (1976).

Moskos, Charles, and J. S. Butler. *All That We Can Be: Black Leadership and Racial Integration the Army Way*. New York: Twentieth Century Fund Book, 1996.

Mullen, Michael. "From the Chairman: Military Must Stay Apolitical." *Joint Forces Quarterly* (2008): 2–3.

Myers, Steven. "Testing of a President: Critics, Marines Scold Officer Who Called Clinton an 'Adulterous Liar' in a Column." *New York Times*, November 14, 1998.

Nielsen, Suzanne. "The Civil Military Relations of the US Army and Military Effectiveness: A Framework for Analysis." Paper presented at the American Political Science Association Conference, Chicago, August 30–September 2, 2001.

Niemi, Richard G. "Collecting Information about the Family: A Problem in Survey Methodology." In *Political Socialization: A Reader in Theory and Research*, edited by Jack Dennis. New York: John Wiley & Sons, 1973.

Noelle-Neumann, Elisabeth. *The Spiral of Silence: Public Opinion—Our Social Skin*. 2nd ed. Chicago: University of Chicago Press, 1993.

Noonan, Peggy. "Untangling Webb: Ronald Reagan's Navy Secretary Runs for Senate as a Standard-Issue Democrat." *OpinionJournal* (2006). http://www.opinionjournal.com/columnists/pnoonan/?id=110008516 (accessed March 23, 2009).

Page, Benjamin I., and Robert Y. Shapiro. *The Rational Public: Fifty Years of Trends in Americans' Policy Preferences*. Chicago: University of Chicago Press, 1992.

Powers, Rod. "FY 2004 Average Annual Salary for Military Personnel." *About.com*. http://usmilitary.about.com/od/fy2004paycharts/l/blsalary.htm (accessed March 23, 2009).

Priest, Robert, Terrence Fullerton, and Claude Bridges. "Personality and Value Changes in West Point Cadets." *Armed Forces & Society* 8, no. 4 (1982): 14.

Rasmussen, Scott. "On Iraq, 50% Trust Dems, 38% Prefer GOP." *Rasmussen Reports* (2007). http://www.rasmussenreports.com/public_content/politics/on_iraq_50_trust_dems_38_prefer_gop (accessed March 23, 2009).

Ricks, Thomas. *Making the Corps: Sixty-one Men Came to Paris Island to Become Marines, Not All of Them Made It*. New York: Scribner, 1997.

———. "The Widening Gap between the Military and Society." *The Atlantic Monthly*, July 1997, 66–78.

Riper, Paul Van, and Darab Unwalla. "Voting Patterns among High-Ranking Military Officers." *Political Science Quarterly* 80, no. 1 (1965): 48–61.

Rohall, David E., Morten G. Ender, and Michael D. Matthews. "The Effects of Military Affiliation, Gender, and Political Ideology on Attitudes toward the Wars in Afghanistan and Iraq." *Armed Forces & Society* 33, no. 1 (2006): 19.

Romer, Daniel, Kate Kenski, Kenneth Winneg, Christopher Adasiewicz, and Kathleen Hall Jamieson. *Capturing Campaign Dynamics, 2000 and 2004: The National Annenberg Election Survey*. Philadelphia: University of Pennsylvania Press, 2006.

Rosiak, Luke. "Troops Deployed Abroad Give 6:1 to Obama." *Capital Eye* (2008).

Rossiter, Clinton. *Conservatism in America*. New York: Vintage Books, 1962.

Roth-Douquet, Kathy, and Frank Schaeffer. *AWOL: The Unexcused Absence of America's Upper Classes from Military Service—and How It Hurts Our Country*. New York: HarperCollins, 2006.

Rustad, Michael. "Review of the Political Education of Soldiers." *Contemporary Sociology* 13, no. 4 (1984): 2.

Samet, Elizabeth D. *Soldier's Heart: Reading Literature through Peace and War at West Point*. New York: Picador, 2007.

Schneider, Jacob. "Students Roughly Split on NROTC Return." *Columbia Spectator*, December 2, 2008.

Schott, Ben. "Op-Art; Who Do You Think We Are?" *New York Times*, February 25, 2007.

Segal, David R. *Recruiting for Uncle Sam: Citizenship and Military Manpower Policy*. Lawrence: University Press of Kansas, 1989.

Segal, David R., Peter Freedman-Doan, Jerald Bachman, and Patrick O'Malley. "Attitudes of Entry-Level Enlisted Personnel: Pro-Military and Politically Mainstreamed." In *Soldiers and Civilians: The Civil-Military Gap and American National Security*, edited by Peter Feaver and Richard Kohn. Cambridge, MA: MIT Press, 2001.

Shapiro, Robert Y., and Yaeli Bloch-Elkon. "Political Polarization and the Rational Public." Paper presented at the Annual Conference of the American Association for Public Opinion Research. Montreal, Canada, May 18–21, 2006.

Silver, Allan. "Why ROTC Should Return to Columbia." *Columbia Spectator,* November 14, 2008.

Skelton, William B. "Officers and Politicians: The Origins of Army Politics in the United States before the Civil War." *Armed Forces & Society* 6, no. 1 (1979).

Snider, Don, and Miranda A. Carlton-Carew, eds. *U.S. Civil-Military Relations: In Crises or in Transition?* Washington, DC: Center for Strategic and International Studies, 1995.

Snider, Don M., and Lloyd J. Matthews, eds. *The Future of the Army Profession.* 2nd ed. Revised and expanded. Boston: McGraw-Hill Primis Custom Publishing, 2005.

Snider, Don, Robert Priest, and Felisa Lewis. "The Civilian-Military Gap and Professional Military Education at the Precommissioning Level." *Armed Forces & Society* 27, no. 2 (2001): 24.

Snider, Don M., Gayle L. Watkins, and Lloyd J. Matthews, eds. *The Future of the Army Profession.* Boston: McGraw-Hill Custom Publishers, 2002.

Stevens, Gwendolyn, Jr., Fred Rosa, and Sheldon Gardner. "Military Academies as Instruments of Value Change." *Armed Forces & Society* 20 (1994): 12.

Stouffer, S. A., et al. *The American Soldier.* Vol. 1, *Adjustment during Army Life.* Vol. 2, *Combat and Its Aftermath.* Princeton: Princeton University Press, 1949.

Sturgis, Patrick. "Analysing Complex Survey Data: Clustering, Stratification and Weights." *Social Research Update,* no. 43 (2004).

Tapper, Jake, and Avery Miller. "Selling the War, through Advertising." *ABCNews.com,* August 22, 2007. http://abcnews.go.com/WN/Story?id=3512978& page=1 (accessed March 23, 2009).

Teigen, Jeremy M. "Veteran's Party Identification, Candidate Affect, and Vote Choice in the 2004 U.S. Presidential Election." *Armed Forces & Society* 33, no. 3 (2007): 24.

Torres-Reyna, Oscar, and Robert Y. Shapiro. "Trends: Defense and the Military." *Public Opinion Quarterly* 66, no. 2 (2002): 279–303.

Traub, James. "The Things They Carry." *New York Times Magazine,* January 4, 2004, 28–33, 41, 52–53.

Tyson, Ann Scott. "A Strident Minority: Anti-Bush US Troops in Iraq." *Christian Science Monitor,* September 21, 2004.

Ulrich, Marybeth. "The Civil-Military Relations Education of the US Army's Senior Officers." Paper presented at the Annual Meeting of the International Studies Association 48th Annual Convention. Chicago, March 2007.

———. "Infusing Civil-Military Relations in the Officer Corps." In *The Future of the Army Profession,* edited by Don Snider, Gayle L. Watkins, and Lloyd J. Matthews, 245–70. Boston: McGraw-Hill Custom Publishers, 2002.

United States Military Academy. "USMA Mission." http://www.usma.edu/mission.asp (accessed March 23, 2009).

U.S. Army. Department of the Army Headquarters. *Field Manual No. 1: The Army.* Washington, DC: U.S. Department of Defense, 2005.

U.S. Department of Defense. "Political Activities by Members of the Armed Forces on Active Duty." Edited by U.S. Department of Defense. 2004.

———. Office of Policy, Planning and Analysis. "United States Military Academy Strategic Vision—2010." United States Military Academy, West Point, NY, 2000.

———. Office of the Under Secretary of Defense, Personnel and Readiness. *Population Representation in the Military Services: Fiscal Year 2004.* 2006.

———. *Population Representation in the Military Services: Fiscal Year 2005.* 2007.

U.S. General Accounting Office. "Gender Issues: Information on DOD's Assignment Policy and Direct Ground Combat Definition." Edited by General Accounting Office. National Security and International Affairs Division, Washington, DC, October 1998.

U.S. Government Accountability Office. "Elections: DOD Expands Voting Assistance to Military Absentee Voters, but Challenges Remain." United States Government Accountability Office, Washington, DC, 2006.

Walsh, Kenneth T. "The Most Consequential Elections in History: Abraham Lincoln's Victory in 1864 Led to the End of the Civil War." *U.S. News and World Report,* July 30, 2008.

Walt, Stephen. "The Renaissance of Security Studies." *International Studies Quarterly* 35 (1991): 30.

Warrant Officer Career Center. "What Is a WO?" United States Army Warrant Officer Career Center. http://usawocc.army.mil/whatiswo.htm (accessed March 23, 2009).

Watkins, Shanea J., and James Sherk. "Who Serves in the U.S. Military? Demographic Characteristics of Enlisted Troops and Officers." Washington, DC: Heritage Foundation, 2008.

Watson, Samuel J. "How the Army Became Accepted: West Point Socialization, Military Accountability, and the Nation-State during the Jacksonian Era." *American Nineteenth Century History* 7, no. 2 (2006): 32.

Webb, James H. "Purple Heartbreakers." *New York Times,* January 18, 2006.

Wesbrook, Stephen D. "Sociopolitical Alienation and Military Efficiency." *Armed Forces & Society* 6 (1980): 20.

Young, Cathy. "The Impact of Academic Bias: Professors Do Lean to the Left—but Are Students Listening?" *reasononline,* March 8, 2007. http://www.reason.com/news/show/119026.html (accessed March 23, 2009).

Zaller, John. *The Nature and Origins of Mass Opinion.* Cambridge: Cambridge University Press, 1992.

Zaller, John, and Dennis Chiu. "Government's Little Helper: U.S. Press Coverage of Foreign Policy Crises, 1946–1999." In *Decisionmaking in a Glass House: Mass Media, Public Opinion, and American and European Foreign Policy in the 21st Century,* edited by Robert Y. Shapiro, Brigitte L. Nacos, and Pierangelo Isernia. Lanham, MD: Rowman and Littlefield, 2000.

Index